LEARNING
SCIENCE

Archie E. Lapointe   Janice M. Askew   Nancy A. Mead

Prepared for the National Center of Education Statistics,
U.S. Department of Education and the National Science Foundation

February 1992   Report No. 22-CAEP-02

The International Assessment
of Educational Progress (ETS) *IAEP*

EDUCATIONAL TESTING SERVICE

Educational Testing Service, (ETS) is a private, not for profit corporation devoted to measurement and research, primarily in the field of education. It was founded in 1947 by the American Council on Education, the Carnegie Foundation for the Advancement of Teaching, and the College Entrance Examination Board.

The Center for the Assessment of Educational Progress (CAEP) is a division of ETS devoted to innovative approaches to the measurement and evaluation of educational progress. The present core activity of CAEP is the administration of the National Assessment of Educational Progress (NAEP), under contract from the U.S. Department of Education. CAEP also carries out related activities, including the International Assessment of Educational Progress (IAEP), state assessments, and special studies such as the National Science Foundation-supported Pilot Study of Higher-Order Thinking Skills Assessment Techniques in Science and Mathematics.

The work upon which this publication is based was performed pursuant to Grant No. SDE-8955070 of the National Science Foundation, and additional funding was provided by the U.S. Department of Education through Interagency Agreement No. IAD-91-0222. Supplementary funds were provided by the Carnegie Corporation of New York.

This report, No. 22-CAEP-02, can be ordered from the Center for the Assessment of Educational Progress at Educational Testing Service, Rosedale Road, Princeton, New Jersey 08541-0001.

Library of Congress Card Number: 91-078081

ISBN: 0-88685-121-1

Educational Testing Service is an equal opportunity/affirmative action employer.

Educational Testing Service, ETS, and (ETS)® are registered trademarks of Educational Testing Service.

Introduction 4

Highlights 12

Chapter One – The Science Performance of 13-Year-Olds 15

Chapter Two – The Curriculum 25

Chapter Three – The Classrooms 45

Chapter Four – Students and Their Homes 61

Chapter Five – Countries and Their Education Systems 75

Chapter Six – The Science Performance of 9-Year-Olds 81

A Final Word 99

The Participants 101

Procedural Appendix 123

Data Appendix 143

Acknowledgments 157

Introduction

Bueno es vivir paraver

It is well to live that one
may learn.

Cervantes

Each of the countries that participated in the second International
Assessment of Educational Progress (IAEP) did so for its own reasons.
Some wanted to compare their results with those of neighbors or
competitors. Others wanted to learn about the educational policies and
practices of countries whose students seem to regularly achieve success in
mathematics and science. Still others wanted to establish a baseline of data
within their own countries against which they can measure progress in the
future.

All participants, however, shared a common interest in identifying
what is *possible* for today's 9- and 13-year-old children to know and to be
able to do in mathematics and science. While critics warn of the dangers of
promoting an educational olympiad, the benefits of comparative data must
be considered. Knowledge of what is *possible* produces new enthusiasm,
raises sights, establishes new challenges, and ultimately can improve
personal and societal performance.

Some might say that a study that compares the United States with
Slovenia or England with São Paulo, Brazil, is inappropriate or irrelevant.
Indeed, education is, in fact, imbedded in each society and culture, and
performance should not be studied or described without considering the
important differences from country to country. The life of a 13-year-old in a
rural Chinese community is very different from that of his or her peer
growing up in a middle-class Paris apartment. And yet, these two young
citizens may well meet in the global marketplace 20 years from now. And if
they do, chances are they will rely on the mathematics and science they
learned in this decade to succeed in the complex business and technological
environment of 2012.

While recognizing the fundamental differences from country to
country, the participants in the second IAEP project assembled tests that
focus on the common elements of their curriculums, and to form the
contexts for interpreting student achievement data, they added sets of

questions about students' home background and classroom experiences and the characteristics of the schools they attend.

This report, then, is organized according to those contexts that surround and affect student performance: the curriculum, classroom practices, home environments, and the characteristics of countries and their education systems. While survey research projects like IAEP cannot establish cause-and-effect relationships, they can provide clues that may help explain high and low performance.

Occasionally, the findings are counter-intuitive. For example, in some countries, less well-trained teachers with large classes and poor-quality instructional materials sometimes produce students who achieve truly exceptional results. In other countries, students of better paid, better trained teachers, who work in schools that are more generously supported, perform less well on the IAEP tests. The results presented in this report will highlight some of these paradoxes.

One possible reaction to this report would be for a country to examine the results and attempt to find out how to become *Number 1* in the world. A more thoughtful course of action would be for each country to use this information to set reasonable goals that are in harmony with its own values and culture.

The achievement results reported here can help identify what is *possible* for 9- and 13-year-olds to achieve and the descriptive information can suggest practices and curriculums that others are using successfully. It seems reasonable to expect that each country may find elements worth emulating in the practices of its neighbors and competitors.

ABOUT THE PROJECT In 1990-91, a total of 20 countries surveyed the mathematics and science performance of 13-year-old students and 14 also assessed 9-year-olds in the same subjects. An optional short probe of the geography achievement of 13-year-olds and an experimental performance-based assessment of 13-year-olds' ability to use equipment and materials to solve mathematics and science problems were also administered by some participants. Their results will be presented in forthcoming reports.

Some countries drew samples from virtually all children in the appropriate age group; others confined their assessments to specific geographic areas, language groups, or grade levels. The definition of populations often followed the structure of school systems, political divisions, and cultural distinctions. For example, the sample in Israel focused on students in Hebrew-speaking schools, which share a common curriculum, language, and tradition. The assessment in Slovenia reflected the needs and aspirations of this recently separated republic of Yugoslavia. The restriction of certain grades in the Portuguese assessment was necessitated by a very dispersed student population resulting from a unique education system that allows students to repeat any grade up to three times. All countries limited their assessment to students who were in school, which for some participants meant excluding significant numbers of age-eligible children. In a few cases, a sizable proportion of the selected schools or students did not participate in the assessment, and therefore results are subject to possible nonresponse bias.[1]

A list of the participants is provided below with a description of limitations of the populations assessed. Unless noted, 90 percent or more of the age-eligible children in a population are in school. For countries where more than 10 percent of the age-eligible children are out of school a notation of *in-school population* appears after the country's name. In Brazil, two separate samples were drawn, one each from the cities of São Paulo and Fortaleza. In Canada, nine out of the 10 provinces drew separate samples of 13-year-olds and four of these drew separate samples of English-speaking and French-speaking schools, for a total of 14 separate samples. Four Canadian provinces — six separate samples — participated in the assessment of 9-year-olds.[2] These distinct Canadian samples coincide with the separate provincial education systems in Canada and reflect their concern for the two language groups they serve.

PARTICIPANTS

BRAZIL	Cities of São Paulo and Fortaleza, restricted grades, in-school population
CANADA	Four provinces at age 9 and nine out of 10 provinces at age 13
CHINA	20 out of 29 provinces and independent cities, restricted grades, in-school population
ENGLAND	All students, low participation at ages 9 and 13
FRANCE	All students
HUNGARY	All students
IRELAND	All students
ISRAEL	Hebrew-speaking schools
ITALY	Province of Emilia-Romagna, low participation at age 9
JORDAN	All students
KOREA	All students
MOZAMBIQUE*	Cities of Maputo and Biera, in-school population, low participation
PORTUGAL	Restricted grades, in-school population at age 13
SCOTLAND	All students, low participation at age 9
SLOVENIA	All students
SOVIET UNION	14 out of 15 republics, Russian-speaking schools
SPAIN	All regions except Cataluña, Spanish-speaking schools
SWITZERLAND	15 out of 26 cantons
TAIWAN	All students
UNITED STATES	All students

---

[1] Percentages of age-eligible children excluded from samples and percentages of sampled schools and students that participated are provided in the Procedural Appendix, pp. 129-130.

[2] Taken together, the Canadian samples represent 94 percent of the 13-year-olds and 74 percent of the 9-year-olds in Canada. An appropriately weighted subsample of responses was drawn from these samples for the calculation of the statistics for Canada.

*Mozambique, one of 20 participants in IAEP, did not assess its students in science.

Typically, a representative sample of 3,300 students from 110 different schools was selected from each population at each age level and half were assessed in mathematics and half in science.[3] A total of about 175,000 9- and 13-year-olds (those born in calendar years 1981 and 1977, respectively) were tested in 13 different languages in March 1991.[4]

Steps to ensure the uniformity and quality of the surveys were taken at all stages of the project. While procedures could not always be followed in exactly the same way in each of the separate assessment centers, overall compliance was very high, as shown in the quality control procedures provided in the figure on the next page.[5] Translations and adaptations of assessment materials were carefully checked for accuracy. All questions were pilot-tested in participating countries before they were used in the final assessment. Comparable sampling designs were used by all participants and the quality of their implementation was carefully checked and documented. Participants were provided with training and computer software to facilitate their tasks and to ensure uniformity and quality. Test administrators were trained to administer the tests to students using the same set of instructions and time limits. The standardization of administration procedures was carefully checked within each country and across countries by an international monitoring team. While the reports of the quality control observers were for the most part completed check lists, some impressionistic observations of international monitoring team members are interspersed throughout this report to give a more personal view of the test administrations in several countries. The accuracy of the database was validated through independent checks of a random selection of completed student test booklets and school questionnaires; the accuracy of the data analysis was validated by comparing the results obtained using different statistical programs and computer equipment.

---

3 The numbers of schools and students in each sample are provided in the Procedural Appendix, pp. 132-133.

4 Because their school year begins in March instead of September, Brazil, and Korea assessed six months earlier in September 1990, and to compensate for the earlier assessment, in Brazil and Korea, they sampled students who were six months older (born between July 1, 1976 through June 30, 1977).

5 Additional documentation of data collection is provided in the Procedural Appendix, pp. 137-139 and in Adam Chu, et al, *IAEP Technical Report*, Princeton, NJ, Educational Testing Service, 1992.

Quality Control Procedures

TRANSLATIONS OF ASSESSMENT MATERIALS INDEPENDENTLY VERIFIED   Achievement and background questions and student directions were adapted and translated within each country and then checked independently by language experts in the United States. All countries used the same artwork and physical page layouts for their tests.

PILOT TEST OF ASSESSMENT QUESTIONS   Achievement and background questions were pilot-tested with groups of students from each participating country (except Slovenia, which joined the project late) to determine which questions would work best in the final assessment.

SAMPLES INDEPENDENTLY VERIFIED   Samples for each population were drawn using agreed-upon procedures and were independently checked in the United States to ensure that procedures were followed accurately and that sampling weights were appropriately calculated.

PROCEDURAL MANUALS AND TRAINING PROVIDED   Procedural manuals were developed for coordinating the project, drawing samples, administering the assessments, conducting a quality control program, and entering results into a database. Regional training sessions were held at which the individuals from each assessment center who actually performed the tasks were provided detailed instructions and hands-on experiences.

COMPUTER SOFTWARE PROVIDED   Specially developed computer software was provided to the participants to facilitate sampling and data entry and to ensure uniformity and quality.

STANDARDIZED TEST ADMINISTRATION   Test booklets were administered to students using the same instructions and the same time limits in each participating country. To ensure procedures were understood, test administrators, usually school personnel, were trained in 20 out of 29 assessment centers.

ON-SITE OBSERVATION OF ASSESSMENTS   Unannounced observations of 10 to 20 percent of the test administrations were conducted by 22 out of 29 assessment centers.

INDEPENDENT QUALITY CONTROL   In all countries except Brazil and Mozambique, an independent, trained observer interviewed the country project manager about all aspects of the project and visited one or more test administration sites. In most cases, the observer was fluent in the language of the assessment.

DATA FILES AND DATA ANALYSIS VALIDATED   The scoring of open-ended mathematics questions was checked in 10 percent of the booklets by 27 out of 29 assessment centers and in all cases, accuracy of scoring was 98 percent or higher. Each country validated its own data files, using software provided by the project, to ascertain their quality and accuracy. Data files were also independently validated by comparing the responses of a random set of 10 student booklets and 10 school questionnaires of each type to the data entered into the databases. If data files contained 1 percent errors or greater, participants were asked to rekey all the responses. This happened in one case. Data analysis procedures were checked by calculating statistics using different programs and computer equipment and comparing the results.

ASSESSMENT QUESTIONS CHECKED FOR CURRICULAR OR CULTURAL BIAS   Assessment results were checked to verify that responses to individual questions could be summarized without misrepresenting curricular or cultural differences within particular countries. Cluster analyses and analyses of differential item functioning (DIF) resulted in the removal of one mathematics question at each age level, two science questions at age 9, and eight at age 13 before final analyses were conducted.

A WORD ABOUT COMPARISONS A major challenge of international studies is to provide fair comparisons of student achievement. Some of the problems faced by these studies are similar to those of any survey research project. For example, samples must be adequately drawn, test administration procedures must be scrupulously adhered to, and care must be taken to produce accurate data files. These concerns are not trivial. However, international studies must also address a number of unique issues that stem from the differences in language, culture, and education systems of the participating countries.[6]

Three areas of concern warrant special attention: the representativeness of the target population, the appropriateness of the measures, and educational and cultural differences. As indicated earlier, some participants confined assessments to particular geographic areas, language groups, or grade levels. In some cases, significant numbers of age-eligible children were not attending school and in other cases, participation rates of schools or students were low. These limitations are described in more detail in the figure on the following page. There is simply no way to measure the bias introduced when certain groups of children are excluded from a sample or when response rates are low; their participation could have raised performance scores, lowered them, or not affected them at all.

To address concerns of representativeness, all populations have been named on all of the figures and in the text in ways that highlight the major limitations of their assessment. For example, Italy is listed in the figures and in the text as "Emilia-Romagna," the actual province that was assessed, and China is listed in the figures as "China-in-school population, restricted grades, 20 provinces and cities," and in the text as "China (in-school population)," their major limitation.

Countries also differ with respect to the appropriateness of the curricular areas the IAEP assessment sought to measure. All countries participated in the development of the mathematics and science frameworks that guided the design of the instruments; curricular experts in each country reviewed all potential questions for their appropriateness for their own students.[7] While acceptable to all, the resulting tests do not match all countries' curricula equally well. Differences in curriculum emphasis are documented alongside the performance of each country in various curricular areas in Chapter Two.

---

[6] A thoughtful treatment of the issues involved in international studies is discussed in Norman M. Bradburn and Dorothy M. Gilford, eds., *A Framework and Principles for International Comparative Studies in Education*, Washington, D.C., National Academy Press, 1990.

[7] A full discussion of the development of frameworks and selection of questions is provided in Center for the Assessment of Educational Progress, *The 1991 IAEP Assessment, Objectives for Mathematics, Science, and Geography*, Princeton, NJ, Educational Testing Service, 1991.

Descriptions of Limited Populations**

	Included			Excluded	
Brazil, Age 13	3%	13-year-olds in grades 5 through 8 in cities of São Paulo and Fortaleza.	97%		13-year-olds in grades other than 5 through 8 in São Paulo (20% of those in school) and in Fortaleza (34% of those in school). 13-year-olds not in school (8% of those in São Paulo and 15% of those in Fortaleza). 13-year-olds in schools in other cities and rural areas.
Canada, Age 9	74%	9-year-olds in English-speaking schools in British Columbia and New Brunswick. 9-year-olds in English- and French-speaking schools in Ontario and Quebec.	26%		9-year-olds in French-speaking schools in New Brunswick. 9-year-olds in six other provinces and territories.
China, Age 13	38%	13-year-olds in 17 provinces and independent cities of Beijing, Tienjing, and Shanghai in middle schools (grades 7 through 9).	62%		13-year-olds below grade 7 in 20 provinces and cities (10% of those in school). 13-year-olds not in school (about 49% of 13-year-olds). 13-year-olds in schools in 9 provinces and autonomous regions with predominantly non-Chinese populations.
Israel, Age 9	71%	9-year-olds in public Hebrew-speaking schools.	29%		9-year-olds in non-public Hebrew-speaking schools (about 7%). 9-year-olds in Arabic schools (about 20% of 9-year-olds).
Israel, Age 13	71%	13-year-olds in public Hebrew-speaking schools.	29%		13-year-olds in non-public Hebrew-speaking schools (about 10%). 13-year-olds in Arabic schools (about 20% of 13-year-olds).
Italy, Age 9	4%	9-year-olds in schools of Emilia-Romagna province.	96%		9-year-olds in 19 other provinces.
Italy, Age 13	6%	13-year-olds in schools in Emilia-Romagna province.	94%		13-year-olds in 19 other Italian provinces.
Mozambique, Age 13	1%	13-year-olds in schools of cities of Maputo and Beira.	99%		13-year-olds not in school (about 75% of 13-year-olds). 13-year-olds in other cities and rural areas.
Portugal, Age 9	81%	9-year-olds in grades 3 and 4.	19%		9-year-olds in grades other than 3 and 4 (about 16%).
Portugal, Age 13	68%	13-year-olds in grades 5 through 9.	32%		13-year-olds in grades other than 5 through 9 (about 18% of those in school). 13-year-olds not in school (about 16%).
Soviet Union, Age 9	63%	9-year-olds in Russian-speaking schools in 14 republics.	37%		9-year-olds in non-Russian-speaking schools in 14 republics. 9-year-olds in schools in Uzbeckistan republic.
Soviet Union, Age 13	60%	13-year-olds in Russian-speaking schools in 14 republics.	40%		13-year-olds in non-Russian-speaking schools in 14 republics. 13-year-olds in schools in Uzbeckistan republic.
Spain, Age 9	80%	9-year-olds in all Spanish-speaking schools except those in the Catalan autonomous community.	20%		9-year-olds in all schools in the Catalan autonomous community. 9-year-olds in exclusively Valencian- and Basque-speaking schools.
Spain, Age 13	80%	13-year-olds in all Spanish-speaking schools except those in the Catalan autonomous community.	20%		13-year-olds in all schools in the Catalan autonomous community. 13-year-olds in exclusively Valencian- and Basque-speaking schools.
Switzerland, Age 13	76%	13-year-olds in German-, French- and Italian-speaking public schools in 15 cantons.	24%		13-year-olds in private and Romansch schools in 15 cantons. 13-year-olds in the remaining 11 cantons.

**Unless noted above, all other populations included 90 percent or more of their age-eligible children.

Furthermore, the testing format — multiple-choice and short-answer questions — is not equally familiar to students from all countries. To address this issue, participants were given the option of administering a practice test to sampled students prior to the assessment. Finally, since countries differ in the age at which students start school and policies for promotion, students at ages 9 and 13 are further along in their schooling in some countries than in others.[8] While all results presented in this report represent performance of all students in each age group, participants were also provided with results broken down by the two most common grade levels for students in each age group.

International results must ultimately be interpreted in light of the educational and cultural context of each country. The countries participating in IAEP are large and small, rich and poor, and have varied ethnic, religious, language, and cultural traditions. Likewise, educational goals, expectations, and even the meaning of achievement vary from nation to nation. As a reminder of these differences among countries, results are presented along with relevant contextual information that is designed to help the reader interpret their significance.

---

[8] See the Procedural Appendix, pp. 134-136 for the distribution of students by grade level.

Highlights

- Factors that impact academic performance, interact in complex ways, and operate differently in various cultures and education systems. There is no single formula for success.

- The IAEP results demonstrate what is *possible* for 9- and 13-year-olds to achieve in science. This information can be instructive for policy makers as they set goals and standards for their own young citizens.

- In almost all 13-year-old populations at least 10 percent of the students performed well (15 points or more above the IAEP average) and at least 10 percent performed poorly (15 points or more below the IAEP average).

- In nearly all populations, 13-year-old boys performed significantly better than girls that age. Nevertheless, in almost all populations, three-quarters or more of the students felt "science is for boys and girls about equally."

- Science tests and quizzes are most frequently used in Taiwan, the Soviet Union (Russian-speaking schools), the United States, and Jordan. From 67 to almost 90 percent of students take tests or quizzes at least once a week compared with fewer than one-half of the students from most other populations.

- Within individual populations, greater frequency of teacher presentations is associated with higher performance for the majority of IAEP participants, suggesting either the importance of the intensity of instruction in general or of this practice in particular.

- The highest-achieving countries with the exception of Taiwan do not practice ability grouping within science classes at age 13. In England(low participation) and Taiwan, more than one-half the schools reported this practice. All other populations were likely to form mixed-ability science classes.

- Thirteen-year-old students in most countries do not spend a great deal of time doing science homework. Between 55 and 90 percent of the students reported spending one hour or less *each week* in all populations except the Soviet Union (Russian-speaking schools) where 59 percent of the students spend four hours or more weekly on science homework.

- Thirteen-year-olds are much more likely to spend their spare time watching television than studying. The most common response is two to four hours of television viewing *each day* in all but two IAEP populations. Twenty percent or more of 13-year-olds from Israel (Hebrew), Scotland, the United States, England (low participation), and Fortaleza (restriced grades) indicated that they watch five hours or more of television each school day.

- Most students in most populations have positive attitudes about science, except students from Korea where only one quarter of these top-performing students exhibited positive attitudes; conversely, students in Jordan, who are relatively lower-performing have the greatest percentage of students with positive attitudes (82 percent).

- The range of average performance across the 14 populations participating in the IAEP assessment at age 9 was 13 points. In almost all populations, at least 10 percent of the students performed well (15 points or more above the IAEP average) and at least 10 percent performed poorly (15 points or more below the IAEP average).

- The difference in performance between 9- and 13-year-olds in each of the 14 populations ranged from 15 to 25 points.

Science Performance
of 13-Year-Olds

CHAPTER ONE

That is what learning is.
You suddenly understand
something you've understood all
of your life, but in a new way.

Doris Lessing, British Writer

The results presented in this chapter reflect some of what 13-year-olds know and can do in science in 19 countries. The percentages displayed in the figures represent the percentages of questions groups of students from the various populations answered correctly. In addition to total group averages, FIGURE 1.1 displays how the best students (top 10 percent) and the least successful (bottom 10 percent) from each population performed on the assessment. Next to each printed statistic, in parentheses, is an estimate of sampling error.[9] It is especially important to consider the imprecision in the estimates when comparing populations with similar results.

Results are presented separately for two groups in the assessment: **Comprehensive populations** and **populations with exclusions or low participation**. Comprehensive populations are those that included virtually all age-eligible students within a defined group, even if that group was

---

[9] The estimate of sampling error provided is a jackknifed standard error. It can be said with 95 percent certainty that for each population of interest the value for the whole population is within ± 2 standard errors of the estimate for the sample.

limited to a specific geographic area or certain language group. Populations with exclusions or low participation are those that excluded a significant proportion (more than 10 percent) of age-eligible students from within the defined group, typically because not all grade levels were assessed or some children were not in-school, or those where participation of the sampled schools and students was low (less than 70 percent).

In the figures that follow, two kinds of data are displayed: the comparative achievement results and some indicators of cultural and educational differences. These cultural and educational characteristics are drawn from referenced international databases, country questionnaires completed by the project directors, school questionnaires completed by school administrators, and student questionnaires completed by the assessed students. The source of each piece of descriptive data is indicated by a footnote.

The descriptive data permit easier and more thoughtful interpretation of the significance of achievement results. Key characteristics of participants, their educational systems, classrooms, homes, and students are presented, along with a graphic representation of achievement, in the attached fold-out CHART. The average percents correct and distributions of scores are repeated in Figure 1.1. After the introduction of overall achievement results in this chapter, they are discussed in more depth, along with contextual information, in the chapters that follow.

OVERALL SCIENCE RESULTS The red bars in Figure 1.1 indicate the average percent correct for each population and take into account the imprecision of these estimates due to sampling. When bars overlap with one another, as they do in many cases, the performance of these populations do not differ significantly.

The average score across comprehensive populations and populations with exclusion or low participation, represented by a vertical dashed line, is 67 percent.[10] Students from seven populations — France, Scotland, Spain (except Cataluña), the United States, England (low participation), and China (in-school population) — performed at or very near this IAEP average. As the overlapping bars on the figure indicate, in many cases, performance levels were essentially the same for these populations.

The highest-performing students were those in Korea, Taiwan, and Switzerland (15 cantons) with average percents correct that ranged between 74 and 78 percent. In Hungary, the Soviet Union (Russian-speaking schools), Slovenia, Emilia-Romagna, Israel (Hebrew), and Canada students achieved between 2 to 6 points above the IAEP average. Students from Ireland and Portugal (restricted grades) each performed 4 percentage points below the IAEP average. Jordan scored lower (with an average of 57 percent) and the two lowest-performing groups were the students assessed in São Paulo (restricted grades) and those in Fortaleza (restricted grades) where students scored 14 and 21 percentage points below the IAEP average, respectively.

As indicated by Figure 1.1 (Part 2), the performance of the individual Canadian populations that contribute to the overall Canada score ranged from 60 to 74 percent correct. However, as the overlapping bars indicate, the scores often are not significantly different from one population to the next. Five of the 14 Canadian populations assessed scored at or very near the IAEP average — Ontario (English), Manitoba (French), New Brunswick (English), Newfoundland, and Saskatchewan (French). The highest-performing Canadian populations, from highest to lowest were Alberta, British Columbia, Quebec (French), Saskatchewan (English), Quebec (English), Nova Scotia, and Manitoba (English). Only two Canadian populations, New Brunswick (French) and Ontario (French), scored below the IAEP average.

---

10 The IAEP average is the unweighted average of the scores of the comprehensive populations and populations with exclusions or low participation. An unweighted average was chosen to describe the midpoint because it is not influenced by the differential weights of very large and very small populations.

Science, Age 13
Distribution of Percent Correct Scores by Population*
Part 1

FIGURE 1.1

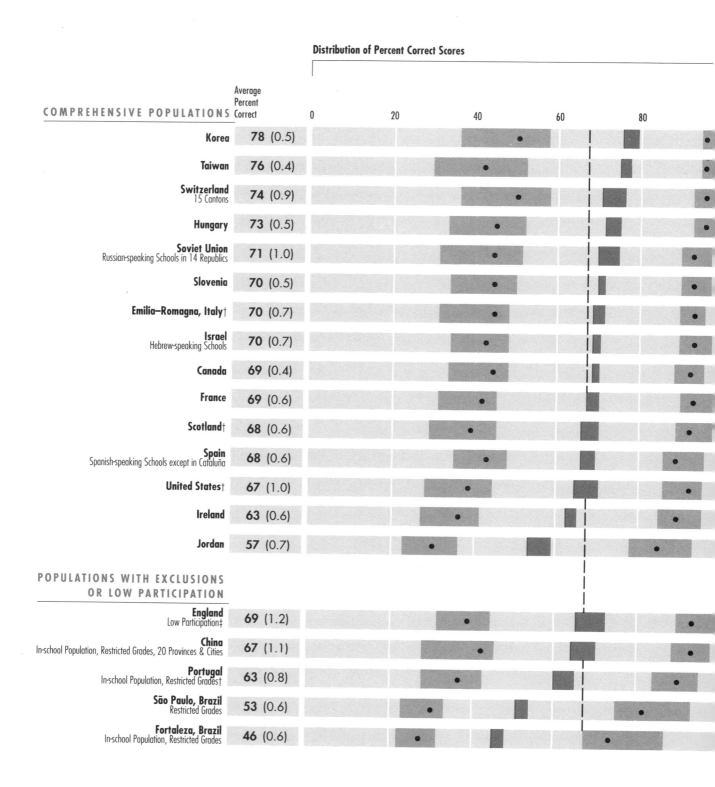

Distribution of Percent Correct Scores

COMPREHENSIVE POPULATIONS	Average Percent Correct						
		0	20	40	60	80	
Korea	78 (0.5)						
Taiwan	76 (0.4)						
Switzerland 15 Cantons	74 (0.9)						
Hungary	73 (0.5)						
Soviet Union Russian-speaking Schools in 14 Republics	71 (1.0)						
Slovenia	70 (0.5)						
Emilia–Romagna, Italy†	70 (0.7)						
Israel Hebrew-speaking Schools	70 (0.7)						
Canada	69 (0.4)						
France	69 (0.6)						
Scotland†	68 (0.6)						
Spain Spanish-speaking Schools except in Cataluña	68 (0.6)						
United States†	67 (1.0)						
Ireland	63 (0.6)						
Jordan	57 (0.7)						

POPULATIONS WITH EXCLUSIONS OR LOW PARTICIPATION

	Average Percent Correct						
England Low Participation‡	69 (1.2)						
China In-school Population, Restricted Grades, 20 Provinces & Cities	67 (1.1)						
Portugal In-school Population, Restricted Grades†	63 (0.8)						
São Paulo, Brazil Restricted Grades	53 (0.6)						
Fortaleza, Brazil In-school Population, Restricted Grades	46 (0.6)						

Average percent correct with simultaneous confidence interval controlling for all possible comparisons among comprehensive populations, populations with exclusions or low participation, and Canadian populations based on the Bonferroni procedure (the average ±2.78 standard errors).
Bullet is 5th and 95th percentile. ▪ are 1st to 10th percentiles and 90th to 99th percentiles.

⋮ IAEP Average

* Jackknifed standard errors are presented in parentheses.
† Combined school and student participation rate is below .80 but at least .70; interpret results with caution because of possible nonresponse bias.
‡ Combined school and student participation rate is below .70; interpret results with extreme caution because of possible nonresponse bias.

Science, Age 13
Distribution of Percent Correct Scores by Population*
Part 2

FIGURE 1.1

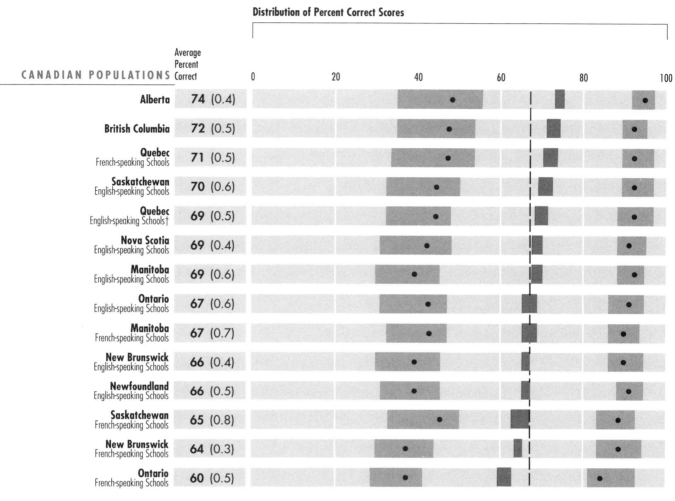

Distribution of Percent Correct Scores

CANADIAN POPULATIONS	Average Percent Correct	
Alberta	**74** (0.4)	
British Columbia	**72** (0.5)	
Quebec French-speaking Schools	**71** (0.5)	
Saskatchewan English-speaking Schools	**70** (0.6)	
Quebec English-speaking Schools†	**69** (0.5)	
Nova Scotia English-speaking Schools	**69** (0.4)	
Manitoba English-speaking Schools	**69** (0.6)	
Ontario English-speaking Schools	**67** (0.6)	
Manitoba French-speaking Schools	**67** (0.7)	
New Brunswick English-speaking Schools	**66** (0.4)	
Newfoundland English-speaking Schools	**66** (0.5)	
Saskatchewan French-speaking Schools	**65** (0.8)	
New Brunswick French-speaking Schools	**64** (0.3)	
Ontario French-speaking Schools	**60** (0.5)	

▬ Average percent correct with simultaneous confidence interval controlling for all possible comparisons among comprehensive populations, populations with exclusions or low participation and Canadian populations based on the Bonferroni procedure (the average ±2.78 standard errors).
● Bullet is 5th and 95th percentile. ▬ are 1st to 10th percentiles and 90th to 99th percentiles.

⋮ IAEP Average

* Jackknifed standard errors are presented in parentheses.
† Combined school and student participation rate is below .80 but at least .70; interpret results with caution because of possible nonresponse bias.

Achievement reflects the percent correct on 64 of 72 questions included in the assessment. Responses to eight questions were removed from the results after a series of data analysis steps demonstrated inconsistency of performance across countries, topics, or individual items. These procedures identified questions that were not functioning in the same way across all populations.[11] These items were not considered *bad items*, they simply did not seem to measure the same content or skill in all of the populations, probably because of curricular differences, or cultural or linguistic idiosyncracies.

___

[11] See the Procedural Appendix, pp. 140 - 141 and the *IAEP Technical Report* for a detailed discussion of cluster and differential item functioning analyses.

HIGH AND LOW ACHIEVERS Averages provide a useful picture of group performance in participating countries. However, the technological leaders of the 21st century will probably come from the highest-performing students in schools today. Figure 1.1 also shows the range of correct responses for the top-performing students from each participating country (the 90th through the 99th percentiles). These data reflect the achievement levels of the best students from each country. Of equal concern is what can be done to improve the results of each country's poorest performers. Also displayed are the range of results for the lowest-performing students in each population assessed (the 1st through the 10th percentiles). The average percents correct for students at the 5th and 95th percentiles are indicated by a bullet inside the shaded bar.[12]

Percentiles represent locations in the distribution of scores. If the average percent correct for the 5th percentile is 30 percent, it means that the 5 percent of the population who are the lowest scorers answered 30 percent or fewer of the questions correctly. If the average percent correct for the 95th percentile is 90, the 5 percent of the population who are the highest scorers answered 90 percent or more of the questions correctly.

The results for high and low achievers tend to mirror the averages, but they also demonstrate that in almost all populations there are some very good students (scoring at least 15 points above the IAEP average) and a number of poor performers (scoring at least 15 points below the IAEP average). Some marked differences can be noted among the participating countries. Korean students and students from Switzerland (15 cantons) in the 10th percentile perform at about the same level as the average Jordanian student. The best-performing students (90th percentile) from Fortaleza (restricted grades) performed just at the IAEP average.

SCIENCE PERFORMANCE BY GENDER FIGURE 1.2 reports the average science performance for males and females at age 13 and the degree to which students agreed that science is equally appropriate for both groups. It is particularly noteworthy that in nearly every population the majority of all students assessed agreed with the statement that "science is important for boys and girls about equally," despite a gender performance gap that was prevalent in nearly all of the populations. The performance of boys and girls is equivalent in only three participating countries, Taiwan, Jordan and England (low participation). In each of the remaining comprehensive populations and populations with exclusions or low participation, there was a significant gender gap favoring males.

---

[12] Performance of students at the very bottom of the distribution (the lowest 1 percent) and at the very top (the highest 1 percent) are not represented on the figure because very few students fall into these categories and their performance cannot be estimated with precision.

Science, Age 13

Percentages of Students Reporting Science Is Equally Important for Boys and Girls and Average Percents Correct*
Part 1

FIGURE 1.2

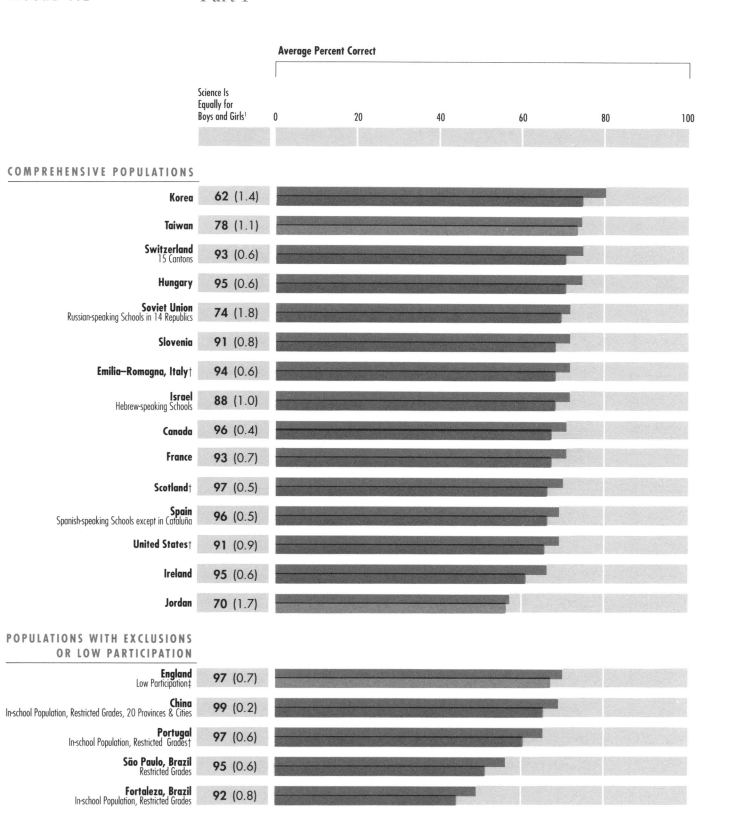

Average Percent Correct

	Science Is Equally for Boys and Girls[1]	Average Percent Correct
COMPREHENSIVE POPULATIONS		
Korea	62 (1.4)	
Taiwan	78 (1.1)	
Switzerland 15 Cantons	93 (0.6)	
Hungary	95 (0.6)	
Soviet Union Russian-speaking Schools in 14 Republics	74 (1.8)	
Slovenia	91 (0.8)	
Emilia–Romagna, Italy†	94 (0.6)	
Israel Hebrew-speaking Schools	88 (1.0)	
Canada	96 (0.4)	
France	93 (0.7)	
Scotland†	97 (0.5)	
Spain Spanish-speaking Schools except in Cataluña	96 (0.5)	
United States†	91 (0.9)	
Ireland	95 (0.6)	
Jordan	70 (1.7)	
POPULATIONS WITH EXCLUSIONS OR LOW PARTICIPATION		
England Low Participation‡	97 (0.7)	
China In-school Population, Restricted Grades, 20 Provinces & Cities	99 (0.2)	
Portugal In-school Population, Restricted Grades†	97 (0.6)	
São Paulo, Brazil Restricted Grades	95 (0.6)	
Fortaleza, Brazil In-school Population, Restricted Grades	92 (0.8)	

Males
Females
Statistically significant difference between groups at the .05 level.
* Jackknifed standard errors are presented in parentheses.
† Combined school and student participation rate is below .80 but at least .70; interpret results with caution because of possible nonresponse bias.
‡ Combined school and student participation rate is below .70; interpret results with extreme caution because of possible nonresponse bias.
[1] IAEP Student Questionnaire, Age 13.

 IAEP

FIGURE 1.2

Science, Age 13
Percentages of Students Reporting Science Is Equally Important for Boys and Girls and Average Percents Correct*
Part 2

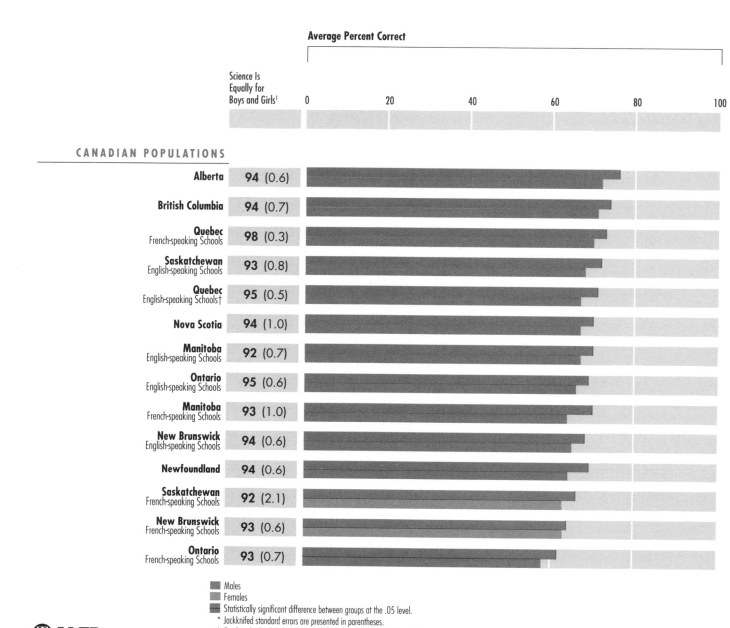

Average Percent Correct

	Science Is Equally for Boys and Girls[1]	0 — 20 — 40 — 60 — 80 — 100

CANADIAN POPULATIONS

Alberta	94 (0.6)	
British Columbia	94 (0.7)	
Quebec French-speaking Schools	98 (0.3)	
Saskatchewan English-speaking Schools	93 (0.8)	
Quebec English-speaking Schools†	95 (0.5)	
Nova Scotia	94 (1.0)	
Manitoba English-speaking Schools	92 (0.7)	
Ontario English-speaking Schools	95 (0.6)	
Manitoba French-speaking Schools	93 (1.0)	
New Brunswick English-speaking Schools	94 (0.6)	
Newfoundland	94 (0.6)	
Saskatchewan French-speaking Schools	92 (2.1)	
New Brunswick French-speaking Schools	93 (0.6)	
Ontario French-speaking Schools	93 (0.7)	

■ Males
■ Females
■ Statistically significant difference between groups at the .05 level.
 * Jackknifed standard errors are presented in parentheses.
 † Combined school and student participation rate is below .80 but at least .70; interpret results with caution because of possible nonresponse bias.
 [1] IAEP Student Questionnaire, Age 13.

IAEP

The largest performance gaps existed in São Paulo (restricted grades) where boys outperformed girls by about 7 percentage points. These findings in some cases support those of other international studies.[13]

It is curious that two countries, Taiwan and Jordan, which were more likely to view science as gender-linked, did not exhibit significant differences in performance by gender. In Taiwan, 20 percent of the

[13] For example, similar results were found for the populations that participated in the first IAEP study: England, Ireland, Korea, Spain, the United States, British Columbia, New Brunswick (English and French), Ontario (English and French), and Quebec (English and French).

students thought science was more for boys and only 2 percent felt it was more for girls; in Jordan, 18 percent of the students felt science was more for boys and 12 percent thought it was more for girls. In England (low participation), although the performance difference of girls and boys appears to be about 3 percentage points, when one considers the standard errors, the difference is not statistically significant.

In Korea less than two-thirds of the students believed science was equally for boys and girls. This was one of few populations where fewer than 90 percent of the students perceived science to be equally appropriate for boys and girls. However, the gap in achievement between Korean boys and girls is no larger than gender differences in Italy or Ireland for instance, where about 95 percent of the students believed science is equally important for boys and girls. A similar relationship exists in the Soviet Union (Russian-speaking schools) where only 74 percent of the students believed science was equally important for boys and girls. The difference in performance by gender for these students was no larger than in other populations where a significant majority had positive attitudes about the utility of science learning for both boys and girls.

During elementary school, both boys and girls are provided essentially the same opportunities to study science as noted in the tracking and ability grouping practices reported in Chapter Three, it is more likely that cultural expectations and socialization contribute to gender performance differences rather than instructional methods or student motivation.

For most Canadian populations, boys outperformed girls by about as much as they did for Canada as a whole. However, two provinces, Saskatchewan (French) and New Brunswick (French) are notable exceptions in that no statistically significant gender differences were apparent.

A FIRST LOOK AT RESULTS While science achievement ranged considerably, from 46 to 78 average percents correct, there is evidence of science capability in almost all populations as demonstrated by the performance of top the 10 percent of students from each population. The data from the bottom 10 percent remind us that even the most successful countries have students that need further help and encouragement.

Most students in most participating countries believe that science is equally important for boys and girls. Still in all but three participating populations, performance does not match attitude and 13-year-old boys achieved significantly better than girls.

While it is tempting to look only at which country is *Number 1*, the IAEP results can only be useful if they inform educators, policy makers, and the public about characteristics of low as well as high performers. To that end, the achievement results are examined in relation to school, home, and societal factors in the chapters that follow.

KOREA   September 20, 1990

A sunny, cold morning in downtown Seoul. The new middle-school building, housing 3,000 students at three different grade levels, along with its soccer field and play areas, is squeezed into a busy urban environment. Students streaming into the building are wearing a variety of international, early-teen-age garb reflecting the fact that this particular school does not require uniforms, a local option.

The noise level in the hallways before class is typical, universal student chatter, excited, interested, secretive, and frantic. At the bell, each classroom fills up with about 60, suddenly self-disciplined, quiet, and attentive young people. The front wall of the spotless room is a backdrop for a framed set of admonitions that translate into "Be Honest," "Be Diligent," "Show Respect to Elders." The rear wall is filled with Korean calligraphy and examples of student work.

At the middle-school levels, students are taught by subject matter specialists. The math teacher, a middle aged man, calls the names of the 13-year-olds in the room who have been selected as part of the IAEP sample. As each name is called, the student stands at attention at his or her desk until the list is complete. Then, to the supportive and encouraging applause of their colleagues, the chosen ones leave to find the large seminar room where the assessment will be administered.

The feeling of self discipline and serious attention to what they are about carries over into the assessment activity. Directions and procedures are scrupulously followed with no distractions by the student participants. Noise from an enthusiastic game on the soccer field is the sole reminder of the physical energy potential in the room.

This level of serious behavior is expected of students at middle school. During their elementary experience, until about age 10, the class sizes are smaller, only about 40 students to a room, and their parents are more heavily involved in the process, visiting schools often, and discussing their work with their children. However, at this age, 12, 13, 14, students are expected to be responsible for their own serious behavior.

ETS Quality Control Observer

The Curriculum

CHAPTER TWO

Könnyebb örökölni, mint tanulni.

It is easier to inherit
than to learn.

Hungarian Proverb

While politicians and the public may be most interested in the overall performance of children from various countries, these findings have only limited utility for educators charged with developing student competence. Knowledge and skills are taught in segments that are usually organized around topics featured in the curriculum and textbooks. Results showing that students performed poorly can only sound a general alarm. Teachers and administrators must know areas of strengths and weakness before they can target their limited time and resources.

While statistical analyses of the data confirm that questions across all of the topic areas can be summarized without masking important differences between countries, results by topics presented in this chapter show some variation.[14] This is understandable because countries differ in their

---

[14] A country-by-topic analysis using Hartigan and Wong's K-Means cluster analysis indicates that the differences in performance from topic to topic do not confound the main effects of overall performance. This means that the relative performance of countries would remain essentially the same if a group of items from a particular topic or topics was removed from the overall summary measure. More details of this analysis are provided in the Procedural Appendix, pp. 140-142 and in the *IAEP Technical Report*.

approaches to teaching science to 13-year-olds. While the IAEP assessment was based on a consensus description of the topics and skills that all countries report were taught in their schools and were appropriate for this age group, the assessment is not aligned with any specific country's curriculum.

The materials included in the assessment are neither given equal emphasis nor taught on the same time schedule in all participating countries. Furthermore, the importance ascribed to what *is not* covered by the IAEP assessment varies from country to country.

The results for 13-year-olds are presented for four content areas typically taught in science: **Life Sciences, Physical Sciences, Earth and Space Sciences,** and **Nature of Science**. All of the questions for the science assessment used a multiple-choice format. FIGURE 2.1 shows the number of questions devoted to each of these topics. All of the questions used a multiple-choice format.

FIGURE 2.1

Science, Age 13:
Number of Questions by Topic

Life Sciences	Physical Sciences	Earth and Space Sciences	Nature of Science	Total
19	25	9	11	64

LIFE SCIENCES At age 13, 19 questions (30 percent of the assessment) focused on Life Sciences. Samples of relatively difficult and relatively easy questions from this category are shown in FIGURE 2.2.[15] Short descriptions of all of the questions in this category and their average difficulty levels are provided in the Data Appendix along with the same information for items in the other three content areas. These questions for 13-year-olds assessed students' basic understanding of the science facts and knowledge that they were likely to encounter in everyday life. The major sub-topic categories in the assessment for Life Sciences are energy transformations, plants, animal behavior, and ecology. The questions required students to classify plants and animals, identify parts of the human anatomy, and make distinctions between mammals and reptiles.

---

[15] The difficulty level for sample questions for this and subsequent topics is an unweighted average of the item percent corrects across the comprehensive populations and populations with exclusions or low participation. These illustrative sample items are broad in context and are not intended to be indicative of all the skills students should possess in science.

FIGURE 2.2

Science, Age 13:
Sample Questions for Life Sciences

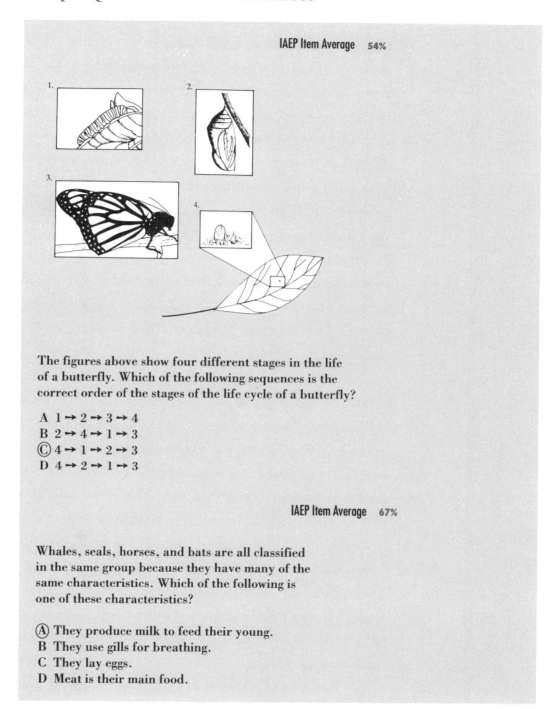

IAEP Item Average 54%

The figures above show four different stages in the life of a butterfly. Which of the following sequences is the correct order of the stages of the life cycle of a butterfly?

A 1 → 2 → 3 → 4
B 2 → 4 → 1 → 3
C 4 → 1 → 2 → 3
D 4 → 2 → 1 → 3

IAEP Item Average 67%

Whales, seals, horses, and bats are all classified in the same group because they have many of the same characteristics. Which of the following is one of these characteristics?

A They produce milk to feed their young.
B They use gills for breathing.
C They lay eggs.
D Meat is their main food.

Comprehensive populations and populations with exclusions or low participation are listed in order of performance across all science questions in FIGURE 2.3. The bars display both the IAEP average across all the populations and the average percent correct for each population for Life Sciences.

In general, the performance of the two groups on this topic mirrors their overall achievement in science. This is shown by the red bars representing the topic averages which generally follow the same pattern as the bars representing overall averages in Figure 1.1 in Chapter One. The patterns of performance were examined to see if the performance of a population in a particular topic area was different from its overall performance and some exceptions were identified. Since the average difficulty level of the questions in the various topics and across all topics differs, performance was examined in relative terms. The difference between a population's topic average and the IAEP topic average was compared with the difference between the population's overall average and the IAEP overall average. If the difference between those deviations was greater than what might be expected due to sampling error, the population's performance on that topic was identified as an exception. In some cases, performance in a topic was identified as higher compared to achievement overall. In some cases it was identified as relatively lower than performance in general.[16]

For example, students in Hungary were identified as performing at relatively higher levels in Life Sciences than they did overall, because in this topic, these students scored 9 points higher than the IAEP Life Sciences average of 68 while they performed 6 points higher than the overall science average of 67. Students assessed in Fortaleza (restricted grades) also performed better in this topic area than they did in science overall. Students assessed in Israel (Hebrew) were identified as performing less well in Life Sciences relative to their performance overall, because they scored 3 points below the IAEP topic average but scored about 3 points above the IAEP average overall. In both cases, these differences, in absolute terms, are greater than would be expected due to sampling error. Ireland and China (in-school population) scored lower in this topic relative to their overall science achievement.

Patterns of instruction vary from country to country, sometimes in ways that are not always congruent with performance. To better understand how these instructional differences may have affected student performance, IAEP asked school administrators in sampled schools to indicate the relative emphasis they placed on several of the subtopics within each of the main topic areas.

---

16 For these analyses of achievement by topic, populations are cited as deviating from their normal pattern if the difference between their deviation from the mean for the topic and their deviation from the overall mean is twice the standard error of the difference between these deviations, or greater. Further details of these analyses is provided in the Procedural Appendix, pp. 140-142 and the *IAEP Technical Report.*

Science, Age 13
Percentages of Schools that Emphasize Life Science Sub-topics and Average Percents Correct*

FIGURE 2.3

	Percent of Schools Emphasizing A Lot[1]			Average Percent Correct					
	Plants	Animals	Human Body	0	20	40	60	80	100

COMPREHENSIVE POPULATIONS

	Plants	Animals	Human Body
IAEP Topic Average			
Korea	47 (7.3)	64 (6.7)	64 (7.3)
Taiwan	15 (2.9)	18 (3.2)	11 (2.8)
Switzerland 15 Cantons	36 (5.5)§	38 (6.9)§	54 (8.3)§
Hungary	66 (6.7)	74 (6.3)	74 (6.0)
Soviet Union Russian-speaking Schools in 14 Republics	47 (4.9)	95 (2.2)	28 (4.8)
Slovenia	4 (1.7)	12 (9.4)	97 (1.8)
Emilia-Romagna, Italy†	18 (3.8)	18 (4.6)	45 (5.1)
Israel Hebrew-speaking Schools	36 (6.8)	37 (5.8)	21 (5.7)
Canada	21 (1.9)	19 (2.1)	11 (1.2)
France	1 (0.7)	1 (0.7)	18 (4.1)
Scotland†	16 (5.6)	18 (5.9)	42 (7.2)
Spain Spanish-speaking Schools except in Cataluña	46 (6.6)	46 (6.9)	74 (5.9)
United States†	25 (***)	25 (***)	23 (***)
Ireland	40 (6.3)	38 (6.2)	60 (5.1)
Jordan	31 (***)	14 (***)	29 (7.8)

POPULATIONS WITH EXCLUSIONS OR LOW PARTICIPATION

	Plants	Animals	Human Body
England Low Participation‡	12 (5.6)	23 (8.0)	28 (7.6)
China In-school Population, Restricted Grades, 20 Provinces & Cities	19 (4.7)	79 (7.0)	11 (3.9)
Portugal In-school Population, Restricted Grades†	42 (7.7)	49 (8.9)	5 (4.3)
São Paulo, Brazil Restricted Grades	12 (4.8)	14 (4.5)	93 (3.0)
Fortaleza, Brazil In-school Population, Restricted Grades	24 (7.8)	31 (8.4)	93 (4.1)

* Jackknifed standard errors are presented in parentheses.
*** Jackknifed standard error is greater than 9.9.
† Combined school and student participation rate is below .80 but at least .70; interpret results with caution because of Iof possible nonresponse bias.
‡ Combined school and student participation rate is below .70; interpret results with extreme caution because of possible nonresponse bias.
§ Results represent percent of classrooms in schools.
[1] IAEP School Questionnaire, Age 13.

School administrators were asked if students in the modal grade for 13-year-olds in their country (typically grade 7 or 8) studied a particular subtopic "a lot," "some," or "not at all" and their responses were examined to determine if high or low emphasis was related to student achievement.[17] For almost all populations across each of the four topic areas — Life Sciences, Physical Sciences, Earth and Space Sciences, and Nature of Science — the emphasis that schools devoted to many of the subtopics varied dramatically but could not consistently be linked to performance. For example, schools in Taiwan reported emphasizing the major subtopics of Life Sciences a lot less than schools in Korea and Hungary, yet Taiwanese students performed just as well as their counterparts in the other two countries.

However, this lack of a clear relationship between curricular emphases and achievement does not imply that what is being emphasized in school does not affect what students know and can do. The results suggest that often the classroom is probably not the only place children learn to apply science skills and that students also extend their skills outside of school. Also, some aspects of science such as the use and integration of skills are not necessarily specific to the science curriculum and are sometimes interdisciplinary in nature.

PHYSICAL SCIENCES The 25 questions for age 13 that focused on the Physical Sciences topic area represent 39 percent of the total assessment questions and measured students' knowledge of fundamental components of the natural universe — space, time, matter, and energy. Students were asked to infer from diagrams, interpret simple graphs, and answer questions about motion, mass, electricity, circuitry, properties of matter, chemical reactions, and changes. FIGURE 2.4 illustrates sample items from the assessment and FIGURE 2.5 shows the emphasis each population assigned to the Physical Sciences subtopics and their performance in this content area.

In every population, students performed in this topic area at relatively the same level as they did in science overall. While students from some populations performed slightly better and others performed slightly worse on items within this area, compared to their performance overall, none of the differences were statistically significant. Emphasis on Physical Sciences subtopics at this age level differed considerably from country to country.

---

[17] Several questions in the IAEP age 13 school questionnaire focused on the teachers and educational program for the grade in which most 13-year-olds are enrolled, or the modal grade. Each country tailored its questionnaire to indicate the appropriate title for that grade — e.g., junior high 2 in Korea and Taiwan, 7th class in German Switzerland, 8th year in French and Italian Switzerland.

FIGURE 2.4

Science, Age 13:
Sample Test Question for Physical Sciences

IAEP Item Average   Question 1: 46%
                                            Question 2: 61%

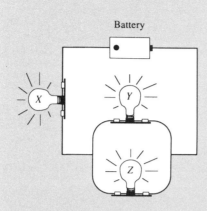

Questions 1 and 2 refer to the diagram of an electrical circuit in which there are three identical light bulbs labeled *X, Y, Z*. Each bulb is glowing.

1. Which bulbs would be equally bright?

   A *X and Y*
   B *X and Z*
   Ⓒ *Y and Z*
   D *X, Y, and Z*

2. If one particular bulb is taken out of this circuit, the others will not light. Which one could be taken out to stop the other bulbs from lighting?

   Ⓐ *X only*
   B *Y only*
   C *Z only*
   D *Either Z or Y*

IAEP Item Average   76%

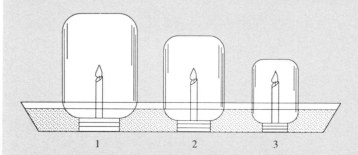

As shown above, jars were placed over identical lighted candles at the same time. Which of the following will happen?

A All flames will go out immediately
B The flames will go out in this order: 1, 2, 3.
Ⓒ The flames will go out in this order: 3, 2, 1.
D The candles will burn awhile, and then all the flames will go out at the same time.

Science, Age 13
Percentages of Schools that Emphasize Physical Science Sub-topics and Average Percent Correct*

FIGURE 2.5

	Percent of Schools Emphasizing A Lot[1]					Average Percent Correct					
	Electricity and Magnetism	Mass Motion and Gravity	Chemical Substances	Light and Sound	Solids, Liquids, and Gases	0	20	40	60	80	100

COMPREHENSIVE POPULATIONS

	Electricity and Magnetism	Mass Motion and Gravity	Chemical Substances	Light and Sound	Solids, Liquids, and Gases	Average Percent Correct
IAEP Topic Average						
Korea	84 (4.4)	10 (3.3)	11 (3.7)	2 (1.4)	19 (4.5)	
Taiwan	11 (3.8)	81 (4.3)	20 (5.4)	7 (2.3)	56 (7.2)	
Switzerland 15 Cantons	16 (5.9)§	17 (3.8)§	7 (4.6)§	7 (2.9)§	10 (3.5)§	
Hungary	80 (5.5)	15 (5.2)	24 (4.8)	3 (1.3)	32 (6.6)	
Soviet Union Russian-speaking Schools in 14 Republics	70 (2.9)	32 (5.7)	87 (3.2)	35 (4.7)	63 (8.5)	
Slovenia	14 (4.2)	31 (7.0)	91 (3.6)	42 (5.5)	75 (7.4)	
Emilia-Romagna, Italy†	62 (6.8)	45 (5.6)	13 (4.6)	34 (5.9)	33 (5.1)	
Israel Hebrew-speaking Schools	59 (7.2)	35 (6.7)	67 (7.4)	13 (4.5)	75 (5.2)	
Canada	17 (1.9)	32 (1.8)	18 (1.9)	9 (1.3)	51 (2.4)	
France	46 (7.4)	3 (1.6)	10 (3.2)	29 (5.2)	12 (3.3)	
Scotland†	42 (6.6)	20 (4.6)	49 (8.0)	41 (7.3)	31 (6.7)	
Spain Spanish-speaking Schools except in Cataluña	46 (6.2)	42 (7.1)	65 (6.2)	35 (5.9)	45 (7.6)	
United States†	19 (***)	40 (9.8)	23 (***)	20 (***)	39 (***)	
Ireland	34 (6.0)	39 (4.8)	36 (6.0)	27 (4.9)	54 (6.1)	
Jordan	74 (6.9)	51 (9.9)	62 (8.4)	10 (5.4)	13 (5.7)	

POPULATIONS WITH EXCLUSIONS OR LOW PARTICIPATION

	Electricity and Magnetism	Mass Motion and Gravity	Chemical Substances	Light and Sound	Solids, Liquids, and Gases	Average Percent Correct
England Low Participation‡	39 (***)	17 (5.3)	45 (***)	26 (8.0)	40 (***)	
China In-school Population, Restricted Grades, 20 Provinces & Cities	14 (6.3)	62 (4.6)	5 (2.2)	15 (4.4)	27 (6.2)	
Portugal In-school Population, Restricted Grades†	37 (8.3)	1 (0.5)	38 (8.1)	5 (2.1)	23 (6.9)	
São Paulo, Brazil Restricted Grades	3 (1.7)	2 (1.5)	4 (2.0)	4 (1.9)	5 (2.3)	
Fortaleza, Brazil In-school Population, Restricted Grades	18 (9.2)	17 (8.9)	21 (8.2)	20 (9.4)	22 (8.9)	

* Jackknifed standard errors are presented in parentheses.
*** Jackknifed standard error is greater than 9.9.
† Combined school and student participation rate is below .80 but at least .70; interpret results with caution because of possible nonresponse bias.
‡ Combined school and student participation rate is below .70; interpret results with extreme caution because of possible nonresponse bias.
§ Results represent percent of classrooms in schools.
[1] IAEP School Questionnaire, Age 13.

At age 13, the Earth and Space Sciences domain included nine questions that represented 14 percent of the assessment and measured students' knowledge of the solar system, water cycles, fossils, and soil erosion.

For most participating countries, the patterns of performance in this topic area generally mirror overall performance. The exceptions were Taiwan and Scotland where students scored lower compared to their performance in science overall. However, relatively few schools in Taiwan and Scotland gave Earth and Space Sciences subtopics much emphasis in their curricula. Students from Jordan and São Paulo (restricted grades) scored higher in this topic area compared with their scores overall in science. Most schools in Jordan devoted a lot of time to two of the major categories for Earth and Space Sciences — weather and climate, and stars and planets — while schools in São Paulo (restricted grades) gave less emphasis to the subtopics in this area. FIGURES 2.6 and 2.7 provide sample items and the emphasis and performance for each population in Earth and Space Sciences.

FIGURE 2.6

Science, Age 13:
Sample Test Questions for Earth and Space Sciences

IAEP Item Average   54%

Sun

○ Moon   ◯ Earth

When the Moon, the Earth, and the Sun are in the same line, as shown above, which of the following would occur?

(A) An eclipse of the Sun would occur.
B An eclipse of the Moon would occur.
C The Moon would be pulled out of its orbit and toward the Sun.
D The spin of the Earth would be speeded up.

IAEP Item Average   78%

The Moon produces no light, and yet it shines at night. What is the best explanation for this?

(A) It reflects the light from the Sun.

B It rotates at a very high speed.

C It is covered with a thin layer of ice.

D It has many craters.

Science, Age 13
Percentages of Schools that Emphasize Earth and Space Sciences Sub-topics and Average Percents Correct*

FIGURE 2.7

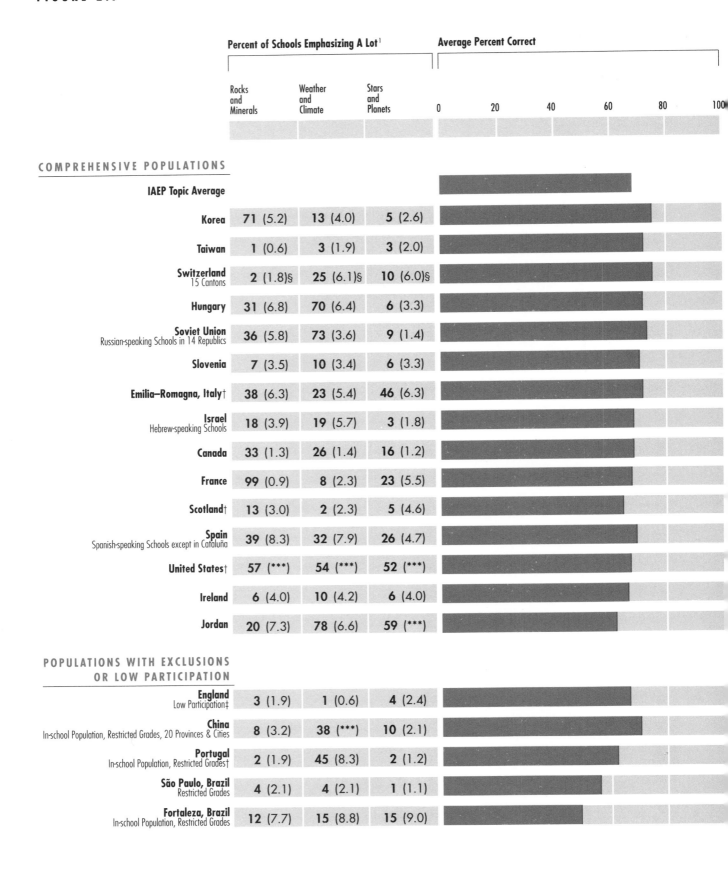

	Percent of Schools Emphasizing A Lot[1]			Average Percent Correct					
	Rocks and Minerals	Weather and Climate	Stars and Planets	0	20	40	60	80	100

COMPREHENSIVE POPULATIONS

	Rocks and Minerals	Weather and Climate	Stars and Planets
IAEP Topic Average			
Korea	71 (5.2)	13 (4.0)	5 (2.6)
Taiwan	1 (0.6)	3 (1.9)	3 (2.0)
Switzerland 15 Cantons	2 (1.8)§	25 (6.1)§	10 (6.0)§
Hungary	31 (6.8)	70 (6.4)	6 (3.3)
Soviet Union Russian-speaking Schools in 14 Republics	36 (5.8)	73 (3.6)	9 (1.4)
Slovenia	7 (3.5)	10 (3.4)	6 (3.3)
Emilia–Romagna, Italy†	38 (6.3)	23 (5.4)	46 (6.3)
Israel Hebrew-speaking Schools	18 (3.9)	19 (5.7)	3 (1.8)
Canada	33 (1.3)	26 (1.4)	16 (1.2)
France	99 (0.9)	8 (2.3)	23 (5.5)
Scotland†	13 (3.0)	2 (2.3)	5 (4.6)
Spain Spanish-speaking Schools except in Cataluña	39 (8.3)	32 (7.9)	26 (4.7)
United States†	57 (***)	54 (***)	52 (***)
Ireland	6 (4.0)	10 (4.2)	6 (4.0)
Jordan	20 (7.3)	78 (6.6)	59 (***)

POPULATIONS WITH EXCLUSIONS OR LOW PARTICIPATION

	Rocks and Minerals	Weather and Climate	Stars and Planets
England Low Participation‡	3 (1.9)	1 (0.6)	4 (2.4)
China In-school Population, Restricted Grades, 20 Provinces & Cities	8 (3.2)	38 (***)	10 (2.1)
Portugal In-school Population, Restricted Grades†	2 (1.9)	45 (8.3)	2 (1.2)
São Paulo, Brazil Restricted Grades	4 (2.1)	4 (2.1)	1 (1.1)
Fortaleza, Brazil In-school Population, Restricted Grades	12 (7.7)	15 (8.8)	15 (9.0)

* Jackknifed standard errors are presented in parentheses.
*** Jackknifed standard error is greater than 9.9.
† Combined school and student participation rate is below .80 but at least .70; interpret results with caution because of possible nonresponse bias.
‡ Combined school and student participation rate is below .70; interpret results with extreme caution because of possible nonresponse bias.
§ Results represent percent of classrooms in schools.
[1] IAEP School Questionnaire, Age 13.

Nature of Science is an overarching topic area that encompasses the fundamentals of scientific literacy. The 11 questions in this area focus on students' ability to interpret data from graphs, charts, and diagrams, to formulate hypotheses, and to deduce results from described experiments (see examples in FIGURE 2.8). Nature of Science questions represent 17 percent of the science assessment at age 13.

FIGURE 2.8

Science, Age 13:
Sample Test Questions for Nature of Science

IAEP Item Average   **54%**

A student did an experiment in which bread mold was grown in three containers kept at three different temperatures. Each container had an equal amount of nutrients for the mold. At the end of four days, the amounts in each container were compared.
The student was testing to see if the amount of bread mold produced depended on which of the following?

A The number of days that the mold grew
Ⓑ The temperature of the container
C The amount of nutrients in each container
D The number of containers used in the experiment

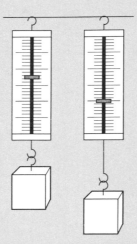

IAEP Item Average   **82%**

The two blocks are attached to identical scales, as shown in the figure above. Which of the following is a correct statement about what can be seen in the picture?

Ⓐ The two blocks have different weights.
B The two block have different volumes.
C The two blocks are hollow.
D The two block are made of the same material.

A large number of exceptions to overall patterns of performance may be seen in FIGURE 2.9. Six populations performed at relatively higher levels in this topic than they did overall: Israel (Hebrew), Canada, France, Scotland, the United States, and Ireland. Students from the following populations performed at lower levels in this topic area compared with their overall performance: Taiwan, the Soviet Union (Russian-speaking schools), Jordan, and São Paulo (restricted grades), and Fortaleza (restricted grades). Less than 20 percent of the schools in Jordan, São Paulo (restricted grades), and Fortaleza (restricted grades) emphasized Nature of Science subtopics at this age level, which may explain their relatively low performance.

Science, Age 13
Percentages of Schools that Emphasize Nature of Science Sub-topics and Average Percents Correct*

FIGURE 2.9

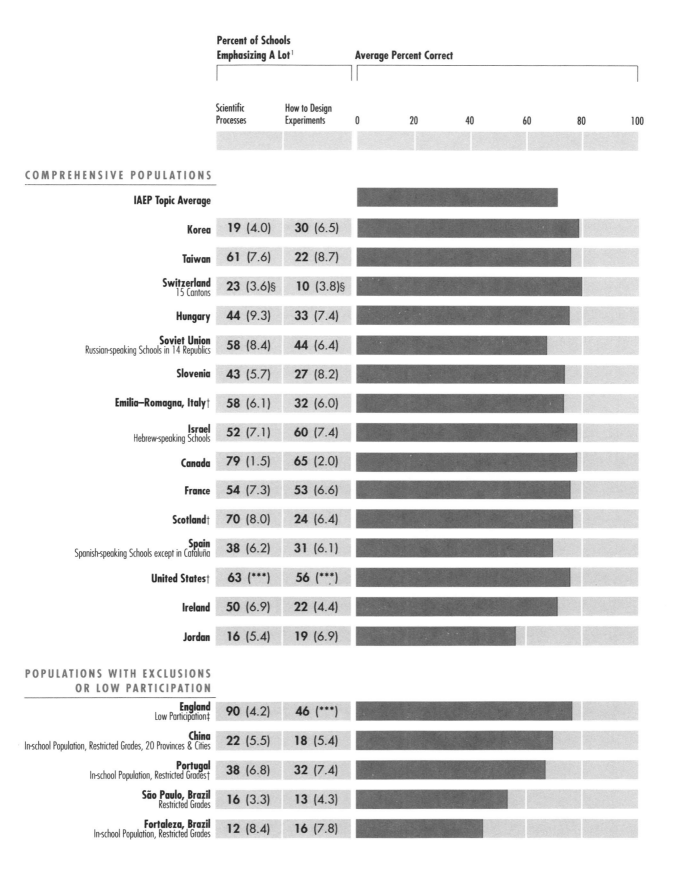

	Percent of Schools Emphasizing A Lot [1]		Average Percent Correct					
	Scientific Processes	How to Design Experiments	0	20	40	60	80	100
COMPREHENSIVE POPULATIONS								
IAEP Topic Average								
Korea	19 (4.0)	30 (6.5)						
Taiwan	61 (7.6)	22 (8.7)						
Switzerland 15 Cantons	23 (3.6)§	10 (3.8)§						
Hungary	44 (9.3)	33 (7.4)						
Soviet Union Russian-speaking Schools in 14 Republics	58 (8.4)	44 (6.4)						
Slovenia	43 (5.7)	27 (8.2)						
Emilia–Romagna, Italy†	58 (6.1)	32 (6.0)						
Israel Hebrew-speaking Schools	52 (7.1)	60 (7.4)						
Canada	79 (1.5)	65 (2.0)						
France	54 (7.3)	53 (6.6)						
Scotland†	70 (8.0)	24 (6.4)						
Spain Spanish-speaking Schools except in Cataluña	38 (6.2)	31 (6.1)						
United States†	63 (***)	56 (***)						
Ireland	50 (6.9)	22 (4.4)						
Jordan	16 (5.4)	19 (6.9)						
POPULATIONS WITH EXCLUSIONS OR LOW PARTICIPATION								
England Low Participation‡	90 (4.2)	46 (***)						
China In-school Population, Restricted Grades, 20 Provinces & Cities	22 (5.5)	18 (5.4)						
Portugal In-school Population, Restricted Grades†	38 (6.8)	32 (7.4)						
São Paulo, Brazil Restricted Grades	16 (3.3)	13 (4.3)						
Fortaleza, Brazil In-school Population, Restricted Grades	12 (8.4)	16 (7.8)						

* Jackknifed standard errors are presented in parentheses.
*** Jackknifed standard error is greater than 9.9.
† Combined school and student participation rate is below .80 but at least .70; interpret results with caution because of possible nonresponse bias.
‡ Combined school and student participation rate is below .70; interpret results with extreme caution because of possible nonresponse bias.
§ Results represent percent of classrooms in schools.
[1] IAEP School Questionnaire, Age 13.

SCIENCE PROCESSES In looking for ways to improve students' science performance, educators are focusing as much on the science processes that students must use as on the content of specific topics. Science specialists in the United States are now recommending that teachers focus on cognitive processes through problem solving, communication, and reasoning tasks.[18]

In an attempt to reflect these emphases, IAEP participants included questions at three levels of cognitive processing: **Knows Science, Uses Science,** and **Integrates Science.** The assessment questions were distributed so that 23 percent of the questions fit into the Knows Science category, 48 percent into Uses Science, and the remaining 28 percent into Integrates Science.[19]

Knows Science questions required students to exhibit basic knowledge of everyday science facts and concepts. For example, students should be able to demonstrate a knowledge of basic scientific terminology and principles, to read simple graphs, and to match distinguishing characteristics of animals and plants. This category generally involved a one-step cognitive approach. To complete Uses Science tasks students had to combine factual knowledge with rules and formulas for a specific purpose. Students who performed these tasks have developed some understanding of simple scientific principles, could interpret data from simple tables, and could make inferences about the outcomes of experimental procedures. This category usually involved a two-step process. Integrates Science tasks involved a multi-step process requiring students to draw conclusions on the basis of available data. Students were to generalize, hypothesize, and reason by synthesizing specific information.

It is difficult to know exactly what processes students use to solve problems. A student who has studied a topic and is familiar with its components may simply recall facts; another student who has no experience with the task may have to use reasoning skills to solve the problem. It is difficult to make distinctions between any of the three cognitive areas considering that students almost certainly need to apply the ability learned from Uses Science, for instance, to successfully complete tasks that are classified as Integrates Science. The classifications of cognitive skills are not meant to be hierarchical; moreover, there are difficult and easy items for each of the process areas.

FIGURE 2.10 (Part 1 and Part 2) presents the results for comprehensive populations and populations with exclusions or low participation by science cognitive abilities.

[18] For example, in the United States see Ina V.S. Mullis et al., *Trends in Academic Progress*, National Assessment of Educational Progress, Educational Testing Service, Princeton, NJ: 1991.

[19] Percentages do not total 100 because of rounding.

Science, Age 13
Average Percents Correct by Cognitive Process
Part 1

FIGURE 2.10

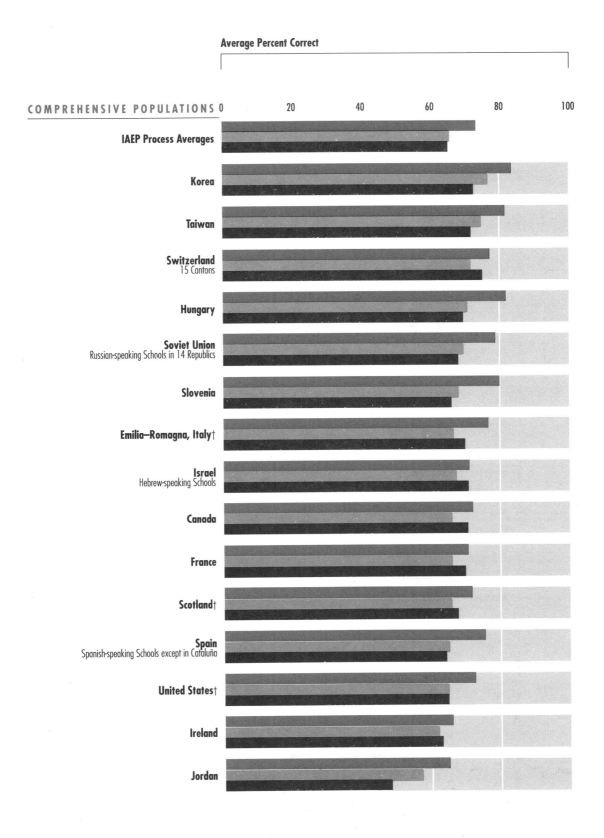

Average Percent Correct

COMPREHENSIVE POPULATIONS

IAEP Process Averages

Korea

Taiwan

Switzerland
15 Cantons

Hungary

Soviet Union
Russian-speaking Schools in 14 Republics

Slovenia

Emilia–Romagna, Italy†

Israel
Hebrew-speaking Schools

Canada

France

Scotland†

Spain
Spanish-speaking Schools except in Cataluña

United States†

Ireland

Jordan

Knows
Uses
Integrates

† Combined school and student participation rate is below .80 but at least .70; interpret results with caution because of possible nonresponse bias.

Students from most all populations performed particularly well in the Knows Science category. However, five populations obtained lower scores in this area relative to their overall performance: Israel (Hebrew), Canada, France, Ireland, and China (in-school population). Students from Hungary, Slovenia, Spain (except Cataluña), Jordan, and Fortaleza (restricted grades) did particularly well in the knowledge items compared with their performance overall.

Science, Age 13
Average Percents Correct By Cognitive Process
Part 2

FIGURE 2.10

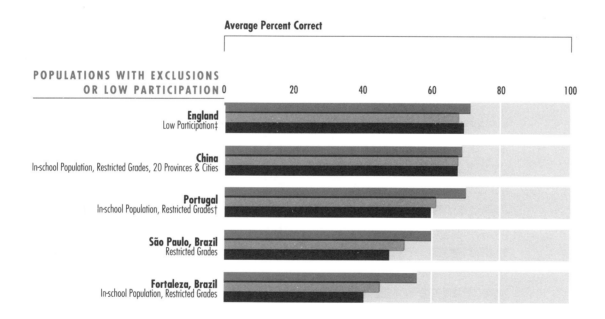

Average Percent Correct

POPULATIONS WITH EXCLUSIONS OR LOW PARTICIPATION

England
Low Participation‡

China
In-school Population, Restricted Grades, 20 Provinces & Cities

Portugal
In-school Population, Restricted Grades†

São Paulo, Brazil
Restricted Grades

Fortaleza, Brazil
In-school Population, Restricted Grades

Knows
Uses
Integrates

† Combined school and student participation rate is below .80 but at least .70; interpret results with caution because of possible nonresponse bias.
‡ Combined school and student participation rate is below .70; interpret results with extreme caution because of possible nonresponse bias.

Typically, performance in Uses and Integrates Science is somewhat lower than performance on the Knowledge items. In all populations, students performed relatively the same on the Uses Science questions as on their performance overall. Patterns of performance on the Integrates Science questions differed from overall performance. Students from Israel (Hebrew), Canada, and France scored relatively higher in this area than they did in science in general and students from Korea, Jordan, São Paulo (restricted grades), and Fortaleza (restricted grades) scored relatively lower than they did overall.

PERFORMANCE OF CANADIAN POPULATIONS The performance of Canadian populations in each of the content and process categories, presented in FIGURE 2.11, mirror their performance overall with only a few exceptions.

Alberta, British Columbia, and New Brunswick (French) performed relatively less well in Life Sciences than they did overall; all Canadian populations performed at relatively the same levels in Physical Sciences as they did overall. In Earth and Space Sciences only Saskatchewan (French) scored relatively higher than overall and every population except Manitoba (French) and New Brunswick (French) performed relatively better than they did overall in Nature of Science.

The achievement levels of the Canadian populations in each of the process categories — Knows Science, Uses Science, and Integrates Science showed some variation from overall achievement.

Science, Age 13
Average Percents Correct by Topics and Cognitive Process for Canadian Populations*

FIGURE 2.11

	Topics				Cognitive Processes		
	Life Sciences	Physical Sciences	Earth and Space Sciences	Nature of Science	Knows	Uses	Integrates
IAEP Averages	68 (0.5)	64 (0.5)	67 (0.7)	71 (0.8)	73 (0.6)	65 (0.4)	65 (0.8)
CANADIAN POPULATIONS							
Alberta	72 (0.5)	71 (0.5)	74 (0.5)	84 (0.5)	76 (0.5)	72 (0.4)	76 (0.6)
British Columbia	70 (0.5)	71 (0.5)	72 (0.6)	81 (0.6)	76 (0.5)	70 (0.5)	74 (0.6)
Quebec French-speaking Schools	73 (0.5)	67 (0.6)	70 (0.6)	80 (0.6)	74 (0.6)	69 (0.5)	74 (0.7)
Saskatchewan English-speaking Schools	71 (0.6)	65 (0.7)	72 (0.7)	80 (0.6)	74 (0.6)	68 (0.5)	70 (0.8)
Quebec English-speaking Schools†	69 (0.5)	65 (0.6)	68 (0.6)	81 (0.6)	73 (0.6)	66 (0.5)	71 (0.7)
Nova Scotia	68 (0.5)	66 (0.4)	69 (0.5)	76 (0.9)	72 (0.4)	68 (0.4)	68 (0.8)
Manitoba English-speaking Schools	68 (0.6)	65 (0.6)	71 (0.6)	77 (0.7)	73 (0.6)	67 (0.5)	68 (0.7)
Ontario English-speaking Schools	66 (0.6)	63 (0.7)	66 (0.6)	78 (0.7)	70 (0.6)	64 (0.6)	69 (0.8)
Manitoba French-speaking Schools	65 (0.8)	64 (0.8)	67 (0.7)	73 (0.9)	70 (0.8)	64 (0.7)	68 (1.0)
New Brunswick English-speaking Schools	66 (0.4)	63 (0.4)	66 (0.5)	75 (0.4)	70 (0.4)	65 (0.4)	67 (0.5)
Newfoundland	65 (0.6)	62 (0.5)	69 (0.7)	75 (0.6)	70 (0.6)	65 (0.5)	66 (0.6)
Saskatchewan French-speaking Schools	64 (1.1)	60 (1.1)	68 (0.9)	74 (1.1)	68 (1.1)	62 (0.8)	67 (1.2)
New Brunswick French-speaking Schools	62 (0.4)	62 (0.4)	65 (0.4)	69 (0.5)	64 (0.5)	63 (0.3)	64 (0.5)
Ontario French-speaking Schools	61 (0.6)	56 (0.6)	61 (0.6)	68 (0.8)	62 (0.7)	59 (0.5)	61 (0.7)

* Jackknifed standard errors are presented in parentheses.
† Combined school and student participation rate is below .80 but at least .70; interpret results with caution because of possible nonresponse bias.

In the Knows Science category, six populations — Alberta, Quebec (French), Nova Scotia, Ontario (English), New Brunswick (French), and Ontario (French) — all scored relatively lower than their overall science performance; the remaining populations were relatively the same as their overall science achievement. In Uses Science, all populations performed at about the same levels compared with their performance overall. Canadian populations performed well in the Integrates Science category with more than half the populations — Alberta, British Columbia, Quebec (French), Quebec (English), Ontario (English), Manitoba (French), Saskatchewan (French) and Ontario (French) — performing relatively higher in this cognitive area than in science overall.

CURRICULUM DOES MAKE A DIFFERENCE Participating countries' school administrators were asked about the level of emphasis their schools placed on the specific topics that were measured and student performance was compared to their reports of high and low emphases. Responses indicate that both across and within participating countries, there is a lot of variation in what subtopics are taught to 13-year-olds and that these differences from topic to topic are not always consistently related to performance.

Only in Nature of Science was there some correspondence between what is being emphasized in the classroom and student performance. In populations that emphasize the Nature of Science topics less often, students tended to perform less well in this topic area and less well on the science assessment overall.

SWITZERLAND   *March 26, 1991*

In a small village in the Canton of Bern, in German Switzerland, there is a lovely school campus — a square of traditional Swiss buildings that house the elementary, middle, and secondary schools. The formal, neatly-landscaped garden in the center is green, yellow, and purple with abundant grass, daffodils, crocuses, and hyacinths. The church next door completes a beautiful picture. If it weren't 7 a.m. on a cold, misty morning in March, I would probably be happy to be here.

When we enter the building marked "Middle School," the impression continues. Everything is neat and orderly, even the temperature inside is Teutonic. The sixteen, 13-year-olds are handsome, alert, and smiling. They and an excited teacher are looking forward to a good time. The teacher explains with some pride that one boy is absent because he is playing soccer in England with the Swiss national youth team.

The booklets are passed out and the cover information is handled in a business-like manner by the teacher. When he instructs the class to read the instructions for the test along with him, there follows a spirited choral reading aloud that commands everyone's attention.

After the exercise, they answer our questions and think the test questions are difficult but interesting. This is a rural, agricultural area and a very small percentage (8 to 12 percent) will go on to universities. Most will follow other paths toward work and apprenticeships.

The National Coordinator and I are both pleased at the efficient and orderly administration with instructions read verbatim and time limits precisely met. the National Coordinator had no idea what to expect and he assured me that the test was typical of the "feedback" he has been getting from all but one or two of the teachers involved.

We thanked the students and the teacher, started back and stopped in the oldest, still-operating restaurant in Switzerland for coffee. The National Coordinator used the time to continue his description of how Swiss education functions. As he progressed, the picture got increasingly confusing, as there was no general rule. There were only exceptions. But it works. The coming year and the European Economic Community (EEC) are pressing some serious questions concerning how the Swiss diplomas/ certificates will stack up against those their graduates will be competing against. They will soon have to decide, altogether, whether to join the EEC, or make some other accommodations.

Classrooms

CHAPTER THREE

옥도 갈아야 빛을 낸다

Even a gem, without polishing,
will not glitter.　　　Korean Proverb

In classrooms around the world, teachers apply their knowledge and skills, employ a variety of teaching methods, make use of available instructional materials, and organize their students for learning. International comparative studies offer unique opportunities to compare and contrast differing classroom factors and to relate them to student performance. IAEP collected information about some of these elements from the students who participated in the study and from their school administrators.

The results reported in this chapter reflect the interpretations of students and their administrators. Responses of others, for example, teachers or curriculum experts, might provide a different perspective of the classroom. Because the nature of schooling differs from country to country — for example, the length of the school week, the number of days of science instruction each week, and the way various instructional practices are used in the classroom—the student and school background questions may take on different meanings from population to population. Some of the possible differences in interpretation of questions are suggested in the discussion of the results.

TEACHING PRACTICES Teaching practices vary from country to country; in some cases, there is even greater variability among regions within a single country. In the hands of a gifted, caring teacher, the particular methods used may be immaterial. Nevertheless, educational experts often promote certain techniques as more effective than others. The descriptive data collected in IAEP highlight the variation in teaching practices across countries. Some of the results are summarized in FIGURE 3.1.

School administrators in a majority of the populations reported that their schools spent between 150 to 200 minutes a week (typically about 30 or 40 minutes a day) on science instruction, in the grade in which most 13-year-olds were enrolled. The average was between 200 to 250 minutes a week in Taiwan, Hungary, and the United States, and higher (283 minutes) in Slovenia. Schools in the Soviet Union (Russian-speaking schools) spent 387 minutes a week or about 75 minutes a day, and China (in-school population) devoted 331 minutes a week to science. In these schools students study more than one science subject at a time. Schools in Korea, Emilia-Romagna, and Fortaleza (restricted grades) spent less than 150 minutes a week on science.

The majority of the students from the Soviet Union (Russian-speaking schools), the United States, and Jordan spent their instructional time listening to their teachers explain science lessons every day, while the majority of their peers from other countries reported listening to teacher presentations less often.

In many participating countries, students do not necessarily have a science class every day and some students may have interpreted "every day" as every school day while others may have interpreted "every day" as every science class.

It is uncommon for students to conduct science experiments on their own in most classrooms in most countries. The exceptions are in Scotland and England (low participation), where more than 80 percent of the students reported conducting experiments at least once a week. About one-half of the students in the Soviet Union (Russian-speaking schools) and in Canada do experiments this often. Experimentation is less prevalent in other partcipating countries with about one quarter of the students in seven populations — Taiwan, Slovenia, France, the United States, Ireland, Jordan, and China (in-school population) — never conducting science experiments at all. In Korea, Switzerland (15 cantons), Hungary, Israel (Hebrew), and São Paulo (restricted grades), one-third of the students reported conducting no experiments; and almost one-half of the students in Emilia-Romagna, Spain (except Cataluña), Portugal (restricted grades), and Fortaleza (restricted grades) reported the same.

Science, Age 13

FIGURE 3.1

Average Percents Correct and Teaching Practices*

COMPREHENSIVE POPULATIONS	Average Percent Correct	Average Minutes of Science Instruction Each Week[1]	Percent of Students Who Listen to Science Lessons Each Day[2]	Percent of Students Who Never Do Experiments[2]	Percent of Students Who Take a Science Test or Quiz at Least Once a Week[2]	Percent of Students Who Spend 4 Hours or More on Science Homework Each Week[2]
Korea	78 (0.5)	144 (2.8)	21 (1.0)	35 (1.7)	21 (1.6)	9 (1.0)
Taiwan	76 (0.4)	245 (***)	25 (1.4)	25 (1.3)	67 (1.2)	10 (0.8)
Switzerland 15 Cantons	74 (0.9)	152 (***)	28 (1.6)	36 (1.7)	18 (1.2)	1 (0.4)
Hungary	73 (0.5)	207 (***)	40 (1.3)	31 (1.7)	27 (1.6)	13 (0.8)
Soviet Union Russian-speaking Schools in 14 Republics	71 (1.0)	387 (6.0)	80 (1.9)	13 (0.8)	88 (1.2)	59 (0.8)
Slovenia	70 (0.5)	283 (7.0)	16 (1.1)	22 (1.5)	18 (1.0)	7 (0.7)
Emilia-Romagna, Italy†	70 (0.7)	138 (3.1)	10 (0.9)	59 (1.9)	9 (1.0)	2 (0.4)
Israel Hebrew-speaking Schools	70 (0.7)	181 (***)	0 (0.2)	35 (1.4)	28 (1.9)	4 (0.5)
Canada	69 (0.4)	156 (1.9)	21 (1.0)	13 (0.7)	26 (1.1)	4 (0.3)
France	69 (0.6)	174 (8.1)	27 (1.4)	20 (1.7)	47 (1.4)	1 (0.2)
Scotland†	68 (0.6)	179 (4.5)	15 (1.2)	3 (0.3)	11 (1.0)	2 (0.4)
Spain Spanish-speaking Schools except in Cataluña	68 (0.6)	189 (7.2)	38 (1.5)	51 (2.3)	42 (2.6)	12 (0.9)
United States†	67 (1.0)	233 (7.9)	66 (1.6)	25 (1.9)	69 (2.0)	7 (0.8)
Ireland	63 (0.6)	159 (4.1)	23 (1.5)	27 (2.1)	18 (1.1)	5 (0.7)
Jordan	57 (0.7)	180 (0.7)	60 (1.8)	26 (1.4)	73 (1.8)	12 (1.0)
POPULATIONS WITH EXCLUSIONS OR LOW PARTICIPATION						
England Low Participation‡	69 (1.2)	194 (4.9)	11 (1.9)	2 (0.6)	8 (0.9)	2 (0.4)
China In-school Population, Restricted Grades, 20 Provinces & Cities	67 (1.1)	331 (***)	23 (2.2)	29 (2.4)	42 (2.2)	16 (1.5)
Portugal In-school Population, Restricted Grades†	63 (0.8)	157 (3.4)	16 (0.9)	48 (1.7)	34 (2.0)	6 (0.7)
São Paulo, Brazil Restricted Grades	53 (0.6)	178 (7.3)	12 (1.0)	35 (1.6)	45 (1.2)	8 (0.8)
Fortaleza, Brazil In-school Population, Restricted Grades	46 (0.6)	124 (3.9)	10 (1.1)	44 (1.9)	55 (1.9)	8 (0.9)

* Jackknifed standard errors are presented in parentheses.
*** Jackknifed standard error is greater than 9.9.
† Combined school and student participation rate is below .80 but at least .70; interpret results with caution because of possible nonresponse bias.
‡ Combined school and student participation rate is below .70; interpret results with extreme caution because of possible nonresponse bias.
§ Results represent percent of classrooms in schools.
[1] IAEP School Questionnaire, Age 13.
[2] IAEP Student Questionnaire, Age 13.

Populations that had few students who reported never conducting experiments — less than 5 percent in Scotland and England — are not among the highest-performing populations on the IAEP assessment. On the other hand, one-third of the students in higher performing populations such as Korea, Switzerland (15 cantons), and Hungary reported never having an opportunity to conduct experiments. However, the IAEP written assessment was not designed to measure laboratory skills or the quality and nature of the experiments that students conducted.

Testing practices vary considerably from country to country. Some countries rely on short-answer and essay forms of testing, others use multiple-choice formats almost exclusively, and some do not administer tests at all on a regular basis.[20] The IAEP results indicate that schools in most countries do not use tests extensively to evaluate student performance in science. Tests are most widely used in Taiwan and the Soviet Union (Russian-speaking schools), both high-performing populations, and in the United States and Jordan, lower-scoring groups. From 67 to almost 90 percent of the students in these four populations reported being tested at least once a week. Less than one-half of the students from most other participating countries reported weekly testing.

Doing more homework is often cited by educators and parents as a means of improving academic performance. Research suggests that many factors contribute to the effectiveness of homework as an instructional activity: the types of assignment, whether the homework is discussed in class, and whether it is graded.[21] IAEP results indicate that most students in most countries do not spend a great deal of time doing homework outside of class. For science, more than one-half of the students from most participating countries reported spending one hour or less each week. The percentage of students doing four hours or more of science homework each week (at least 45 minutes a night) is quite low among all IAEP populations except in the Soviet Union (Russian-speaking schools) where 59 percent of the students spend four or more hours each week on science homework. Nevertheless, as shown later in this chapter, students who do spend a lot of time on their science homework may be the highest achievers within each individual country.

[20] George Madaus and Thomas Kellaghan, *Student Examination Systems in the European Community: Lessons for the United States.* Contractor Report, Office of Technology Assessment, United States Congress. 1991.

[21] Herbert J. Walberg, Synthesis of Research on Time and Learning, *Educational Leadership,* Vol. 45, No.6, 1988.

Characteristics of teaching practices do not seem to distinguish between high- and low-performing populations. However it should be noted, for example, that it may not be the number of minutes of science instruction that is important, but how that time is used; or it may not be the number of hours devoted to homework, but how the homework is used in instruction. IAEP was designed to provide information on a broad set of classroom variables, but it cannot make finer distinctions concerning how specific instructional methods are used within the classroom to foster student achievement.

RELATIONSHIP OF CLASSROOM FACTORS AND SCIENCE PERFORMANCE

The findings describing classroom factors highlight the variation in practices among countries. They do not identify any particular practices and characteristics common to all high-performing populations that are absent from low-performing populations. On the contrary, in many cases, both high- and low-achieving countries had high values on the variables examined. This lack of strong interpretable patterns underlines the importance of looking at other areas to understand differences in performance — for example, students' home environments, the countries' cultural factors, and the structure of national educational systems may all play a role and these will be discussed in subsequent chapters.

While the frequency information presented in Figure 3.1, may not show explicit cross-populations trends, it is possible to find more consistent relationships between classroom variables and science achievement within individual participating countries. Analyses of this type are summarized in FIGURE 3.2. If the relationship between levels of a particular variable and achievement within a population is positive, a "+" is shown, if the relationship is negative, a "-" is shown, and if a linear relationship does not exist, a "0" is shown.[22] For example, if the students in a particular population who spent more time on science homework did better on the assessment than the students who spent less time, a "+" appears for the population in the homework column; if the students who reported conducting experiments more frequently did less well on the assessment than those who did them less frequently, a "-" appears in the experiments column.

---

[22] These analyses did not look for curvilinear or other types of nonlinear trends that may be present in the data. The analyses tested for the presence of a statistically significant linear relationship between levels of the background variable and achievement. An estimated slope at least 2 standard errors (of the slope) larger than 0 was taken to indicate a positive relationship; a slope at least 2 standard errors less than 0 was taken to indicate a negative relationship; slopes less than 2 standard errors in absolute value were considered not to be statistically significant. More details of these analyses are provided in the Procedural Appendix, p. 142, and the *IAEP Technical Report*.

Science, Age 13
Relationship of Classroom Factors and
Average Percents Correct within Populations

FIGURE 3.2

COMPREHENSIVE POPULATIONS	Amount of Listening to Science Lessons[1]	Amount of Student Conducted Experiments[1]	Amount of Science Testing[1]	Amount of Time Spent on Science Homework[1]
Korea	+	−	−	−
Taiwan	+	0	+	+
Switzerland 14 Cantons	0	0	0	−
Hungary	0	−	0	+
Soviet Union Russian-speaking Schools in 14 Republics	+	0	+	+
Slovenia	+	−	−	0
Emilia-Romagna, Italy†	0	0	−	0
Israel Hebrew-speaking Schools	+	−	0	0
Canada	0	+	+	0
France	+	−	0	−
Scotland†	0	0	0	0
Spain Spanish-speaking Schools except in Cataluña	0	−	0	+
United States†	0	−	0	0
Ireland	+	0	0	+
Jordan	+	−	0	0

POPULATIONS WITH EXCLUSIONS OR LOW PARTICIPATION

England Low Participation‡	−	0	−	+
China In-school Population, Restricted Grades, 20 Provinces & Cities	+	0	0	0
Portugal In-school Population, Restricted Grades†	0	−	0	0
São Paulo, Brazil Restricted Grades	0	−	−	0
Fortaleza, Brazil In-school Population, Restricted Grades	0	−	0	+

+ Statistically significant positive linear relationship.
− Statistically significant negative linear relationship.
0 No statistically significant linear relationship.
† Combined school and student participation rate is below .80 but at least .70; interpret results with caution because of possible nonresponse bias.
‡ Combined school and student participation rate is below .70; interpret results with extreme caution because of possible nonresponse bias.
[1] IAEP Student Questionnaire, Age 13.

IAEP

Current educational research in the United States indicates that classroom instruction is often dominated by teacher lectures, traditional workbook and textbook material that is often mostly drill-and-practice, and that little time is left for students to participate actively in the learning enterprise.[23] IAEP results indicate that science instruction dominated by frequent teacher presentations is not negatively associated with performance, except in England (low participation) where student performance tended to decline with more frequent teacher presentations. In Korea, Taiwan, the Soviet Union (Russian-speaking schools), Slovenia, Israel (Hebrew), France, Ireland, Jordan, and China (in-school population), students who reported high amounts of teacher presentations displayed higher performance than those who reported less.

IAEP examined how often students reported conducting science experiments by themselves or in small groups. The results showed that in nearly all populations fewer than one-half of the students conducted science experiments at least once a week. The greatest percentage of students who reported performing science experiments were in Scotland and England (low participation) where extensive performance-based instruction is part of their curricula. Nevertheless, only in one participating country— Canada — was hands-on activities positively related to science performance. In 11 populations the relationship between conducting experiments and science performance was negative and in the remaining populations, the relationship was neither positive nor negative. This finding is particularly dissatisfying considering the efforts many countries are now making to include performance-based instruction and testing in their science programs. Hands-on activities in the classroom are still relatively new for many of the participating countries and more experience may be needed to understand how best to implement performance-based curricula.

Survey instruments such as IAEP cannot fully test some of the things students know and can do as a result of their classroom experiences. Some of the goals of science education such as the ability to carry out sustained experimental work simply cannot be assessed through traditional paper and pencil tests administered to large numbers of students. Different results may have been obtained if the assessment measured performance tasks.

---

23 John Goodlad, *A Place Called School.* McGraw-Hill Book Co., NY: New York 1984.

Iris R. Weiss, *Report of the 1985-86 National Survey of Science and Mathematics Education.* Research Triangle Park, NC: Research Triangle Institute, 1987.

The descriptive results suggest that testing is relatively infrequent among most IAEP participants, and even among those countries that use tests more frequently — Taiwan, the Soviet Union (Russian-speaking schools), the United States, and Jordan — the relationship between frequent testing and performance is not consistent. In Taiwan, the Soviet Union (Russian-speaking schools), and Canada frequent testing is associated with higher science performance. In five populations, Korea, Slovenia, Emilia-Romagna, England (low participation), and São Paulo (restricted grades) the relationship between the amount of testing and student performance was negative, and in the remaining populations, the relationship was neither positive nor negative.

Generally, the majority of students from most populations reported spending very few hours on science homework. The norm for almost all countries is between zero and one hour each week. In only seven populations — Taiwan, Hungary, the Soviet Union (Russian-speaking schools), Spain (except Cataluña), Ireland, England (low participation), and Fortaleza (restricted grades) — there was a positive relationship between amount of time spent on science homework and performance. In three populations — Korea, Switzerland (15 cantons), and France — the relationship was negative. In the remaining populations, the amount of time spent on homework was not linearly related to science performance to a statistically significant degree.

Results of time spent on science homework and science performance, which are summarized in FIGURES 3.1 and 3.2, are provided in detail in FIGURE 3.3. This figure gives the percentages of students who reported spending various amounts of time on science homework each week — 0 to 1 hour, 2 to 3 hours, and 4 or more hours — and next to each category those students' average percent correct on the science assessment is indicated by a bar. The differences in the length of the bars show the magnitude of the increase and the percentages of students who answered in each category show how many students are represented in the increase.

For example, in Taiwan there is a moderate increase in performance for students who spent 2 to 3 hours on science homework each week (25 percent of the students) and a larger increase for students who spent 4 hours or more on homework weekly (10 percent of the students).

Science, Age 13
Percentages of Students Reporting Amounts of Weekly Science Homework and Average Percents Correct by Homework Categories*
Part 1

FIGURE 3.3

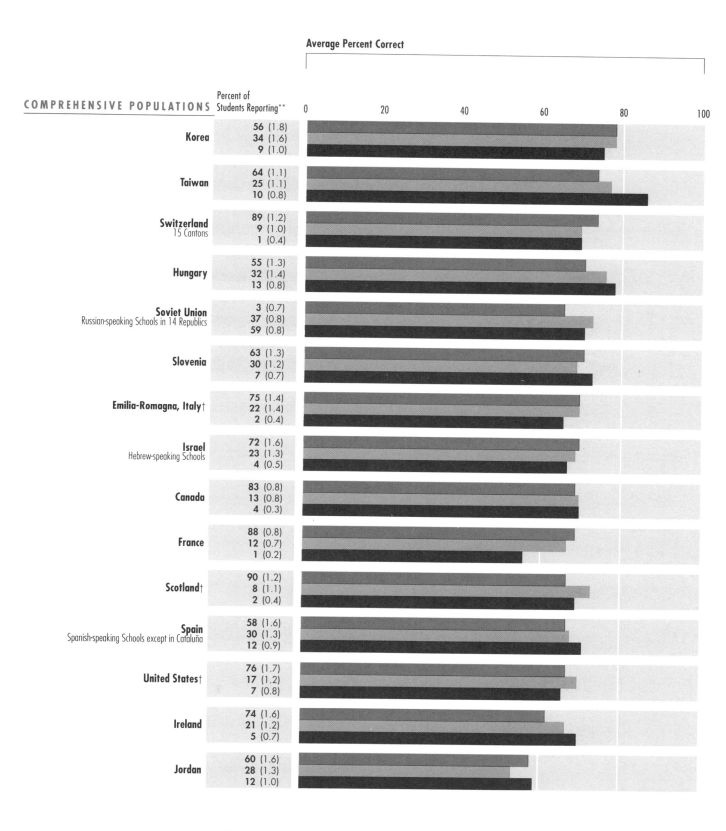

Average Percent Correct

COMPREHENSIVE POPULATIONS	Percent of Students Reporting**
Korea	56 (1.8) / 34 (1.6) / 9 (1.0)
Taiwan	64 (1.1) / 25 (1.1) / 10 (0.8)
Switzerland 15 Cantons	89 (1.2) / 9 (1.0) / 1 (0.4)
Hungary	55 (1.3) / 32 (1.4) / 13 (0.8)
Soviet Union Russian-speaking Schools in 14 Republics	3 (0.7) / 37 (0.8) / 59 (0.8)
Slovenia	63 (1.3) / 30 (1.2) / 7 (0.7)
Emilia-Romagna, Italy†	75 (1.4) / 22 (1.4) / 2 (0.4)
Israel Hebrew-speaking Schools	72 (1.6) / 23 (1.3) / 4 (0.5)
Canada	83 (0.8) / 13 (0.8) / 4 (0.3)
France	88 (0.8) / 12 (0.7) / 1 (0.2)
Scotland†	90 (1.2) / 8 (1.1) / 2 (0.4)
Spain Spanish-speaking Schools except in Cataluña	58 (1.6) / 30 (1.3) / 12 (0.9)
United States†	76 (1.7) / 17 (1.2) / 7 (0.8)
Ireland	74 (1.6) / 21 (1.2) / 5 (0.7)
Jordan	60 (1.6) / 28 (1.3) / 12 (1.0)

Legend:
- ■ 0 to 1 Hour
- ■ 2 to 3 Hours
- ■ 4 Hours or More

* Jackknifed standard errors are presented in parentheses.
** Percentages may not total 100 due to rounding.
† Combined school and student participation rate is below .80 but at least .70; interpret results with caution.

 IAEP

Science, Age 13
Percentages of Students Reporting Amounts
of Weekly Science Homework and Average Percents
Correct by Homework Categories*
Part 2

FIGURE 3.3

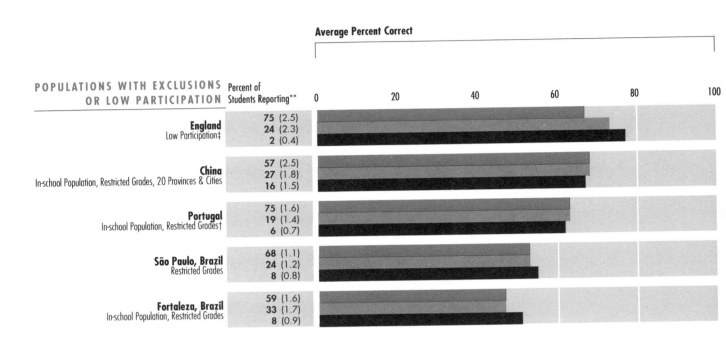

Average Percent Correct

POPULATIONS WITH EXCLUSIONS OR LOW PARTICIPATION	Percent of Students Reporting**
England Low Participation‡	75 (2.5) 24 (2.3) 2 (0.4)
China In-school Population, Restricted Grades, 20 Provinces & Cities	57 (2.5) 27 (1.8) 16 (1.5)
Portugal In-school Population, Restricted Grades†	75 (1.6) 19 (1.4) 6 (0.7)
São Paulo, Brazil Restricted Grades	68 (1.1) 24 (1.2) 8 (0.8)
Fortaleza, Brazil In-school Population, Restricted Grades	59 (1.6) 33 (1.7) 8 (0.9)

■ 0 to 1 Hour
▨ 2 to 3 Hours
■ 4 Hours or More
   * Jackknifed standard errors are presented in parentheses.
 ** Percentages may not total 100 due to rounding.
   † Combined school and student participation rate is below .80 but at least .70; interpret results with caution.
   ‡ Combined school and student participation rate is below .70; results should be interpreted with extreme caution.

In nine populations: Taiwan, Hungary, Slovenia, Spain (except
Cataluña), Ireland, Jordan, England (low participation), São Paulo
(restricted grades), and Fortaleza (restricted grades) performance increased
for students who spent 4 hours or more on science homework. However a lot
fewer students (only 2 to 13 percent) spent this amount of time weekly on
science homework.

TEACHING MATERIALS As the use of technology increases around the world, mathematics and science educators are advocating expanded use of computers and hands-on activities, such as work in science laboratories. Many educators believe these kinds of experiences are central to learning and can help students understand and develop scientific skills. However, as shown in FIGURE 3.4, access to science laboratory facilities varies vastly from country to country and some students have fewer opportunities than others to engage in science experiments. In seven populations, Switzerland (15 cantons), Hungary, Canada, Ireland, Jordan, China (in-school population), and São Paulo (restricted grades), about one quarter to one-half of the schools reported having no science facilities at all for 13-year-olds, and in Fortaleza (restricted grades) 88 percent of the schools reported none. Still, the majority of schools in most countries indicated they had separate general purpose or specialized laboratories that were available for 13-year-olds. Science laboratories are virtually universal in Taiwan, Scotland, and England (low participation). Some schools indicated they provide science facilities within the regular classroom.

As might be expected, computer availability is even more rare than access to science laboratories. In almost all populations, school administrators indicated having few computers that 13-year-olds could use for school work. Only three populations had on average 20 or more computers in schools that students can use for instruction: Scotland, the United States, and England (low participation).

Science, Age 13
Average Percents Correct and Teaching Materials*

FIGURE 3.4

COMPREHENSIVE POPULATIONS	Average Percent Correct	Percent of Schools with No Science Laboratories[1]	Percent of Schools with General or Specialized Science Laboratories in One or More Classrooms[1]	Average Number of Computers in Schools[1]
Korea	78 (0.5)	0 (0.0)	87 (7.4)	15 (1.5)
Taiwan	76 (0.4)	1 (1.0)	99 (1.1)	15 (1.2)
Switzerland 14 Cantons	74 (0.9)	45 (8.8)§	48 (8.3)§	4 (1.4)§
Hungary	73 (0.5)	32 (5.5)	34 (3.8)	6 (0.3)
Soviet Union Russian-speaking Schools in 14 Republics	71 (1.0)	3 (2.1)	94 (3.1)	2 (0.4)
Slovenia	70 (0.5)	7 (3.8)	50 (5.5)	5 (0.4)
Emilia-Romagna, Italy†	70 (0.7)	10 (4.1)	40 (9.1)	7 (0.7)
Israel Hebrew-speaking Schools	70 (0.7)	7 (4.1)	76 (5.6)	14 (1.1)
Canada	69 (0.4)	25 (3.1)	62 (2.9)	17 (0.8)
France	69 (0.6)	4 (2.6)	93 (3.5)	13 (0.6)
Scotland†	68 (0.6)	0 (0.0)	100 (0.0)	40 (2.8)
Spain Spanish-speaking Schools except in Cataluña	68 (0.6)	16 (4.4)	69 (5.9)	3 (0.4)
United States†	67 (1.0)	14 (5.2)	76 (6.8)	24 (6.0)
Ireland	63 (0.6)	23 (5.9)	77 (5.9)	9 (0.7)
Jordan	57 (0.7)	22 (6.5)	65 (7.2)	1 (0.4)

POPULATIONS WITH EXCLUSIONS OR LOW PARTICIPATION				
England Low Participation‡	69 (1.2)	0 (0.0)	100 (0.0)	26 (2.5)
China In-school Population, Restricted Grades, 20 Provinces & Cities	67 (1.1)	31 (7.8)	68 (7.9)	2 (0.7)
Portugal In-school Population, Restricted Grades†	63 (0.8)	14 (***)	79 (***)	2 (0.5)
São Paulo, Brazil Restricted Grades	53 (0.6)	49 (5.7)	36 (6.3)	2 (0.7)
Fortaleza, Brazil In-school Population, Restricted Grades	46 (0.6)	88 (3.0)	12 (3.0)	0 (0.2)

* Jackknifed standard errors are presented in parentheses.
*** Jackknifed standard error is greater than 9.9.
† Combined school and student participation rate is below .80 but at least .70; interpret results with caution because of possible nonresponse bias.
‡ Combined school and student participation rate is below .70; interpret results with extreme caution because of possible nonresponse bias.
§ Results represent percent of classrooms in schools.
[1] IAEP School Questionnaire, Age 13.

 IAEP

TEACHER PREPARATION AND CLASSROOM ORGANIZATION Increasingly, science educators are concerned about the academic background and training of the teachers responsible for teaching science. IAEP asked school administrators whether science classes for 13-year-olds were taught by someone who teaches science most or all of the time or by a classroom teacher who also teaches other subjects. Administrators were also asked how many of these teachers had taken post-secondary courses in science instruction. IAEP also collected information from participating schools on classroom organization. The results are presented in FIGURE 3.5.

In all but three of the populations assessed, 13-year-old students are taught by a teacher who teaches science most or all of the time in a majority of the schools. Regular classroom teachers are responsible for teaching science in 71 percent of the schools in Switzerland (15 cantons), 92 percent of the schools in Emilia-Romagna, and 63 percent of the schools in Canada.

Schools also reported the percentages of science teachers who have taken post-secondary science courses other than courses in how to teach science. In 10 populations, at least one-half of the schools reported that all of their science classroom teachers had taken advanced science courses. In the remaining populations, 25 to about 47 percent of the schools reported that all their science classroom teachers have taken advanced content courses except for Korea. Eighty-four percent of the schools in Korea, the top-performing country, reported that *none* of their teachers had taken college-level courses in science.

The efficacy of grouping students by ability is strenuously debated and grouping practices vary from country to country, as shown in FIGURE 3.5. While assigning students to science classes by ability may give teachers an opportunity to design their instruction according to the specific achievement level of their students, it may mean that some students are exposed to only lower-level content and skills while others are exposed to a more enriched curriculum.[24] Among IAEP participants, only Taiwan and England (low participation) were likely to organize science classes on the basis of ability. More than half the schools in these countries reported this practice. About one-third of the schools in the United States, Ireland, and Fortaleza (restricted grades) practiced ability grouping; and the remaining populations were more likely to form mixed-ability science classes. The highest-achieving populations, with the exception of Taiwan, do not group by ability.

---

24 Jeannie Oakes, *Unequal opportunities: The Effects of Race, Social Class, and Ability Grouping and Access to Science and Mathematics Education.* Palo Alto, CA: The RAND Corp., 1989.

Jeannie Oakes, *Multiplying Inequalities: The Effect of Race, Social Class, and Ability Grouping on Students' Opportunity to Learn Mathematics and Science.* Santa Monica, CA: The RAND Corp., 1990.

Science, Age 13
Average Percents Correct, Teacher Background, and Classroom Organization*

FIGURE 3.5

COMPREHENSIVE POPULATIONS	Average Percent Correct	Percent of Schools with Teachers Who Teach Science Most or All the Time[1]	Percent of Schools Where All Science Teachers Have Taken Some Post-Secondary Science Courses[1]	Percent of Schools Where Science Classes are Based on Ability[1]
Korea	**78** (0.5)	**89** (3.1)	**10** (2.4)	**1** (0.6)
Taiwan	**76** (0.4)	**100** (0.0)	**38** (7.7)	**57** (7.4)
Switzerland 15 Cantons	**74** (0.9)	**29** (5.3)§	**25** (3.6)§	**17** (7.3)§
Hungary	**73** (0.5)	**59** (***)	**79** (5.7)	**0** (0.0)
Soviet Union Russian-speaking Schools in 14 Republics	**71** (1.0)	**85** (4.3)	**66** (***)	**13** (3.0)
Slovenia	**70** (0.5)	**95** (2.7)	**96** (2.2)	**0** (0.0)
Emilia-Romagna, Italy†	**70** (0.7)	**8** (2.8)	**26** (6.0)	**14** (4.1)
Israel Hebrew-speaking Schools	**70** (0.7)	**89** (3.3)	**45** (7.6)	**14** (3.5)
Canada	**69** (0.4)	**37** (1.8)	**50** (2.0)	**5** (0.8)
France	**69** (0.6)	**90** (3.6)	**25** (8.4)	**11** (3.8)
Scotland†	**68** (0.6)	**95** (2.3)	**75** (5.6)	**3** (2.4)
Spain Spanish-speaking Schools except in Cataluña	**68** (0.6)	**66** (5.6)	**43** (5.5)	**0** (0.0)
United States†	**67** (1.0)	**79** (***)	**62** (***)	**29** (***)
Ireland	**63** (0.6)	**99** (1.2)	**69** (6.0)	**38** (5.1)
Jordan	**57** (0.7)	**87** (6.7)	**72** (7.9)	**10** (3.8)
POPULATIONS WITH EXCLUSIONS OR LOW PARTICIPATION				
England Low Participation‡	**69** (1.2)	**100** (0.0)	**70** (9.8)	**58** (***)
China In-school Population, Restricted Grades, 20 Provinces & Cities	**67** (1.1)	**74** (6.5)	**28** (7.1)	**1** (0.8)
Portugal In-school Population, Restricted Grades†	**63** (0.8)	**95** (3.7)	**47** (7.3)	**6** (3.7)
São Paulo, Brazil Restricted Grades	**53** (0.6)	**99** (0.8)	**69** (5.4)	**12** (3.5)
Fortaleza, Brazil In-school Population, Restricted Grades	**46** (0.6)	**81** (4.8)	**44** (5.4)	**35** (6.6)

* Jackknifed standard errors are presented in parentheses.
*** Jackknifed standard errors are greater than 9.9.
† Combined school and student participation rate is below .80 but at least .70; interpret results with caution because of possible nonresponse bias.
‡ Combined school and student participation rate is below .70; interpret results with extreme caution because of possible nonresponse bias.
§ Results represent percent of classrooms in schools.
[1] IAEP School Questionnaire, Age 13.

Although classroom factors impact on student performance more directly than do home and societal variables, relationships between these variables and achievement are not consistent across the participating IAEP countries, reenforcing the notion that effective instructional practices may vary from culture to culture.

Generally, the results suggest that the typical current practice of frequent teacher presentations is an effective and efficient way of imparting science knowledge to students.

While it is disappointing that frequent use of experimentation in the classroom is positively related to science performance in only one country — Canada — it is too early to tell if those techniques that are just now being introduced into more 13-year-old classrooms will make significant contributions in the future, once their implementation is perfected.

SLOVENIA   March 17, 1991

An ornate, wooden bridge that crossed a roaring mountain torrent framed a pair of graceful, elegant Slavic/German church steeples that rose from the village of about 200 white-stuccoed, red-roofed homes. The setting, against the dark green mountains and snowy Alpine peaks, completed the postcard.

As we pulled into the school's diminutive parking area, it seemed reasonable that both a playground and a small vineyard occupied the property. An internationally-recognizable school custodian led us to a large, airy, teachers' room and produced an enthusiastic, yellow-sweatered headmaster, a bearded school psychologist, and three cups of espresso. As I shook hands with a half-dozen young, designer-jeaned, frilly-bloused teachers, one friendlier than the next, I imagined how pleasant it must be going to school there.

Suddenly, it was time. We paraded, the headmaster, the psychologist, a senior teacher, the test administrator, and I, through noisy hallways to the classroom. There awaited 36 smiling, excited students born between January 1 and December 31, 1977. The headmaster made a speech, the school psychologist spoke, and I was asked if I had anything to say. Why not? I told the three dozen attractive faces that there were 115,000,000 13-year-olds on the planet, many of whom were taking the very same mathematics and science tests this month in Madrid, Seoul, Moscow, Paris, and New York. I told them that in 10 years, when they were 23, they would be in charge of the earth, and it was important for them, and for us, that we be sure that they would be ready to assume those responsibilities. I also told them that this particular group of 36 were the most important 13-year-olds in the world. (This was probably an exaggeration, but it seemed an appropriate thing to say at the time!)

The administrator opened the sealed package of tests, and, with the help of all the adults, distributed the booklets: yellow for math, pink for science. He read the instructions verbatim, and the students turned seriously to their tasks. As the session proceeded, I carefully recorded events on the quality-control checklist, wondering if the church bells that rang every 15 minutes constituted an important distraction or not. The sound came through the wide-open windows along with the refreshing mountain air. I was distracted by the fact that the sun had finally climbed over an Alp and its rays were glistening off some mountain snow and shimmering on the lake's deep green surface.

Suddenly, the students were around me saying "Good bye, Sir!" and shaking my hand. One asked if he could take a picture with my camera, assembled a group of his giggling colleagues, stood on a chair, and snapped the shot.

A tour of the classroom, a visit to the library, and lots of handshakes got us out of the building and into the sunshine.

ETS Quality Control Observer

Students and Their Homes

CHAPTER FOUR

*Das ist aber meine Lehre: wer einst
fliegen lernen will, der muß erst
stehn und gehn und laufen und
klettern und tanzen lernen: - man
erfliegt das Fliegen nicht!*

He who would learn to fly one day
must first learn to stand and walk
and run and climb and dance: one
cannot fly into flying.

Friedrich Nietzsche
Thus Spake Zarathustra

The rhetoric of politicians and the realities faced by educators are often at odds with one another. The images of happy, loved, motivated children arriving at school ready to meet the challenges of the day conflict with the sometimes harsh realities of poverty, child abuse, drugs, and crime that also manage to pass through the schoolhouse door. Teachers and schools are asked to somehow reconcile these conflicting views, to accept children with a wide range of abilities and readiness, and to transmit to them the knowledge, skills, tradition, and values held dear by the society.

To find out more about the backgrounds of the students in the assessment and to provide a broader context for the achievement results, IAEP collected descriptive information about the students themselves and their families. Some of the background questions were included because they tap some of the inevitable variation in social and economic advantage; others were included because they explore some of the ways in which families, rich and poor alike, may foster or perhaps hinder academic development. Finally, a number of questions examined how students spend some of their time outside of school in ways that may either enhance or detract from their in-school performance.

HOME CHARACTERISTICS Information on the language spoken in the home, size of family, and the number of books in the home can provide indications of students' social and economic advantage as well as of other factors that might contribute more directly to their academic development. Language minority groups are often at a disadvantage within a dominant culture and students from these families often have the further handicap of receiving instruction in a language that is different from that which is spoken in the home. Size of the family is often negatively correlated with disposable income, and students from large families often have less opportunity for individual attention from parents than those with fewer brothers and sisters. The number of books in the home is considered a general indicator of social and economic status and their presence also provides children with opportunities for expanding their academic horizons.

The IAEP data related to these socioeconomic and academic factors are displayed in FIGURE 4.1. The percentages of language minority students participating in the assessment are low in all of the populations. A number of participants excluded language minority students from their samples or excluded geographic areas where large numbers of language minority students live.

More than 10 percent of the students living in Switzerland (15 cantons), the Soviet Union (Russian-speaking schools), Israel (Hebrew), and Canada reported that a different language from the one used in school was spoken at home. Some of these students had no choice but to attend schools where instruction is provided in the dominant language. Others could attend schools that teach in different languages and could choose an instructional program given in a language other than that spoken in their homes.

The IAEP results indicate that family size is relatively small in most industrialized nations. Only in Jordan did a large percentage of students (88 percent) indicate that they had four or more brothers and sisters. Ireland is unusual among its European neighbors, with about one-third of its students coming from large families.

Responses to the question on the number of books in the home also differed between more and less industrialized participating countries. Close to one-half of the students from Jordan, São Paulo (restricted grades), and Fortaleza (restricted grades) reported that they had fewer than 25 books at home. In most other IAEP populations, fewer than 25 percent of the students fell into this category.

Science, Age 13
Average Percents Correct and Home Characteristics*

FIGURE 4.1

		Percent of Students					
COMPREHENSIVE POPULATIONS	Average Percent Correct	Same Language Spoken at Home as at School[1]	Have 4 or More Brothers and Sisters[1]	Have Less Than 25 Books at Home[1]	Parents are Interested in Science[1]	Talk with Someone at Home About Science Class[1]	Receive Help at Home with Science Homework[1]
Korea	78 (0.5)	98 (0.4)	21 (1.2)	25 (1.3)	28 (1.2)	53 (1.2)	44 (1.1)
Taiwan	76 (0.4)	—	12 (1.0)	35 (1.2)	19 (0.9)	59 (1.2)	45 (1.1)
Switzerland 14 Cantons	74 (0.9)	79 (1.3)	4 (0.5)	16 (1.1)	49 (1.6)	54 (1.7)	26 (1.4)
Hungary	73 (0.5)	99 (0.2)	3 (0.5)	10 (0.8)	54 (1.4)	75 (1.2)	61 (1.5)
Soviet Union Russian-speaking Schools in 14 Republics	71 (1.0)	87 (2.2)	11 (1.6)	11 (1.5)	31 (1.7)	67 (0.5)	26 (1.0)
Slovenia	70 (0.5)	96 (0.9)	3 (0.4)	17 (1.3)	43 (1.5)	84 (0.9)	59 (1.7)
Emilia-Romagna, Italy†	70 (0.7)	95 (1.0)	2 (0.4)	24 (1.6)	56 (1.5)	67 (1.1)	14 (1.0)
Israel Hebrew-speaking Schools	70 (0.7)	87 (1.0)	18 (1.4)	10 (0.9)	39 (1.1)	56 (1.2)	31 (1.3)
Canada	69 (0.4)	88 (1.0)	7 (0.5)	14 (0.7)	36 (0.8)	47 (1.1)	47 (1.0)
France	69 (0.6)	92 (0.9)	11 (1.0)	25 (1.2)	44 (1.3)	62 (1.1)	44 (1.5)
Scotland†	68 (0.6)	95 (0.7)	8 (1.0)	23 (1.4)	38 (1.3)	60 (1.4)	47 (1.6)
Spain Spanish-speaking Schools except in Cataluña	68 (0.6)	91 (1.1)	11 (0.9)	21 (1.4)	63 (1.4)	72 (1.5)	61 (1.5)
United States†	67 (1.0)	94 (1.0)	15 (1.4)	18 (1.5)	35 (1.9)	50 (1.5)	53 (1.8)
Ireland	63 (0.6)	96 (0.8)	36 (1.5)	24 (1.5)	38 (1.4)	59 (1.5)	44 (1.9)
Jordan	57 (0.7)	98 (0.5)	88 (1.0)	48 (2.2)	55 (1.4)	79 (1.4)	40 (1.7)

POPULATIONS WITH EXCLUSIONS OR LOW PARTICIPATION

England Low Participation‡	69 (1.2)	97 (1.0)	9 (1.2)	15 (1.8)	38 (2.2)	61 (1.6)	60 (2.4)
China In-school Population, Restricted Grades, 20 Provinces & Cities	67 (1.1)	97 (0.5)	12 (1.5)	30 (2.4)	62 (1.8)	80 (1.1)	40 (1.8)
Portugal In-school Population, Restricted Grades†	63 (0.8)	99 (0.3)	8 (0.9)	31 (1.7)	44 (2.2)	63 (1.9)	37 (2.1)
São Paulo, Brazil Restricted Grades	53 (0.6)	97 (0.6)	17 (1.1)	45 (1.7)	41 (1.4)	65 (1.4)	39 (1.5)
Fortaleza, Brazil In-school Population, Restricted Grades	46 (0.6)	98 (0.4)	34 (1.8)	46 (1.6)	45 (1.5)	68 (1.4)	39 (1.5)

* Jackknifed standard errors are presented in parentheses.
† Combined school and student participation rate is below .80 but at least .70; interpret results with caution because of possible nonresponse bias.
‡ Combined school and student participation rate is below .70; interpret results with extreme caution because of possible nonresponse bias.
[1] IAEP Student Questionnaire, Age 13.
- Information is not available.

PARENTAL INVOLVEMENT The home characteristics just discussed may be viewed as proxies for socioeconomic indicators and also as variables that contribute to academic development. Parental involvement can have an important impact on a child's success in school regardless of social or economic status. When asked if they thought their parents were interested in science, in most countries about 30 to 60 percent of the students gave positive responses. It is noteworthy that only about 20 percent of the high-performing Taiwanese students felt that their parents were interested in science.

When students were asked if someone at home talked to them about science class, the responses varied considerably from population to population. Between 75 and 85 percent of the students from Hungary, Slovenia, Jordan, and China (in-school population) reported that someone at home asked them about their science class. About one-half of the students from Canada and the United States indicated this type of discussion at home.

Parents were more likely to ask their children about their science class than to help them with their science homework. Help with homework is less prevalent in Switzerland (15 cantons), the Soviet Union (Russian-speaking schools), and Emilia-Romagna than in other populations with about 15 to 25 percent of the students reporting this type of parental involvement. Hungary, Slovenia, Spain (except Cataluña), and England (low participation) are notable in that about 60 percent of their students indicated that their parents help them with homework.

RELATIONSHIP OF HOME CHARACTERISTICS AND SCIENCE PERFORMANCE

The descriptive data about home characteristics show some predictable variation between industrialized and non-industrialized countries and contribute to an understanding of low performance among some of the non-industrialized countries. This variation is further substantiated when home characteristics are examined in relationship to achievement *within* individual populations. FIGURE 4.2 provides this type of analysis. For each population, it indicates with pluses, minuses and zeros whether the relationship between increasing levels of a particular home-related variable and science achievement is positive, negative, or not related in a linear fashion to a statistically significant degree.

Science, Age 13
Relationship of Home Characteristics and Average Percents Correct within Populations

FIGURE 4.2

COMPREHENSIVE POPULATIONS	Number of Brothers and Sisters[1]	Number of Books in the Home[1]	Parents Are Interested in Science[1]
Korea	−	+	+
Taiwan	0	+	0
Switzerland 14 Cantons	−	+	0
Hungary	−	+	0
Soviet Union Russian-speaking Schools in 14 Republics	−	+	0
Slovenia	−	+	0
Emilia-Romagna, Italy†	0	+	0
Israel Hebrew-speaking Schools	0	+	+
Canada	−	+	+
France	−	+	+
Scotland†	−	+	+
Spain Spanish-speaking Schools except in Cataluña	−	+	0
United States†	−	+	+
Ireland	0	+	+
Jordan	0	+	0

POPULATIONS WITH EXCLUSIONS OR LOW PARTICIPATION			
England Low Participation‡	−	+	+
China In-school Population, Restricted Grades, 20 Provinces & Cities	−	+	0
Portugal In-school Population, Restricted Grades†	−	+	0
São Paulo, Brazil Restricted Grades	−	+	0
Fortaleza, Brazil In-school Population, Restricted Grades	−	+	0

+ Statistically significant positive linear relationship.
− Statistically significant negative linear relationship.
0 No statistically significant linear relationship.
† Combined school and student participation rate is below .80 but at least .70; interpret results with caution because of possible nonresponse bias.
‡ Combined school and student participation rate is below .70; interpret results with extreme caution because of possible nonresponse bias.
[1] IAEP Student Questionnaire, Age 13.

ETS IAEP

The importance of socioeconomic factors is confirmed by the within-population results. Science achievement is positively related with the number of books in the home in every population and is negatively related to family size in 15 populations.

The data about parents are more difficult to interpret. About 30 to 60 percent of the students in most countries reported their parents were interested in science. The level of parental involvement is relatively high in some high-performing populations, such as Hungary, but the same is true for some lower-performing populations as well, such as Spain. Within individual populations, parental interest in science was positively related with achievement in only eight instances.

STUDENTS' OUT-OF-SCHOOL ACTIVITIES While education is often cited as the dominant activity of school-aged children, young people actually spend much more of their time outside of school. Some of this out-of-school activity is clearly directed at furthering academic development — for example, doing homework and leisure reading. However, time spent watching television may or may not be supportive of learning. IAEP asked students how much time they spend in these non-school activities and probed their attitudes toward science as a subject area. These descriptive results are presented in FIGURE 4.3.

While reading for fun is not directly related to science performance, consistent readers tend to be high achievers in many academic areas. Varying amounts of students (about 20 to 45 percent) reported reading for fun almost every day in each of the participating countries. The lowest percentages of daily readers were in Korea, 11 percent, and Taiwan, 17 percent, and the highest percentages were in Switzerland (15 cantons), 49 percent, the Soviet Union (Russian-speaking schools), 48 percent and Portugal (restricted grades), 47 percent.

Populations varied more in the amount of time students spend doing homework across all school subjects each day. The most common response of students in 10 of the IAEP countries was one hour of homework each school night across all school subjects. In the remaining populations, close to 50 percent or more of the students reported doing two or more hours of homework each day: Hungary, the Soviet Union (Russian-speaking schools), Emilia-Romagna, Israel (Hebrew), France, Spain (except Cataluña), Ireland, Jordan, São Paulo (restricted grades), and Fortaleza (restricted grades). Students from Emilia-Romagna spent the most time doing homework, with close to 80 percent reporting two hours or more of homework daily.

FIGURE 4.3

Science, Age 13
Average Percents Correct and Home Activities*

COMPREHENSIVE POPULATIONS	Average Percent Correct	Percent of Students Who Read for Fun Almost Every Day[1]	Percent of Students Who Spend 2 Hours or More on All Homework Every Day[1]	Percent of Students Who Watch Television 5 Hours or More Every Day[1]	Percent of Students Who Have Positive Attitudes Towards Science[1,2]
Korea	78 (0.5)	11 (0.8)	38 (1.5)	10 (0.8)	27 (1.3)
Taiwan	76 (0.4)	17 (1.1)	44 (1.3)	7 (0.7)	51 (1.2)
Switzerland 14 Cantons†	74 (0.9)	49 (1.2)	21 (1.3)	7 (0.6)	59 (1.5)
Hungary	73 (0.5)	44 (1.3)	61 (1.5)	16 (1.1)	69 (1.2)
Soviet Union Russian-speaking Schools in 14 Republics	71 (1.0)	48 (1.1)	52 (1.6)	19 (1.3)	66 (1.4)
Slovenia	70 (0.5)	43 (1.5)	27 (1.4)	5 (0.6)	78 (1.2)
Emilia-Romagna, Italy†	70 (0.7)	45 (1.4)	78 (1.2)	7 (0.8)	73 (1.4)
Israel Hebrew-speaking Schools	70 (0.7)	40 (1.4)	49 (1.4)	20 (1.2)	62 (1.6)
Canada	69 (0.4)	36 (0.9)	26 (0.9)	15 (0.7)	62 (1.0)
France	69 (0.6)	39 (1.5)	55 (1.6)	4 (0.5)	55 (1.3)
Scotland†	68 (0.6)	37 (1.4)	15 (1.5)	23 (1.3)	66 (1.2)
Spain Spanish-speaking Schools except in Cataluña	68 (0.6)	34 (1.5)	62 (1.9)	11 (0.9)	78 (1.4)
United States†	67 (1.0)	29 (1.4)	31 (1.6)	22 (1.7)	57 (2.1)
Ireland	63 (0.6)	40 (1.3)	66 (1.6)	9 (0.9)	57 (1.4)
Jordan	57 (0.7)	22 (1.0)	54 (2.0)	10 (0.9)	82 (1.0)

POPULATIONS WITH EXCLUSIONS OR LOW PARTICIPATION

	Average Percent Correct	Read for Fun	Homework	Television	Positive Attitudes
England Low Participation‡	69 (1.2)	36 (1.8)	26 (2.8)	23 (1.7)	66 (2.9)
China In-school Population, Restricted Grades, 20 Provinces & Cities	67 (1.1)	28 (1.4)	35 (2.1)	2 (0.4)	74 (1.7)
Portugal In-school Population, Restricted Grades†	63 (0.8)	47 (1.2)	30 (1.7)	11 (0.9)	71 (1.4)
São Paulo, Brazil Restricted Grades	53 (0.6)	31 (1.1)	48 (1.9)	18 (1.1)	69 (1.3)
Fortaleza, Brazil In-school Population, Restricted Grades	46 (0.6)	41 (1.2)	50 (2.0)	20 (1.5)	74 (1.3)

* Jackknifed standard errors are presented in parentheses.
† Combined school and student participation rate is below .80 but at least .70; interpret results with caution because of possible nonresponse bias.
‡ Combined school and student participation rate is below .70; interpret results with extreme caution because of possible nonresponse bias.
[1] IAEP Student Questionnaire, Age 13.
[2] Attitudes toward science is a composite score based on responses to four attitude questions.

Some television programming is clearly targeted at developing the academic abilities of children and some countries provide more of this type of programming than do others. However, for many students, the content of the television watched has little academic value and consumes valuable hours that could be devoted to activities requiring more intellectual effort. Among all but two of the populations, the most common response of students was two to four hours of television viewing each school day. Eighty-two percent of the Chinese students reported watching little or no television on a daily basis, probably reflecting the fact that many of these students have only limited access to television. Forty-eight percent of French students reported watching one hour or less of television each day and the same percentage reported watching two to four hours daily.

At the other extreme, 20 percent or more of the 13-year-olds from Israel (Hebrew), Scotland, the United States, England (low participation), and Fortaleza (restricted grades) indicated they watch five hours or more of television each school day and 19 percent of their peers from the Soviet Union (Russian-speaking schools) and 18 percent from São Paulo (restricted grades) also reported this amount of television viewing.

ATTITUDES TOWARD SCIENCE Students bring to school certain attitudes toward education in general and toward specific school subjects. These attitudes contribute to, and are a product of, academic success. Students who approach a school subject enthusiastically are more likely to do well in that subject and conversely, students who succeed in a content area are more likely to develop positive attitudes toward it.

Students in the assessment were asked to what extent they agreed with the following statements:

- *Much of what is learned in science is useful in everyday life.*
- *It is important to know some science in order to get a good job.*
- *I am good at science.*
- *My parents are interested in science.*

Their responses were combined to form an index of attitudes toward science; students were categorized as generally expressing positive, negative, or neutral attitudes. As shown in FIGURE 4.3, the majority of 13-year-olds in all participating countries except one expressed positive attitudes toward science, with more than three-quarters of the students from Slovenia, Spain (except Cataluña), and Jordan giving favorable responses. Korean students were a notable exception: only 27 percent of these top-performing students exhibited positive attitudes toward science.

RELATIONSHIP OF HOME ACTIVITIES AND SCIENCE PERFORMANCE

An examination of the relationship between home activities and science performance within populations confirms the importance of how students spend their time outside of school. For each population, FIGURE 4.4 indicates with pluses, minuses, and zeros whether the relationship between achievement and a particular home activity is positive, negative, or not related in a linear fashion to a statistically significant degree. There is a positive relationship between leisure reading and science achievement in 16 populations. Time spent on homework across all school subjects is positively related to performance in 9 populations, and the amount of time spent watching television is negatively related in 10 populations. Positive student attitudes towards science are related to higher science performance in 15 populations.

FIGURE 4.4

Science, Age 13
Relationship of Home Activities and
Average Percents Correct within Populations

COMPREHENSIVE POPULATIONS	Amount of Leisure Reading[1]	Amount of Time Spent on All Homework[1]	Amount of Time Spent Watching Television[1]	Students' Attitudes Towards Science[1,2]
Korea	+	O	–	+
Taiwan	+	+	–	+
Switzerland 15 Cantons	+	O	–	+
Hungary	+	+	–	+
Soviet Union Russian-speaking Schools in 14 Republics	+	+	O	O
Slovenia	+	O	O	+
Emilia-Romagna, Italy†	+	O	O	+
Israel Hebrew-speaking Schools	O	O	O	O
Canada	+	–	–	+
France	+	+	–	+
Scotland†	+	+	–	+
Spain Spanish-speaking Schools except in Cataluña	+	O	O	+
United States†	+	O	–	+
Ireland	+	+	–	+
Jordan	O	+	O	+

POPULATIONS WITH EXCLUSIONS OR LOW PARTICIPATION				
England Low Participation‡	+	+	O	+
China In-school Population, Restricted Grades, 20 Provinces & Cities	+	O	–	+
Portugal In-school Population, Restricted Grades†	+	O	+	O
São Paulo, Brazil Restricted Grades	O	O	O	O
Fortaleza, Brazil In-school Population, Restricted Grades	–	+	O	O

+ Statistically significant positive linear relationship.
– Statistically significant negative linear relationship.
O No statistically significant linear relationship.
† Combined school and student participation rate is below .80 but at least .70; interpret results with caution because of possible nonresponse bias.
‡ Combined school and student participation rate is below .70; interpret results with extreme caution because of possible nonresponse bias.
[1] IAEP Student Questionnaire, Age 13.
[2] Attitudes toward science is a composite score based on responses to four attitude questions.

ETS IAEP

Results of students' attitudes towards science and science performance, which are only summarized in Figures 4.3 and 4.4, are provided in detail in FIGURE 4.5. This figure gives the percentage of students who generally expressed positive, negative or undecided attitudes about science and next to each category is those students' average percent correct on the science assessment is indicated by a bar.

The figure demonstrates that achievement decreased (i.e., the bars become shorter) for students with negative attitudes in nearly every population. The differences in the length of the bars show the magnitude of the decrease and the percentages of students in each category indicate how many students are represented in the decrease. A majority of the Korean students were undecided about science, but their performance was only slightly lower than those with positive attitudes (27 percent of the students). Even those with negative attitudes toward science (19 percent) scored only 1 percentage point below those who were undecided.

Science, Age 13
Percentages of Students Reporting Various Attitudes Towards Science and Average Percents Correct By Attitude Categories*

FIGURE 4.5

Part 1

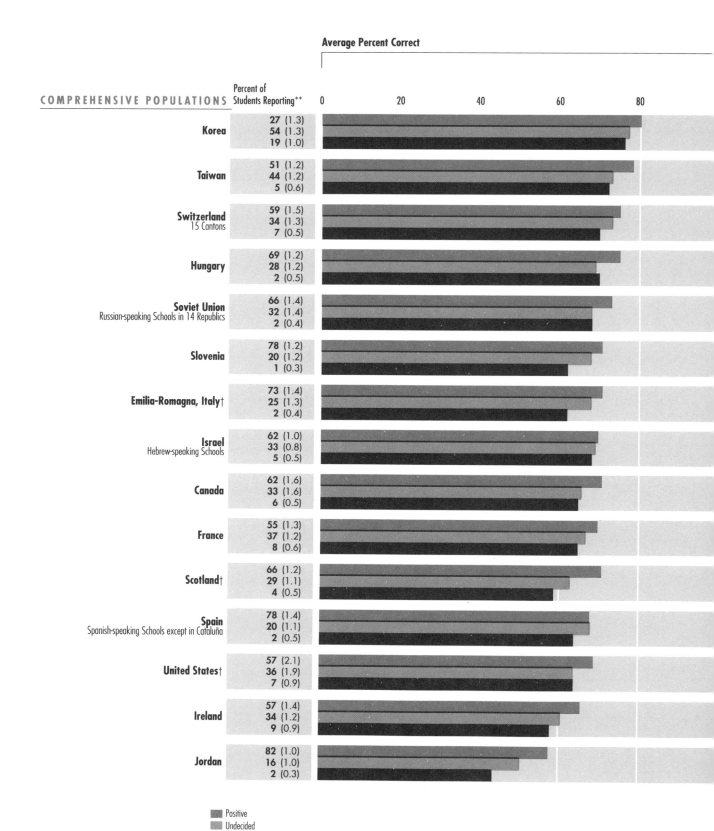

Average Percent Correct

COMPREHENSIVE POPULATIONS	Percent of Students Reporting**
Korea	27 (1.3) / 54 (1.3) / 19 (1.0)
Taiwan	51 (1.2) / 44 (1.2) / 5 (0.6)
Switzerland 15 Cantons	59 (1.5) / 34 (1.3) / 7 (0.5)
Hungary	69 (1.2) / 28 (1.2) / 2 (0.5)
Soviet Union Russian-speaking Schools in 14 Republics	66 (1.4) / 32 (1.4) / 2 (0.4)
Slovenia	78 (1.2) / 20 (1.2) / 1 (0.3)
Emilia-Romagna, Italy†	73 (1.4) / 25 (1.3) / 2 (0.4)
Israel Hebrew-speaking Schools	62 (1.0) / 33 (0.8) / 5 (0.5)
Canada	62 (1.6) / 33 (1.6) / 6 (0.5)
France	55 (1.3) / 37 (1.2) / 8 (0.6)
Scotland†	66 (1.2) / 29 (1.1) / 4 (0.5)
Spain Spanish-speaking Schools except in Cataluña	78 (1.4) / 20 (1.1) / 2 (0.5)
United States†	57 (2.1) / 36 (1.9) / 7 (0.9)
Ireland	57 (1.4) / 34 (1.2) / 9 (0.9)
Jordan	82 (1.0) / 16 (1.0) / 2 (0.3)

■ Positive
■ Undecided
■ Negative

* Jackknifed standard errors are presented in parentheses.
** Percentages may not total 100 due to rounding.
† Combined school and student participation rate is below .80 but at least .70; interpret results with caution.

IAEP

Science, Age 13

Percentages of Students Reporting Various Attitudes
Towards Science and Average Percents
Correct By Attitude Categories*

FIGURE 4.5 Part 2

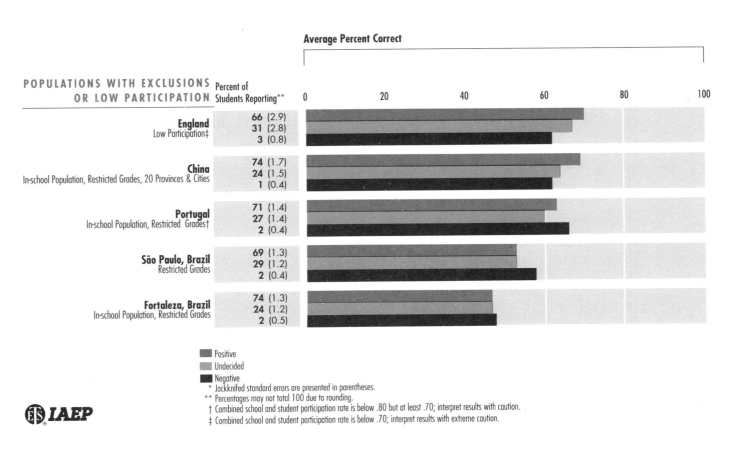

Average Percent Correct

POPULATIONS WITH EXCLUSIONS OR LOW PARTICIPATION	Percent of Students Reporting**						
		0	20	40	60	80	100
England Low Participation‡	66 (2.9) 31 (2.8) 3 (0.8)						
China In-school Population, Restricted Grades, 20 Provinces & Cities	74 (1.7) 24 (1.5) 1 (0.4)						
Portugal In-school Population, Restricted Grades†	71 (1.4) 27 (1.4) 2 (0.4)						
São Paulo, Brazil Restricted Grades	69 (1.3) 29 (1.2) 2 (0.4)						
Fortaleza, Brazil In-school Population, Restricted Grades	74 (1.3) 24 (1.2) 2 (0.5)						

■ Positive
■ Undecided
■ Negative

* Jackknifed standard errors are presented in parentheses.
** Percentages may not total 100 due to rounding.
† Combined school and student participation rate is below .80 but at least .70; interpret results with caution.
‡ Combined school and student participation rate is below .70; interpret results with extreme caution.

ETS IAEP

BEYOND THE SCHOOLHOUSE DOOR The factors influencing learning are not restricted to school variables. Family and out-of-school activity play an important role in promoting in-school success. Some aspects of home life, such as number of books in the home and family size, are often cited as indicators of social and economic advantage and in IAEP these variables are related to science achievement in predictable ways. These factors help explain low performance in some non-industrialized countries, but do not suggest why some countries appear to succeed in spite of difficult conditions.

Perhaps parental involvement, which can influence a child's academic performance regardless of a family's socioeconomic status, is another element that should be considered. Significant amounts of parental involvement were found in some high-performing IAEP populations but not in others.

What students do with their time after school seems to be another important home factor that affects academic performance. In many IAEP populations, high science performance was positively associated with large amounts of time spent on leisure reading and homework in all school subjects and small amounts of time spent watching television. Trends were not consistent across all populations, however, which suggests once again that the factors may operate differently from culture to culture.

Countries and Their Education Systems

CHAPTER FIVE

Starejša kot knjiga je glava.

Older than the book, is the head.

Slovenian Proverb

While it is difficult to tie social, cultural, and economic global differences to the science performance of students, these factors clearly play a role in determining the characteristics of education systems. Each country makes decisions about the education of its citizens and the roles schools play in strengthening the national identity and economy. These choices are rooted in the physical, demographic, and socioeconomic characteristics of the country as well as in its values and cultural traditions.

COUNTRY CHARACTERISTICS The countries participating in IAEP represent a broad range of physical, demographic, and socioeconomic characteristics: large and small, homogeneous and heterogeneous, urban and rural, rich and poor, highly educated and poorly educated. Some of these characteristics are presented in FIGURE 5.1; these data reflect the participating countries in their entirety and not just the republics, provinces, or cities that were sampled in the survey.

Science, Age 13

FIGURE 5.1

Average Percents Correct and Country Characteristics*

COMPREHENSIVE POPULATIONS	Average Percent Correct	Population (in Thousands)[1]	Ethnic Homogeneity (90 Percent or More from One Group)[1]	Percent Urban[1]	Per Capita Gross National Product (U.S. $)[2]	Percent of Gross National Product Spent on Education[2]	Percent Literate[1]
Korea	78 (0.5)	42,793	Yes	70	3,883	4.5	93
Taiwan	76 (0.4)	20,221	No	74	4,355	3.6	92
Switzerland 15 Cantons	74 (0.9)	6,756	No	60	27,693	4.8	100
Hungary	73 (0.5)	10,437	Yes	62	2,490	5.7	99
Soviet Union Russian-speaking Schools in 14 Republics	71 (1.0)	290,122	No	66	8,728	7.0	99
Slovenia	70 (0.5)	1,948	Yes[3]	74[3]	7,233[3]	3.4[3]	99[3]
Emilia-Romagna, Italy†	70 (0.7)	57,512	Yes	65	13,814	4.0	97
Israel Hebrew-speaking Schools	70 (0.7)	4,666	No	89	8,882	10.2	92
Canada	69 (0.4)	26,620	No	76	17,309	7.4	96
France	69 (0.6)	56,647	Yes	73	16,419	6.1	99
Scotland†	68 (0.6)	5,094	Yes[4]	92[4]	10,917[4]	5.2[4]	100[4]
Spain Spanish-speaking Schools except in Cataluña	68 (0.6)	39,618	No	76	8,078	3.2	93
United States†	67 (1.0)	251,394	No	77	19,789	7.5	96
Ireland	63 (0.6)	3,509	Yes	57	7,603	6.7	100
Jordan	57 (0.7)	3,169	Yes	70	1,527	7.1	77

POPULATIONS WITH EXCLUSIONS OR LOW PARTICIPATION							
England Low Participation‡	69 (1.2)	47,536	Yes[4]	92[4]	10,917[4]	5.2[4]	100[4]
China In-school Population, Restricted Grades, 20 Provinces & Cities	67 (1.1)	1,133,683	Yes	26[5]	356	2.7	73
Portugal In-school Population, Restricted Grades†	63 (0.8)	10,388	Yes	30	3,740	4.4	84
São Paulo, Brazil Restricted Grades	53 (0.6)	150,368	No	75	2,245	3.3	81
Fortaleza, Brazil In-school Population, Restricted Grades	46 (0.6)	150,368	No	75	2,245	3.3	81

* Jackknifed standard errors are presented in parentheses.
† Combined school and student participation rate is below .80 but at least .70; interpret results with caution because of possible nonresponse bias.
‡ Combined school and student participation rate is below .70; interpret results with extreme caution because of possible nonresponse bias.
[1] *1991 Britannica Book of the Year.* Chicago: Encyclopedia Britannica, Inc, 1991. Data reflect entire country.
[2] *P.C. Globe.* Tempe, AZ: P.C. Globe, Inc., 1990. Data reflect entire country.
[3] *Annual Statistical Report of Slovenia,* Central Statistics Office, Ljubljana, Slovenia, 1990.
[4] Data are for the United Kingdom.
[5] National Population Census Office, *Major Figures of the Fourth National Population Census of China.* Beijing: China Statistical Publishing House, 1991.

While most of these country characteristics are not closely related to achievement of 13-year-old students, they provide an important context for understanding the relative performance of participants. China, the Soviet Union, and the United States, are the largest populations in IAEP with about 1.1 billion, 300 million, and 250 million people, respectively. Alongside these giants stand the 4.5 million of Israel, 3.5 million of Ireland, 3 million of Jordan, and 2 million of Slovenia. Clearly, large and small countries face different problems in the administration of national educational programs.

The degree of a country's cultural homogeneity also influences how educational programs are formulated and implemented. Eleven of the 19 participating countries have populations that are dominated by a single ethnic group: Korea, Hungary, Slovenia, Italy, France, Scotland, Ireland, Jordan, England, China, and Portugal. Similarities in language, religion, and values tend to reflect ethnic similarities. More than 10 percent of the populations in the remaining eight countries comes from one or more ethnic minority groups.

Most of the participating countries' populations are urbanized and have industrialized economies. All but two of the countries' populations are at least 50 percent urban. China and Portugal are still at least 70 percent rural, which must influence their orientation toward education. Among participants, the variation in national wealth, as measured by per-capita gross national product (in U.S. dollars), is startling and can explain or confuse our understanding of differences in science performance. Among the poorest countries are Jordan, one of the lowest-performing populations, Hungary, one of the highest-performing populations, and China, which performed at about average on the science assessment. In per-capita terms, the wealthiest populations are Switzerland, followed by the United States, Canada, and France.

Some countries can compensate for limited resources by spending a greater share of their wealth on education. Among the IAEP countries, Israel spends the greatest percentage of its gross national product on education — more than 10 percent. China spends the smallest percentage — less than 3 percent.

Statistics indicate that literacy rates are fairly high (90 percent or greater) in all IAEP countries except Jordan, China, Portugal, and Brazil where between 16 and 27 percent of the adult population are still categorized as illiterate.

Basic descriptive characteristics about countries illustrate some of the grave problems that developing countries such as Jordan and Brazil face in the education of their young people. The data, however, fail to explain why some poor countries manage to achieve phenomenal success in education and why some rich and powerful nations fail to perform at the same high levels.

EDUCATION SYSTEMS Differences in country characteristics are often translated into differences in education systems. Predominantly urban countries are more likely to have large schools and large classes. Countries with strong centralized governments tend to centralize educational policy as well. Poor countries have a higher incidence of problems in their schools, such as overcrowding, inadequate facilities, insufficient textbooks. Some of these characteristics of education systems are summarized in FIGURE 5.2.

Although countries vary with respect to the age at which children are required to start school, in most countries, children are six years old when they begin compulsory schooling. Children in Scotland and England start first grade earlier, at the age of five, and those in the German part of Switzerland, parts of the Soviet Union, Slovenia, parts of China, and Brazil do not start until age seven. Countries also vary in terms of the availability of nursery schools and kindergartens and the inclusion of academic content in those programs. Furthermore, since academic development often proceeds along with physical and mental maturation, one cannot assume that by age 9 or 13 that students who started school at age seven are two years behind those who started at age five.

Likewise, one must also be careful in comparing countries with respect to the number of days in the school year. In many locations, festivals, sports events, and other non-academic activities are integrated into the school-year calendar. Trying to get a more precise measure of time spent on school activities, IAEP asked school administrators to indicate the number of days specifically devoted to student instruction in the school year. The results are reported in Figure 5.2. Variation among countries is evident in this indicator as well. The average for most populations is from 175 to about 199 days a year. Schools in France, Ireland and Portugal (restricted grades) provide fewer than 175 days of instruction annually. The average in China (in-school population) is dramatically higher (251 days) and Korea, Taiwan, Switzerland (15 cantons), Emilia-Romagna, and Israel (Hebrew), reported averages from 200 to 225 days a year.

To obtain a full picture of instructional time, one needs also to know the number of minutes spent on instruction each school day, excluding time spent for homeroom, lunch, recess, study hall, or moving to and from classes. Most IAEP countries devote, on average, between 240 and 360 minutes (four to six hours) to instruction each day. France spends the most time on instruction, 370 minutes daily. Two populations provide less than 240 minutes daily: Hungary and Fortaleza (restricted grades).

Science, Age 13
Average Percents Correct and Education Systems*

FIGURE 5.2

COMPREHENSIVE POPULATIONS	Average Percent Correct	Age Start School[1]	Average Days of Instruction in Year[2]	Average Minutes of Instruction in School Each Day[2]	Average Class Size for Modal Grade[2]	National Curriculum[1]	Percent of Schools with One or More Serious Problems[2]
Korea	**78** (0.5)	6	**222** (0.4)	**264** (2.4)	**49** (0.7)	Yes	**24** (4.9)
Taiwan	**76** (0.4)	6	**222** (2.5)	**318** (6.9)	**44** (0.6)	Yes	**10** (2.8)
Switzerland 14 Cantons	**74** (0.9)	6 or 7	**207** (3.2)§	**305** (7.4)§	**18** (0.7)§	No	**11** (3.5)§
Hungary	**73** (0.5)	6	**177** (1.5)	**223** (1.3)	**27** (0.8)	Yes	**32** (4.2)
Soviet Union Russian-speaking Schools in 14 Republics	**71** (1.0)	6 or 7	**198** (2.1)	**243** (2.6)	**22** (1.1)	Yes	**72** (5.1)
Slovenia	**70** (0.5)	7	**190** (1.5)	**248** (2.5)	**25** (0.4)	Yes	**50** (5.3)
Emilia-Romagna, Italy†	**70** (0.7)	6	**204** (0.5)	**289** (5.0)	**21** (1.9)	Yes	**18** (5.1)
Israel Hebrew-speaking Schools	**70** (0.7)	6	**215** (2.2)	**278** (6.5)	**32** (0.7)	Yes	**46** (6.7)
Canada	**69** (0.4)	6	**188** (0.2)	**304** (0.8)	**25** (0.3)	No	**13** (1.3)
France	**69** (0.6)	6	**174** (1.7)	**370** (3.4)	**25** (0.6)	Yes	**29** (4.9)
Scotland†	**68** (0.6)	5	**191** (0.9)	**324** (2.3)	**24** (0.7)	Yes	**23** (4.0)
Spain Spanish-speaking Schools except in Cataluña	**68** (0.6)	6	**188** (2.3)	**285** (3.2)	**29** (0.7)	Yes	**33** (5.0)
United States†	**67** (1.0)	6	**178** (0.4)	**338** (5.0)	**23** (1.3)	No	**5** (2.2)
Ireland	**63** (0.6)	6	**173** (0.9)	**323** (4.4)	**27** (0.7)	Yes	**39** (5.8)
Jordan	**57** (0.7)	6	**191** (1.6)	**260** (2.9)	**27** (1.5)	Yes	**63** (5.3)

POPULATIONS WITH EXCLUSIONS OR LOW PARTICIPATION

England Low Participation‡	**69** (1.2)	5	**192** (1.8)	**300** (4.4)	**22** (1.7)	Yes	**24** (8.3)
China In-school Population, Restricted Grades, 20 Provinces & Cities	**67** (1.1)	6.5 or 7	**251** (2.1)	**305** (7.1)	**48** (0.8)	Yes	**43** (6.3)
Portugal In-school Population, Restricted Grades†	**63** (0.8)	6	**172** (1.1)	**334** (6.5)	**25** (0.8)	Yes	**56** (7.9)
São Paulo, Brazil Restricted Grades	**53** (0.6)	7	**181** (0.2)	**271** (9.3)	**38** (1.8)	No	**60** (4.6)
Fortaleza, Brazil In-school Population, Restricted Grades	**46** (0.6)	7	**183** (1.1)	**223** (9.8)	**32** (2.1)	No	**62** (5.3)

* Jackknifed standard errors are presented in parentheses.
† Combined school and student participation rate is below .80 but at least .70; interpret results with caution because of possible nonresponse bias.
‡ Combined school and student participation rate is below .70; interpret results with extreme caution because of possible nonresponse bias.
§ Results represent percent of classrooms in schools.
[1] IAEP Country Questionnaire. Data reflect entire country.
[2] IAEP School Questionnaire, Age 13.

While large class sizes do not hinder many types of instruction, they do limit opportunities for individual attention, small group discussions, and hands-on activities. School administrators in 10 populations indicated the average class size for the grade in which most 13-year-olds are enrolled is between 25 and 34 students. Schools in Switzerland (15 cantons), the Soviet Union (Russian-speaking schools), Emilia-Romagna, Scotland, the United States, and England (low participation) have smaller classes, ranging from 18 to 24 students. Very large classes of more than 45 students are the norm in Korea and China (in-school population), while classes average 38 and 44 students in São Paulo (restricted grades) and Taiwan, respectively.

Four IAEP countries encourage local or regional control over curricular matters: Switzerland, Canada, the United States, and Brazil which does not set the educational programs for São Paulo and Fortaleza. Of this group, the United States is actively discussing centralization. The remaining populations have a national curriculum. In England (low participation), the centralization of educational goals and objectives is only two years old. In the other countries, a strong national ministry of education is a long-established tradition.

School administrators were asked to what extent they face problems of overcrowded classrooms, inadequate facilities and maintenance, shortages of textbooks and other educational materials. Student absenteeism, lack of discipline, and vandalism of school property were also surveyed. Their responses to eight questions listing these problems were combined into an index of serious problems. In only six populations did at least one-half of the schools report one or more serious problems: the Soviet Union (Russian-speaking schools), Slovenia, Jordan, Portugal (restricted grades), São Paulo (restricted grades), and Fortaleza (restricted grades).

NO SINGLE SOLUTION Education systems vary from country to country but not necessarily in patterns that explain high and low science achievement. It does not seem to matter greatly whether students begin school at an early or late age and while some high-performing countries have a longer school year or a longer school day, these characteristics were also present among some low-achieving groups. While no one would advocate the benefits of increasing class size, several education systems demonstrated success despite large class sizes. Finally, some countries succeed, in some cases, in spite of serious problems in school.

The Science Performance of 9-Year-Olds

CHAPTER SIX

Мир освещен Солнцем,
а человек - Знанием.

**The World is lighted by the Sun,
a human being – by knowledge.**

Russian Proverb

Fourteen of the 19 countries participated in an optional assessment of 9-year-olds. Some countries sampled students from the entire age cohort and others excluded some segments of the total age-eligible population or had low school and student participation rates. The results of these two sets of countries are reported separately as comprehensive populations and populations with exclusions or low participation.

OVERALL SCIENCE PERFORMANCE The average percent correct and distribution of scores for each population are presented in FIGURE 6.1. The red bars indicate the average percent correct and take into account the imprecision of these estimates due to sampling. When the bars overlap with one another, as they do in many cases, performance is not significantly different. The shaded bars indicate the range of scores for the best students (those in the 90th through the 99th percentile) and for the lowest-performing students (those in the 1st through the 10th percentiles). The average percents correct for students in the 5th and 95th percentiles are marked by bullets within the shaded bars.[25]

The range of average percents correct across the 14 comprehensive populations and populations with exclusions or low participation at age 9 is only 13 points, and in all populations some students performed very well and others performed poorly. The difference between the highest- and lowest-performing groups was much greater at age 13, but when considering just these populations that participated in the assessment at both age levels, the difference was only 15 points.

The average score across the two population groups, represented by a vertical dashed line, is 62 percent correct.[26]

Nine-year-olds from Canada (four provinces), Hungary, Spain (except Cataluña), the Soviet Union (Russian-speaking schools), Israel (Hebrew), England (low participation), and Scotland (low participation) performed about the same as the IAEP average. The highest-performing populations were in Korea, Taiwan, the United States, and Emilia-Romagna (low participation) with average percents correct of 68, 67, 65, and 67, respectively. As the overlapping bars on the figure illustrate, performance of these four groups are essentially the same.

The remaining comprehensive populations and populations with exclusions or low participation scored below the IAEP average. These included, Slovenia, Ireland, and Portugal (restricted grades); and when sampling error is taken into account, their performance levels are equivalent.

Four Canadian populations scored about at the IAEP average: Quebec (English), Quebec (French), Ontario (English), and New Brunswick (English). Of the remaining Canadian populations, British Columbia scored above the IAEP average with 66 percent correct and Ontario (French) scored below the average with 56 percent correct. The range of scores for the Canadian populations is only 10 points, and in many cases performance is equivalent from one population to another.

Achievement reflects the percent correct on 58 questions. Responses to two questions included in the assessment were removed from the results after a series of data analysis steps determined they were not functioning the same way across all populations.[27]

---

25 Performance of students at the very bottom of the distribution (the lowest 1 percent) and the very top (the highest 1 percent) are not represented on the figure because very few students fall into these categories and their performance cannot be estimated with precision.

26 The IAEP average is the unweighted average of scores of the comprehensive populations, populations with exclusions or low participation, and Canadian populations. An unweighted average has been chosen to describe the midpoint because it is not influenced by the differntial weights of very large and very small populations.

27 See the Procedural Appendix pp. 140-141, and the *IAEP Technical Report* for a detailed discussion of cluster and differential item functioning analysis.

FIGURE 6.1

Science, Age 9
Distribution of Percent Correct Scores by Country*

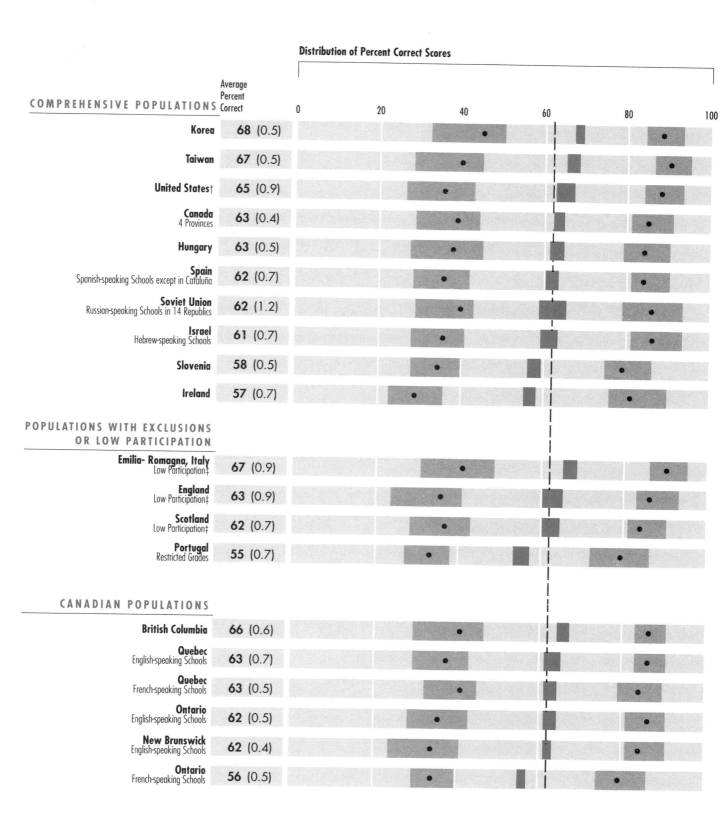

Distribution of Percent Correct Scores

COMPREHENSIVE POPULATIONS	Average Percent Correct
Korea	**68** (0.5)
Taiwan	**67** (0.5)
United States†	**65** (0.9)
Canada 4 Provinces	**63** (0.4)
Hungary	**63** (0.5)
Spain Spanish-speaking Schools except in Cataluña	**62** (0.7)
Soviet Union Russian-speaking Schools in 14 Republics	**62** (1.2)
Israel Hebrew-speaking Schools	**61** (0.7)
Slovenia	**58** (0.5)
Ireland	**57** (0.7)

POPULATIONS WITH EXCLUSIONS OR LOW PARTICIPATION

Emilia- Romagna, Italy Low Participation‡	**67** (0.9)
England Low Participation‡	**63** (0.9)
Scotland Low Participation‡	**62** (0.7)
Portugal Restricted Grades	**55** (0.7)

CANADIAN POPULATIONS

British Columbia	**66** (0.6)
Quebec English-speaking Schools	**63** (0.7)
Quebec French-speaking Schools	**63** (0.5)
Ontario English-speaking Schools	**62** (0.5)
New Brunswick English-speaking Schools	**62** (0.4)
Ontario French-speaking Schools	**56** (0.5)

■ Average percent correct with simultaneous confidence interval controlling for all possible comparisons among comprehensive populations, populations with exclusions or low participation, and Canadian populations based on the Bonferroni procedure (the average ±2.62 standard errors).

● Bullet is 5th and 95th percentile. ■ are 1st to 10th percentiles and 90th to 99th percentiles.

┊ IAEP Average

* Jackknifed standard errors are presented in parentheses.

† Combined school and student participation rate is below .80 but at least .70; interpret results with caution because of possible nonresponse bias.

‡ Combined school and student participation rate is below .70; interpret results with extreme caution because of possible nonresponse bias.

IAEP

The patterns of performance for males and females at age 9, shown in FIGURE 6.2, are not the same as those seen at age 13. A gender gap is prevalent in more than half of the populations, with males outperforming females by significant margins in Korea, Taiwan, Canada (4 provinces), Hungary, Spain (except Cataluña), Israel (Hebrew), Ireland, and Portugal (restricted grades). In the case of Canada and Hungary the gender differences are not as large as the difference seen in other populations, but the differences are still statistically significant. The largest gap occurred in Korea where boys, on average, achieved scores that were 5 percentage points higher than those for girls. In Scotland (low participation), girls at age 9 appear to perform slightly better than boys. However, when the standard errors are considered, the difference in performance is not statistically significant.

The population results were not always consistent at the two age levels. While there were no significant gender differences at age 9 in the United States, the Soviet Union (Russian-speaking schools), Slovenia, Emilia-Romagna (low participation), and Scotland (low participation), boys scored significantly higher than girls at age 13 as seen in Chapter One. In Taiwan at age 13, there was no gender gap, but at age 9, boys outperformed girls.

Figure 6.2 also indicated that most students in most populations agreed with the statement "science is appropriate for boys and girls equally," as was seen at age 13. Only in Korea did significant numbers of students view science as gender-linked. In Korea 31 percent of the students believed science was more for boys and 26 percent believed it was more important for girls.

Performance levels of boys and girls were about the same in each Canadian population except for Quebec (English) and Ontario (English) where boys performed significantly better than girls. In Ontario (French), 15 percent of the students thought science was more appropriate for boys, while 18 percent said it was more for girls.

Sciences, Age 9

Percentages of Students Reporting Science Is Equally Appropriate for Boys and Girls and Average Percents Correct by Gender*

FIGURE 6.2

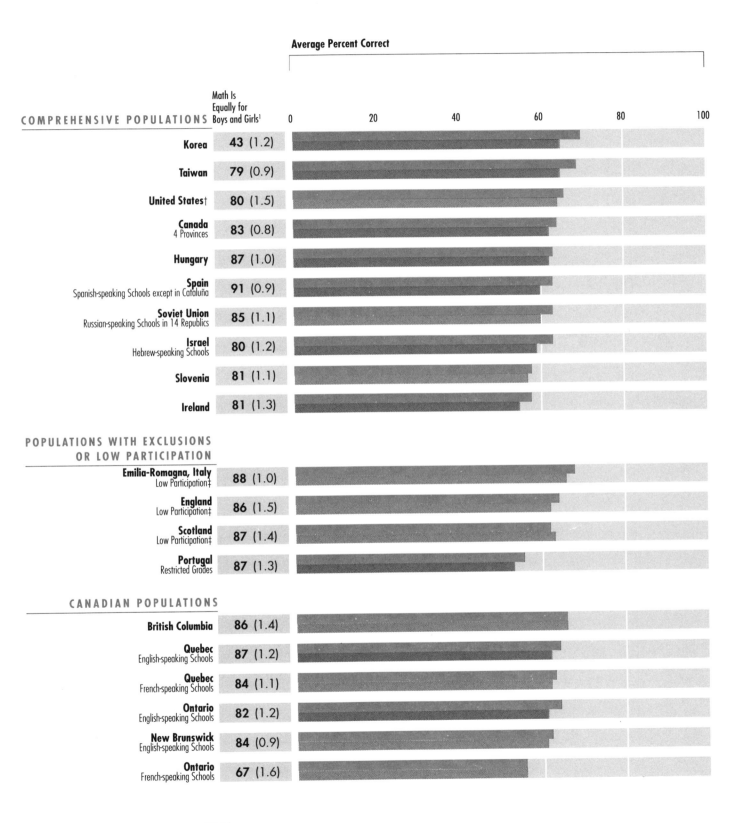

Average Percent Correct

COMPREHENSIVE POPULATIONS	Math Is Equally for Boys and Girls[1]
Korea	**43** (1.2)
Taiwan	**79** (0.9)
United States†	**80** (1.5)
Canada 4 Provinces	**83** (0.8)
Hungary	**87** (1.0)
Spain Spanish-speaking Schools except in Cataluña	**91** (0.9)
Soviet Union Russian-speaking Schools in 14 Republics	**85** (1.1)
Israel Hebrew-speaking Schools	**80** (1.2)
Slovenia	**81** (1.1)
Ireland	**81** (1.3)

POPULATIONS WITH EXCLUSIONS OR LOW PARTICIPATION

Emilia-Romagna, Italy Low Participation‡	**88** (1.0)
England Low Participation‡	**86** (1.5)
Scotland Low Participation‡	**87** (1.4)
Portugal Restricted Grades	**87** (1.3)

CANADIAN POPULATIONS

British Columbia	**86** (1.4)
Quebec English-speaking Schools	**87** (1.2)
Quebec French-speaking Schools	**84** (1.1)
Ontario English-speaking Schools	**82** (1.2)
New Brunswick English-speaking Schools	**84** (0.9)
Ontario French-speaking Schools	**67** (1.6)

■ Males
■ Females
■ Statistically significant difference between groups at the .05 level.
* Jackknifed standard errors are presented in parentheses.
† Combined school and student participation rate is below .80 but at least .70; interpret results with caution because of possible nonresponse bias.
‡ Combined school and student participation rate is below .70; interpret results with extreme caution because of possible nonresponse bias.
[1] IAEP Student Questionnaire, Age 9.

Summaries of science performance merely begin to describe the variation that exists from country to country. Of more importance to educators is a description of performance in the various science content areas that are taught in school. While statistical analyses of the IAEP data confirm that questions across all topics can be legitimately summarized without masking important differences between countries, results by topic categories do show some variation.[28] The results for age 9 students are presented for four topics, which are listed in FIGURE 6.3 along with the number of questions in each category. All of the questions used a multiple-choice format.

FIGURE 6.3

Science, Age 9:
Numbers of Questions by Topics

Life Sciences	Physical Sciences	Earth and Space Sciences	Nature of Science	Total
23	17	10	8	58

The performance of the comprehensive populations and populations with exclusions or low participation in each of the four topics is presented in FIGURE 6.4. The patterns of performance were examined to see if the achievement of a population in a particular topic area was different from its overall achievement. In general, the relative performance of the two groups in each of the topics mirrors their overall achievement in science. However, there were some exceptions. Since the average difficulty levels of the questions in the various topics and across all topics differ, performance was examined in relative terms. This was done by comparing the difference between a population's topic average and the IAEP topic average with the difference between the population's overall average and the IAEP overall average.[29]

---

[28] A country-by-topic interaction analysis using Hartigan and Wong's K-Means analysis technique indicates that the differences in performance from topic to topic do not confound the main effects of overall performance. This means that the relative performance of countries would remain essentially the same if a group of items from a particular topic or topics were removed from the overall summary measure. More details of this analysis is provided in the Procedural Appendix, p. 140 and in the *IAEP Technical Report*.

[29] For these analyses of achievement by topic, populations are cited as deviating from their normal pattern if the difference between their deviation from the mean for the topic and their deviation from the overall mean is twice the standard error of the difference between these deviations, or greater. Further details of these analyses are provided in the Procedural Appendix, pp. 141-142, and the *IAEP Technical Report*.

Science, Age 9

FIGURE 6.4

Average Percents Correct by Topic

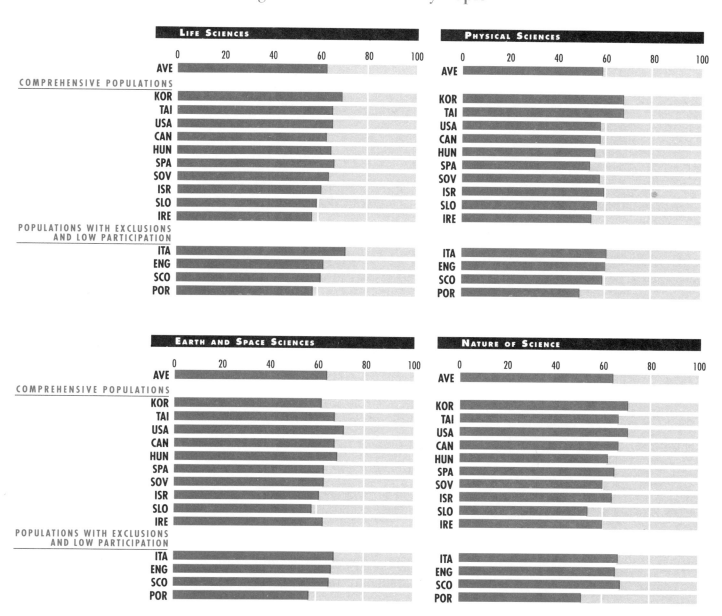

KEY

AVE   IAEP Topic Average
KOR   Korea
HUN   Hungary
TAI   Taiwan
SOV   Soviet Union – Russian-speaking Schools in 14 Republics
ISR   Israel – Hebrew-speaking Schools
SPA   Spain – Spanish-speaking Schools Except in Cataluña
IRE   Ireland
CAN   Canada – 4 Provinces
USA   United States †
SLO   Slovenia
ITA   Emilia-Romagna, Italy – Low Participation‡
SCO   Scotland – Low Participation‡
ENG   England – Low Participation‡
POR   Portugal – Restricted Grades

† Combined school and student participation rate is below .80 but at least .70; interpret results with caution because of possible nonresponse bias.
‡ Combined school and student participation rate is below .70; interpret results with extreme caution because of possible nonresponse bias.

The performance of comprehensive populations and populations with exclusions or low participation in Life Sciences, which accounts for 40 percent of the assessment, was relatively the same across all science questions except that students from Spain (except Cataluña) and Emilia-Romagna (low participation) performed relatively better in this area than they did overall; while students from Ireland performed relatively lower than their overall science score. In Physical Sciences — 29 percent of the assessment — Korea, Taiwan, and Slovenia performed better compared with their overall scores, while students from the United States, Hungary, and Spain (except Cataluña) did less well compared to their achievement overall. About 17 percent of the assessment was devoted to Earth and Space Sciences questions and in this category, three comprehensive populations and populations with exclusions or low participation performed relatively better than they did overall: the United States, Hungary, and Ireland. Korea scored lower compared with their overall achievement level. Performance of populations varied from the norm in the Nature of Science — 14 percent of the assessment — with students from the United States, Canada (four provinces), and Scotland (low participation) receiving relatively higher scores than they did overall; and students from Slovenia and Portugal (restricted grades) receiving relatively lower scores than they did on all science items.

In addition to the science topics discussed, IAEP measured three categories of science processes: Knows Science, Uses Sciences, and Integrates Science. The performance for nearly all populations was fairly consistent across the science process areas as indicated by FIGURE 6.5.

Achievement on Knows Science questions mirrored overall performance except Spain (except Cataluña) performed relatively better and Taiwan scored relatively less well than they did overall. In the Uses Science category, all populations had scores that were not statistically different from their overall averages. Finally, in Integrates Science Scotland (low participation) scored higher and Emilia-Romagna (low participation) lower, compared to their performance overall.

The performance of the Canadian populations in the various topics and process categories shown in FIGURE 6.6 was also fairly consistent. Most of the exceptions occur in the topic areas of Earth and Space Sciences and Nature of Science.

FIGURE 6.5

Science, Age 9
Average Percents Correct by Cognitive Process

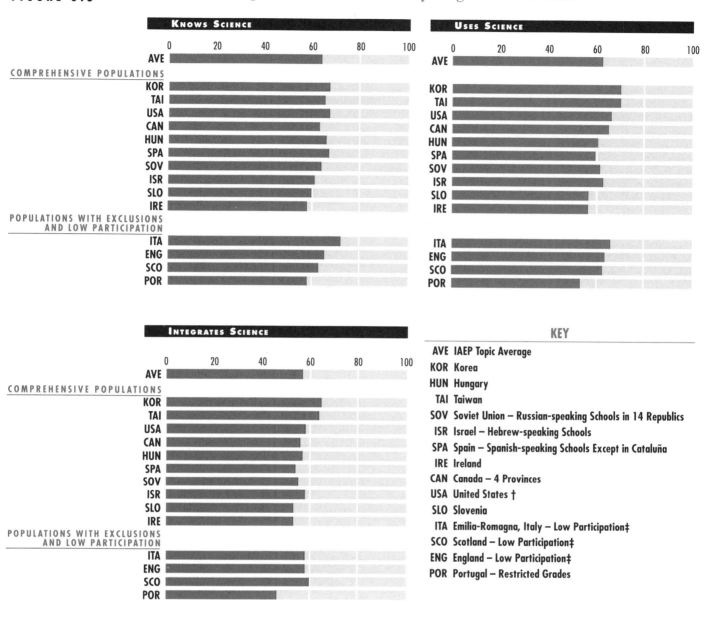

KEY

AVE	IAEP Topic Average
KOR	Korea
HUN	Hungary
TAI	Taiwan
SOV	Soviet Union – Russian-speaking Schools in 14 Republics
ISR	Israel – Hebrew-speaking Schools
SPA	Spain – Spanish-speaking Schools Except in Cataluña
IRE	Ireland
CAN	Canada – 4 Provinces
USA	United States †
SLO	Slovenia
ITA	Emilia-Romagna, Italy – Low Participation‡
SCO	Scotland – Low Participation‡
ENG	England – Low Participation‡
POR	Portugal – Restricted Grades

† Combined school and student participation rate is below .80 but at least .70; interpret results with caution because of possible nonresponse bias.
‡ Combined school and student participation rate is below .70; interpret results with extreme caution because of possible nonresponse bias.

In Earth and Space Sciences, three populations scored relatively better than they did overall: British Columbia, Ontario (English), and New Brunswick (English); and in Nature of Science, two populations — Quebec (English) and Quebec (French) received relatively higher scores than they did overall. In the remaining topic areas, Ontario (French) performed relatively lower than their overall achievement in Life Sciences and British Columbia performed less well in Physical Sciences compared to its score in science overall. The performance of the other Canadian populations mirrored in these two topics their overall averages.

In the science process areas, the scores were the same relative to their scores overall for most populations. The only exceptions were Quebec (French) and Ontario (French) which performed less well in Knows Science, and better in Uses Science questions compared with their achievement levels in general.

Science, Age 9
Average Percents Correct by Topic and Cognitive Process for Canadian Populations*

FIGURE 6.6

	Topics				Cognitive Processes		
	Life Sciences	Physical Sciences	Earth and Space Sciences	Nature of Science	Knows Science	Uses Science	Integrates Science
IAEP Topic Averages	63 (0.6)	59 (0.5)	64 (0.7)	64 (0.8)	64 (0.6)	63 (0.5)	57 (0.7)
CANADIAN POPULATIONS							
British Columbia	66 (0.7)	60 (0.7)	72 (0.6)	70 (0.8)	68 (0.6)	67 (0.6)	59 (0.8)
Quebec English-speaking Schools†	64 (0.8)	57 (0.6)	67 (0.8)	68 (0.8)	65 (0.8)	64 (0.6)	56 (0.8)
Quebec French-speaking Schools	63 (0.6)	59 (0.6)	63 (0.6)	69 (0.7)	61 (0.5)	67 (0.6)	58 (0.6)
Ontario English-speaking Schools	63 (0.6)	57 (0.5)	68 (0.6)	66 (0.7)	64 (0.6)	64 (0.5)	55 (0.5)
New Brunswick English-speaking Schools	61 (0.4)	57 (0.4)	67 (0.5)	65 (0.5)	63 (0.4)	63 (0.4)	54 (0.5)
Ontario French-speaking Schools	55 (0.5)	54 (0.5)	61 (0.5)	60 (0.7)	55 (0.5)	60 (0.5)	52 (0.6)

* Jackknifed standard errors are presented in parentheses.
† Combined school and student participation rate is below .80 but at least .70; interpret results with caution because of possible nonresponse bias.

CONTEXTS AND ACHIEVEMENT Collecting background information from 9-year-olds is often a challenge. Children at this age often do not understand difficult questions and cannot make fine distinctions in their responses. For these reasons, the IAEP assessment asked only a few questions about their home and school experiences. Also, because the educational environment varies from country to country, students may interpret questions in different ways.

Many of the answers of 9-year-olds mirror the responses of their 13-year-old schoolmates. Information obtained about language spoken in the home, family size, and number of books in the home is essentially the same at both ages. The differences that occur may be due to misunderstandings by some of the younger students.

Classroom activities at age 9 differ from country to country. As shown in FIGURE 6.7, in most populations, about one quarter to one-third of the students indicated that they often read books about science in class. In Taiwan and Portugal (restricted grades) less than 20 percent of the students read science books often and in Spain (except Cataluña) and Slovenia about 40 percent of the students reported the same. Sizable percentages of students have never conducted science experiments at age 9. Fifty percent of the students from Ireland and Emilia-Romagna (low participation) reported that they never conduct experiments, followed by about 40 percent of the 9-year-olds in Hungary, Spain (except Cataluña), and the Soviet Union. About one quarter of the students from the United States, Canada, Scotland (low participation), Portugal (restricted grades), and Slovenia have never conduct experiments on their own. The exceptions are Israel and England where close to one-third of the students reported conducting experiments often.

The amount of student-conducted experiments is not consistently related to achievement. For example, 50 percent of the students from Ireland and Emilia-Romagna (low participaton) reported never conducting experiments. Students from Emilia-Romagna (low participaton) performed above the IAEP average and students from Ireland performed below the average.

FIGURE 6.7

Science, Age 9
Average Percents Correct, Classroom and Home Activities*

COMPREHENSIVE POPULATIONS	Average Percent Correct	Percent of Students Who Read About Science in School Often[1]	Percent of Students Who Never Conduct Experiments[1]	Percent of Students Who Read For Fun Almost Every Day[1]	Students Who Spend 2 Hours or More on All Homework Every Day[1]	Percent of Percent of Students Who Watch Television 5 Hours or More Every Day[1]
Korea	68 (0.5)	21 (1.1)	19 (1.1)	25 (1.4)	20 (1.2)	10 (0.8)
Taiwan	67 (0.5)	17 (1.0)	10 (0.8)	32 (1.3)	29 (1.4)	12 (0.8)
United States†	65 (0.9)	32 (1.5)	22 (1.3)	47 (1.8)	19 (1.4)	25 (1.6)
Canada	63 (0.4)	20 (0.7)	27 (1.0)	48 (0.9)	12 (0.6)	22 (0.7)
Hungary	63 (0.5)	36 (1.3)	40 (1.3)	52 (1.5)	29 (1.5)	15 (1.2)
Spain Spanish-speaking Schools except in Cataluña	62 (0.7)	39 (1.7)	40 (2.2)	54 (1.9)	28 (1.6)	20 (1.8)
Soviet Union Russian-speaking Schools in 14 Republics	62 (1.2)	33 (2.2)	44 (1.2)	65 (1.8)	27 (1.8)	17 (1.1)
Israel Hebrew-speaking Schools	61 (0.7)	27 (1.3)	14 (1.1)	55 (1.3)	36 (1.7)	24 (1.2)
Slovenia	58 (0.5)	40 (1.5)	21 (1.1)	61 (1.2)	15 (1.2)	10 (0.8)
Ireland	57 (0.7)	24 (1.3)	50 (2.0)	50 (1.5)	16 (1.3)	22 (1.6)
POPULATIONS WITH EXCLUSIONS OR LOW PARTICIPATION						
Emilia-Romagna, Italy Low Participation‡	67 (0.9)	22 (1.6)	50 (1.8)	50 (1.6)	27 (1.2)	9 (1.1)
England Low Participation‡	63 (0.9)	21 (2.0)	11 (1.3)	49 (1.8)	10 (1.1)	22 (1.9)
Scotland Low Participation‡	62 (0.7)	22 (1.5)	28 (2.6)	46 (2.1)	5 (0.8)	24 (1.4)
Portugal Restricted Grades	55 (0.7)	18 (1.9)	22 (1.6)	62 (1.6)	22 (1.6)	18 (1.6)

IAEP

* Jackknifed standard errors are presented in parentheses.
† Combined school and student participation rate is below .80 but at least .70; interpret results with caution because of possible nonresponse bias.
‡ Combined school and student participation rate is below .70; interpret results with extreme caution because of possible nonresponse bias.
[1] IAEP Student Questionnaire, Age 9.

The responses to IAEP student questionnaires indicate that the out-of-school activities of 9-year-olds differ somewhat from those of their older schoolmates. Nine-year-olds are more likely to read books for fun, to watch television on a daily basis, and to spend less time doing homework than 13-year-olds. A major portion of young students — between 45 and 65 percent — of the 9-year-olds indicated that they read for fun almost every day in all populations except in Korea and Taiwan, where only about one quarter and one-third, respectively, reported daily leisure reading.

The norm for time spent on homework in all school subjects for 9-year-olds in all populations was one hour or less on a typical school day, except England, where the majority of students reported no homework was assigned. Heavy concentration on homework at age 9 was very rare in Scotland (low participation) and England (low participation), with 10 percent or fewer reporting two hours or more nightly. About 25 to 35 percent of the students in Taiwan, Hungary, Spain (except Cataluña), the Soviet Union (Russian-speaking schools), Israel (Hebrew), and Emilia-Romagna (low participation), reported spending at least two hours on homework a night at age 9.

About one-half or more of the students in all participating countries reported watching two to four hours of television each school day. Heavy television viewing, five hours or more daily, was more prevalent at age 9 than it was among older students. Heavy television viewing was most common in the United States, Canada (four provinces), Israel (Hebrew), Ireland, England (low participation), and Scotland (low participation) where about one quarter of the 9-year-olds reported watching television five hours or more each day.

The relationship between science performance and classroom and home factors at age 9, shown in FIGURE 6.8, confirms many of the same findings at age 13. However, as at age 13, the results are not always consistent across all populations and some counter examples are also evident. In the figure, the pluses, minuses, and zeros indicate whether the relationship between achievement and increasing values of a particular background variable for each population is positive, negative, or not related in a linear fashion to a statistically significant degree.

The descriptive data indicate that 9-year-olds tend to spend more time reading books about science than doing science experiments in school. For the majority of IAEP populations, science performance is not linearly related to reading science books in school. For one-half of the populations science performance is negatively related to doing science experiments in school and for the remaining populations, performance is unrelated to experimental work. These findings do not suggest that hands-on science experiments cannot be used successfully to build science skills.

Science, Age 9
Relationship of Classroom and Home Factors and Average Percents Correct within Populations

FIGURE 6.8

COMPREHENSIVE POPULATIONS	Amount of Science Book Reading[1]	Amount of Student Experiments[1]	Amount of Leisure Reading[1]	Amount of Time Spent on All Homework[1]	Amount of Time Spent Watching Television[1]
Korea	+	0	+	+	−
Taiwan	+	0	+	+	−
United States†	+	0	+	−	0
Canada	0	0	+	−	−
Hungary	−	−	+	0	−
Spain Spanish-speaking Schools except in Cataluña	0	−	+	0	0
Soviet Union Russian-speaking Schools in 14 Republics	0	−	+	0	0
Israel Hebrew-speaking Schools	0	0	+	+	+
Slovenia	0	−	0	0	−
Ireland	0	−	+	+	0

POPULATIONS WITH EXCLUSIONS OR LOW PARTICIPATION					
Emilia-Romagna, Italy Low Participation‡	0	−	+	0	0
England Low Participation‡	0	0	+	−	0
Scotland Low Participation‡	0	0	+	−	0
Portugal Restricted Grades	0	−	0	0	0

+ Statistically significant positive linear relationship.
− Statistically significant negative linear relationship.
0 No statistically significant linear relationship.
† Combined school and student participation rate is below .80 but at least .70; interpret results with caution because of possible nonresponse bias.
‡ Combined school and student participation rate is below .70; interpret results with extreme caution because of possible nonresponse bias.
[1] IAEP Student Questionnaire, Age 9.

 IAEP

However, educators continue to discuss how science experiments should be integrated into instruction and what the nature of those experiments should be.

The relationship between out-of school activities and achievement is not as consistent at age 9 as at age 13. Nine-year-olds reported spending more time than their older schoolmates reading for fun and those who read more often performed better on the science assessment. This was true in 12 populations. However, the amount of time 9-year-olds spent doing homework across all school subjects appears to be unrelated to science performance in almost half the populations at age 9, probably because homework is not prevalent at this age. However, the amount of homework is positively related in two higher-performing populations — Korea and Taiwan — as well as in Israel (Hebrew) and Ireland, which performed relatively less well in science. Spending more time watching television is also unrelated to achievement in eight of the populations, negatively related to achievement in five, and positively related in one.

COMPARISONS OF 9- AND 13-YEAR-OLDS' PERFORMANCE Collecting data at two ages allows comparisons of levels of performance of equivalent samples on equivalent assessment tasks. In science, a set of 13 questions covering a range of science topics and processes was administered to both age groups.

The average percents correct across the common items are presented for each age group for comprehensive populations and populations with exclusions or low participation in FIGURE 6.9. The difference in scores at the two age levels range from 17 to 25 percentage points. The smallest differences are seen in students from the higher-performing population of Emilia-Romagna (low participation) with a point spread of about 16 and the largest for students from the lower-performing population of Slovenia, where 13-year-olds scored 25 percentage points higher than their 9-year-old counterparts. This probably reflects the fact that there is more room for growth among lower-achieving groups.

FIGURE 6.9

Science, Ages 9 and 13
Average Percents Correct for Common Questions*

COMPREHENSIVE POPULATIONS	Age 9	Age 13	Difference
Korea	**64** (0.7)	**85** (0.5)	21
Taiwan	**64** (0.7)	**83** (0.4)	19
United States†	**61** (1.0)	**78** (1.0)	17
Canada	**59** (0.5)	**79** (0.4)	20
Hungary	**61** (0.7)	**82** (0.5)	21
Spain Spanish-speaking Schools except in Cataluña	**61** (0.8)	**81** (0.6)	20
Soviet Union Russian-speaking Schools in 14 Republics	**58** (1.4)	**80** (0.9)	22
Israel Hebrew-speaking Schools	**60** (0.8)	**78** (0.6)	18
Slovenia	**57** (0.6)	**82** (0.4)	25
Ireland	**53** (0.8)	**74** (0.6)	21

POPULATIONS WITH EXCLUSIONS OR LOW PARTICIPATION

	Age 9	Age 13	Difference
Emilia-Romagna, Italy Low Participation‡	**64** (1.1)	**80** (0.6)	16
England Low Participation‡	**59** (1.1)	**78** (1.0)	19
Scotland Low Participation‡	**57** (0.7)	**77** (0.6)	20
Portugal Restricted Grades	**53** (1.0)	**76** (0.8)	23

* Jackknifed standard errors are presented in parentheses.
† Combined school and student participation rate is below .80 but at least .70; interpret results with caution because of possible nonresponse bias.
‡ Combined school and student participation rate is below .70; interpret results with extreme caution because of possible nonresponse bias.

The sample questions shown in FIGURE 6.10 give three examples of the types of tasks that most 13-year-olds can do and most 9-year-olds cannot.[30] It is not surprising that younger students do not understand the steps necessary required to explain a water cycle in the first example. Nine-year-olds had some difficulty with the second item, with only 45 percent responding correctly. The last example demonstrates a routine science experiment that required the student to synthesize the given information and make a determination of what hypothesis is being tested. This is a higher-level, problem-solving task that may be familiar to 13-year-olds but would probably be an unusual task for their younger schoolmates.

FIGURE 6.10

Science, Ages 9 and 13:
Sample Test Questions

IAEP Item Average   Age 9: 45%
                                             Age 13: 72%

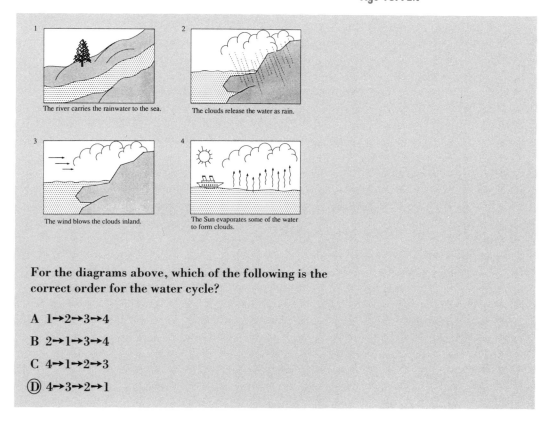

1. The river carries the rainwater to the sea.

2. The clouds release the water as rain.

3. The wind blows the clouds inland.

4. The Sun evaporates some of the water to form clouds.

For the diagrams above, which of the following is the correct order for the water cycle?

A 1→2→3→4

B 2→1→3→4

C 4→1→2→3

Ⓓ 4→3→2→1

IAEP Item Average   Age 9: 50%
                                             Age 13: 75%

Which of the following is NOT a mammal?

A Whale

B Lion

Ⓒ Pigeon

D Bat

---

[30] The difficulty level for the sample questions is in an unweighted average of the item percents correct across the comprehensive populations and populations with exclusions or low participation.

Ten plants were placed in sandy soil and ten others were placed in clay soil. Both groups of plants were kept at room temperature, given the same amount of water, and placed in a sunny room. This experiment tests the effect of which of the following?

(A) Different soils on plant growth

B Temperature on plant growth

C Sunlight on plant growth

D Water on plant growth

LAYING THE FOUNDATIONS FOR LEARNING During the primary school years, students are taught simple scientific facts and are introduced to the basic concepts of the natural sciences, of earth science and physical elements of science. While the range of science performance among participating countries is not as great as it is at age 13, some populations clearly outperform others.

In the classrooms, 9-year-olds tended to spend more time reading about science than they spent actively doing science. At home, these children tended to spend more time reading for fun and watching television and less time doing homework across all school subjects than their 13-year-old peers.

A Final Word

The task of reporting the achievement results in science from 19 countries as diverse as China, the Soviet Union, the United States, Switzerland, Israel, and Brazil is a challenge and a unique opportunity. Because one must interpret the academic performance of such a varied group of populations within the educational and cultural context of each participant, achievement data have been presented together with descriptive information about curriculua, classrooms, home environments, and country characteristics.

While it would have been satisfying to observe clear patterns between the characteristics of high-and low-performing countries, the data rarely suggest a universal answer to the question of what factors contribute to effective schooling and high performance. Although consistent relationships between certain background characteristics and achievement were often noted for a majority of populations, counter examples were almost always cited. And perhaps this is one of the obvious but important findings of the study: factors that impact on academic performance interact in complex ways and operate differently in different cultures and education systems.

The second important finding relates to the actual levels of achievement that were documented. The IAEP results provide educators, policymakers, and parents with a view of what students in 19 countries know and can do at ages 9 and 13. Unfortunately, the IAEP data may lead some individuals to focus on the academic horse race and others may decide that all comparisons are unfair. Still, international comparative achievement data can provide a picture of educational accomplishments that expands the value of national findings. As policymakers attempt to set goals and standards for their own young citizens, it can be instructive to know what levels of achievement are *possible* as demonstrated by the performance of students in other societies.

CHINA   March 9, 1991

The school is sponsored by the National Department of Railroads for the children of railroad workers. Constructed of cement and brick, it was several stories high and was indistinguishable from many of the other buildings in downtown Beijing.

I was warmly welcomed into the reception room and invited to sit at the head of the room in the seat of honor. Glasses of tea and soft drinks appeared. The principal seated at my side, repeatedly asked what he could do to help with my assignment. The student dean and a host of teachers and proctors sat quietly against the side walls. We all chatted at length about the differences between schools in China and those in the West. The principal was reluctant to give up his role as host and dismiss the group. Finally, I stood up a bit nervously, reminding him that the assessment would begin soon.

In the classroom, the children were already seated in absolute silence. On each desk was a plastic pen and pencil sharpener set — "a momento of gratitude from their teachers for their hard work," one teacher advised me.

After the session, one 13-year-old girl told me that this math test was different from her regular exams because it tested "more skill and thinking," whereas her regular exams only asked about "basic knowledge from the textbooks."

When all the papers had been collected, I was given a thorough tour of the four-storied building by the obviously proud supervisor. Most impressive was a shiny new computer lab with over 30 personal computers and several Macintosh computers. Nearby was a dark but spotless specimen room, containing shelves filled to the ceiling with hundreds of biological specimens, guarded by a rather large human skeleton.

ETS Quality Control Observer

The Participants

The thrust of this report has been to put achievement results into context. Results have been displayed and discussed together with background information about the curriculum, classroom practices, students' home environments, and the characteristics of the society and education system of each participating country. These presentations of results have, in some instances, identified factors that are characteristic of high- or low-performing populations. But in many cases, the data have reinforced the notion that many of these variables operate differently from country to country and cannot be interpreted in the same way in all cultures.

Then what does make a difference in performance levels from country to country? The answer must lie in a deeper understanding of the interactions among the variables that were studied and in a recognition of the significance of other factors that cannot be assessed in a survey project such as IAEP. Among these are historical traditions, cultural values, systems of reward, expectations, and motivation, which are most profitably studied using methods of observation and interview and reported in the form of verbal descriptions rather than data tables and graphs.

IAEP attempted to capture some of these difficult-to-measure qualities in a country questionnaire completed by project directors. Most of the questions asked for descriptive responses as opposed to multiple-choice or numerical answers. The following short summaries of each country drew upon those descriptions and describe some of the factors that are difficult to quantify.

These descriptions can only highlight some of the unique characteristics and current challenges that each country faces and, different topics are addressed for each situation. Typical themes include: demographic characteristics, cultural values, educational systems, the role of testing, and current educational reform movements.

A separate, follow-up study will conduct a series of ethnographic studies of several of these environments in an attempt to describe, rather than quantify, the qualities of these societies that motivate parents and students to value learning and to seek knowledge. Its results will be published in 1993.

BRAZIL

No. of 13-year-olds in country	3,383,600
% of 13-year-olds in IAEP frame	3%
Per Capita GNP (US $)	$2,245
% of GNP spent on education	3.3%

One of the largest countries in the world, with an area over 8.5 million square kilometers and a population of 150 million, it presents some problems which are typical of developed countries and others which are common to underdeveloped regions. In spite of its expanse and of the influence of different ethnic groups (Europeans, Africans, and Asians), it has managed, throughout its history, to maintain its linguistic unity in spite of its cultural diversity.

Regular education in Brazil consists of pre-school, for children under 7, which is not compulsory, elementary school from 7 to 14 years of age, and secondary school from 15 to 18 years of age. Access to higher education is achieved by means of highly selective examination.

The complexity of the education system presents problems as in almost all Latin American countries. The major national concern in elementary school is a cycle of repeating grades culminated by students dropping out. Even in the first grade, 52 percent of the students fail to complete the requirements. Failure rates are particularly high in grades 4 through 7. Although elementary school is available to all, it only reaches 87 percent of the 30 million children between the ages of 7 and 14. The great majority of children do not manage to finish the eight years of schooling required by law. The illiteracy rate, which was 26.0 percent in 1980 dropped to 18.8 percent in 1989; the largest pockets of illiteracy occur in the northeastern part of Brazil (36.5 percent).

Another current problem concerns the training of 1.2 million teachers for elementary school. Approximately 230,000 teachers, mainly in the rural and poorer areas, do not have formal teacher training.

There is great concern over investment in the various levels of the educational system. Constitutionally, the federal government must invest 18 percent of its national budget in education. While many state and municipal governments must invest 25 percent each of their budgets, some municipal governments are already investing up to 30 or 40 percent because they consider education an important national challenge.

CANADA

No. of 13-year-olds in country	**361,600**
% of 13-year-olds in IAEP frame	**94%**
Per Capita GNP (US $)	**$17,309**
% of GNP spent on education	**7.4%**

An enormous land mass occupying well over one-half of the North American continent, Canada's population of 26.5 million includes more than 6.5 million whose primary language is French. About 15 percent of the total population are "New Canadians," immigrants who have recently arrived from Asia, Europe, Central and South America, and Africa. This significant population of students who speak different languages and who reflect different cultures represents a major challenge to the educational system.

Each of the 10 provinces has its unique demographics, its own distinctive economy, which range from rural agricultural to highly developed industrial and financial centers, and its own traditions. Canada refers to itself as a mosaic, an apt description.

Each province considers education to be its own responsibility and not that of the federal government. Nine of the 10 provinces (except for Prince Edward Island, population 130,000) participated in IAEP and each of the nine provincial ministers of education agreed to having its results become part of an all-Canada statistic.

Descriptions of each province's educational priorities can be found on pages 116 through 121.

No. of 13-year-olds in country	18,474,000
% of 13-year-olds in IAEP frame	38%
Per Capita GNP (US $)	$356
% of GNP spent on education	2.7%

About 74 percent of the Chinese population lives in rural areas. Although great attention is paid to education, the conditions in many schools are not suitable for specific subject instruction, especially for science education.

Children start school at 6.5 or 7 years of age and a few of them have preschool education. Nine years of compulsory education are divided into 6 years of primary school and 3 years of middle school. Students may enter 3 years of senior middle school (general or vocational), if they pass a highly competitive entrance test.

All students have to take at least one test for each subject at the end of each semester. Groups of students from China regularly attend international competitions in chemistry, physics, and mathematics (the International Mathematics Olympics) and perform with distinction.

The current curriculua were designed in 1982. Since the intense entrance tests competition places a heavy burden on students, a reform of school practice is underway. The goals of the reform are: to reduce or eliminate some non-basic knowledge from textbooks and to supplement basic vocational knowledge in middle school.

No. of 13-year-olds in country	591,900
% of 13-year-olds in IAEP frame	96%
Per Capita GNP (US $)	$10,917
% of GNP spent on education	5.2%

England, the largest of the four countries that comprise the United Kingdom, has a population of 47.5 million. About 92 percent of its people live in cities and towns and England is one of the most densely populated countries in the world. About 2 million English people are from ethnic minority communities with Asian or African-Caribbean origins.

All but a small percentage of schools are maintained by governmental authorities. Under the new Education Reform Act of 1988, schools may seek permission to remove themselves from the control of local authority and can be funded directly by the Department of Education and Science. The Education Reform Act of 1988 also introduced a national curriculum which specifies for separate subject areas, "attainment targets" at 10 different levels and requires testing of all students at ages 7, 11, 14, and 16. Vocational education is also receiving more prominence.

The goal of education is to develop fully the potential and abilities of all individuals. Overall, current educational policies have sought to raise standards at all levels of ability, increase parental choice, make higher education more widely accessible and more responsive to the needs of the economy, and, generally, to the needs of a multi-ethnic society.

No. of 13-year-olds in country	**771,700**
% of 13-year-olds in IAEP frame	**98%**
Per Capita GNP (US $)	**$16,419**
% of GNP spent on education	**6.1%**

A recent law governing education, enacted in 1989 reaffirms the tradition that elementary schools should give priority attention to the development of the basic skills of reading, writing, and mathematics. These are viewed as essential in order to pursue higher levels of academic achievement. It is anticipated that by the year 2000, 80 percent of the students will reach their senior year of secondary school (12th grade).

It is a widely held belief that today's youth are less well educated than their predecessors. In the view of many, the present educational system places too much emphasis on studies of the classics with insufficient stress on pre-professional and scientific preparation. This criticism is leveled at both secondary and post-secondary institutions.

Free, public education is considered to be a right of all children regardless of socioeconomic conditions and faithful attendance is a civic responsibility. Access to a university education is obtained through success at the Baccalaureat examination after secondary studies. A successful student may select from most of the universities except medical and special advanced institutions which have further entrance requirements.

Today's teachers, once highly regarded, are accorded much less prestige even though their recruitment criteria and training are still very rigorous. There are many other career options for competent university graduates especially those skilled in mathematics and the sciences.

School funding is shared by the national government (65 percent), the local community (20 percent), industry (5 percent), and families (10 percent). The curriculum goals are set at the national level but local schools and teachers have increasing freedom to plan the sequence and methodology of instruction. Families are increasingly involved in their children's education and most families help with homework and course selection.

No. of 13-year-olds in country	**152,000**
% of 13-year-olds in IAEP frame	**99%**
Per Capita GNP (US $)	**$2,490**
% of GNP spent on education	**5.7%**

An industrialized country of close to 10.5 million people (97 percent of which are ethnic Hungarian), Hungary has a long and successful history of valuing education and schooling. Culture and education have always enjoyed high esteem throughout the society.

Like many other Eastern European countries, Hungary is emerging aggressively from Marxist frameworks. Indeed, its efforts to radically change education during the 1980s created as much confusion as it did new direction.

Traditionally, Hungary has had a strong, centralized, and controlled system. Changes in educational legislation and policy in 1985 and 1989 have opened the system to new groups of stakeholders: teachers, unions, employers, and parents. There are strong differences of opinion and debates are underway, but the movement is clearly toward western ideas. Severe budget constraints are slowing the pace of reform and change.

The priorities of the emerging system have been set: changing the foreign language requirements from Russian to other languages, introducing a "new moral basis for learning" that aims at higher education standards and competition, strengthening local control of education, and encouraging and supporting religious institutions.

No. of 13-year-olds in country	**70,130**
% of 13-year-olds in IAEP frame	**93%**
Per Capita GNP (US $)	**$7,603**
% of GNP spent on education	**6.7%**

Ireland is a small country of 3.5 million people, where agriculture and food production are vital components of its economy. Over the past thirty years the industrial and technological sectors have grown in importance so that today, more than one half of the population resides in urban areas.

About 55 percent of 4 year olds and 99 percent of 5 year olds are enrolled in primary school. Education is compulsory between the ages of 6 and 15. At age 18, the student enrollment decreases to 40 percent.

Education is centralized and all primary-school teachers follow a common set of curriculum guidelines. In 1971, there was a move to a child-centered curriculum and guidelines were established for all subjects including religion and physical education. Mathematics occupies an important role in the curriculum, but science is taught as part of Social and Environmental Studies, and does not receive as much emphasis.

For post-primary schools, the department of education prescribes curricula for a broad range of subjects that lead to public examination — the Junior Certificate after three years and the Leaving Certificate after two additional years.

The teaching profession is highly regarded in Ireland. Students entering teacher-education programs have traditionally been among the most able. There are limited opportunities for advancement, however, and there is concern at the growing imbalance between males and females in the teaching force.

The goal of the educational system is to provide young people with the necessary skills and academic preparation for further personal development, for working life, for leisure, and for living in the community.

ISRAEL

No. of 13-year-olds in country	**91,900**
% of 13-year-olds in IAEP frame	**71%**
Per Capita GNP (US $)	**$8,882**
% of GNP spent on education	**10.2%**

Israel's short history is a record of rapid and constant change. Its Jewish population is increasing rapidly due to the regular arrival of large numbers of immigrants. The total population of 4.5 million is about 18 percent Arabic. Currently there is a surplus of highly trained people in the society.

The chief goals of Israel's educational policy are the closing of the educational gaps among various segments of the population, promoting social integration, raising the general level of achievement to strengthen the productive sectors of the economy, and promoting Jewish-Zionist consciousness.

The differences among schools in socioeconomic status and scholastic achievement are relatively high and issues of equity, equality, and excellence are currently under discussion. Compensatory extracurricular activities are provided to more than 30 percent of the student population from disadvantaged backgrounds.

All children are legally bound to attend school from ages five to 15. More than 90 percent of the children aged three and four are enrolled in preschool programs. More than 50 percent of the high-school students are enrolled in vocational, technological, and comprehensive secondary education. Others are enrolled in academic education. At age 18, anyone who passes entrance examinations may attend universities. Loans and financial aid are available for higher education, especially to those from poor backgrounds.

Reforms are geared toward decentralization, free choice for parents, and increased community involvement.

ITALY

No. of 13-year-olds in country	669,600
% of 13-year-olds in IAEP frame	6%
Per Capita GNP (US $)	$13,814
% of GNP spent on education	4.0%

Italy has only been a country for slightly more than 130 years. It is still going through the process of becoming a single society. Although the cultural backgrounds of the various regions are different, the national media have had a strong homogenizing effect.

Economic development is most successful in the northern third of the country where Emilia-Romagna is located and is least evident in the South. About 65 percent of the population lives and works in cities. Even though a host of new values have changed the way people think, certain cultural traditions are still important, as evidenced by the importance of extended families, cooperative societies, and volunteer charitable organizations.

School learning continues to be held in high respect since school certificates and degrees provide access to good jobs and careers. The school system is centralized at the national level but legislation is being considered that will increase the financial and organizational autonomy of local schools. There is a good network of well-equipped vocational and technical schools.

Elementary school teachers increasingly participate in in-service training but this is much less common among secondary school faculty members. The main objective of the fairly strong teachers' associations is to protect their autonomy and areas of responsibility.

The primary school's program is relatively new, established in 1985, and the middle school curriculum, installed in 1979, has been kept current. Secondary schools are being encouraged to conduct research and to use innovative instructional practices. The current economic crisis imposes severe limitations on what is possible but the concern about future international competition is a constant stimulus for educational improvement. Public schools are under public pressure to improve the quality of general education, to delay student specialization, and to increase counseling services.

JORDAN

No. of 13-year-olds in country	83,000
% of 13-year-olds in IAEP frame	96%
Per Capita GNP (US $)	$1,527
% of GNP spent on education	7.1%

Jordan is a fast-developing country of about 3 million, mostly Moslems with a small percentage of Christians. About 70 percent of the population is accommodated in urban areas.

Education policy is strictly centralized and uniform for the whole country. Since 1964, the aim of the national education system has been to integrate elements of Arabic and Western thought, technology, and scientific development. It also aims at helping every student grow intellectually, socially, physically, and emotionally in order to become an ideal citizen, capable of self-support and of making a positive contribution to society. Focus is centered on the diversification of secondary education (academic and vocational) and on in-service teacher training. School enrollment at the various educational levels has become one of the highest in the world.

However, the quantitative expansion has been at the expense of quality. The ever-increasing use of technology in all aspects of life has prompted a new, 10-year Education Reform Plan (1989-1999). The plan aims at producing graduates equipped with high-quality general education geared towards problem solving, critical thinking, analytical skills, and the ability to apply information in creative and productive ways in order to give Jordan the skill- and knowledge-intensive workforce it needs to develop its domestic technological capacity and to maintain its competitive advantage in the region-wide labor market.

Basic education has been extended to 10 years. Graduates can continue into higher education after passing the General Secondary Education examination.

KOREA

No. of 13-year-olds in country	811,700
% of 13-year-olds in IAEP frame	97%
Per Capita GNP (US $)	$3,883
% of GNP spent on education	4.5%

Korea is an increasingly industrialized nation of 43 million people with a growing economy and a highly centralized government. The population, which is homogeneous in both language and ethnic origins, is growing at a slower pace than in the 1950s and is more than 90 percent literate.

The Education Act of 1948 stipulates that the purpose of education is to "enable every citizen to perfect his personality, uphold the ideals of universal fraternity, develop a capability for self-support in life, and enable him to work for the development of a democratic state and for the common prosperity of all humankind."

Curriculum and instructional reforms in the 1970s decreed that lectures and textbooks be supplemented by multiple-learning materials and extensive use of radio and television programs. Diagnostic tests and student workbooks guide student activity to mastery.

Middle school students study mathematics and science four hours per week in each subject the first year, then three to four hours per week during the second and third years. There are generally 40 to 55 students in a classroom with teachers rather than students rotating rooms.

PORTUGAL

No. of 13-year-olds in country	151,400
% of 13-year-olds in IAEP frame	68%
Per Capita GNP (US $)	$3,740
% of GNP spent on education	4.4%

Fifteen percent of the Iberian peninsula is home to Portugal's 10.5 million citizens. With historical roots in the Roman, Moslem, and Christian cultures, Portugal has recently joined the European Economic Community (EEC) and is becoming an industrialized country.

Since 1974, in response to the growing demand for secondary education, the country has made energetic and creative efforts to increase the literacy levels of its population through an enormous school literacy program and through the improvement of adult basic education courses.

Nine years of schooling are compulsory for all children. Secondary schools provide optional programs that are predominantly vocational or academic. After their secondary education, students can either enter the work force or go on to universities.

Assessment of student achievement in basic and secondary education is the responsibility of the schools and is accomplished through continuous and final assessments. If students do not attain the necessary results, they are required to repeat a grade level. There are no national examinations.

The ministry of education is responsible for pedagogic, administrative, financial, and disciplinary control of all primary and secondary schools. Since 1987, important measures have been instituted to decentralize, and as a consequence, the schools' autonomy has been increased.

Pre-primary and elementary teachers are trained during a three- or four-year course that includes practice teaching. Secondary-school teachers must hold university degrees in their areas of specialization. There are programs in place to complete the training of uncertified teachers.

The new educational policy envisions the modernization of the country to enable it to meet the challenges of participation in the EEC.

SCOTLAND

No. of 13-year-olds in country	62,100
% of 13-year-olds in IAEP frame	99%
Per Capita GNP (US $)	$10,917
% of GNP spent on education	5.2%

Scotland's tradition of support for a strong and broad educational system is a proud one. There are 750,000 pupils in its primary and secondary schools who are required to continue their education until age 16. Ninety percent of them are in comprehensive schools.

Educational policy is the responsibility of the Scottish education department and 12 local education authorities. Evaluation of the education system is the major responsibility of Her Majesty's Inspectors of Schools, who routinely report on educational institutions.

School teachers are trained for at least four years at the post-secondary level and are traditionally respected members of society, though some feel they are less valued today than in the past. School size ranges widely in terms of number of pupils. There are many very small primary schools reflecting the sparse population in certain parts of the country. A recent development has been the introduction of local school boards, which include both parent and teacher representatives.

A major curriculum and assessment development program is underway for ages 5 through 14 following the successful introduction of new certificate examinations for all pupils at age 16. The emphasis in these examinations and in other assessments is on valid measurement of all relevant knowledge and skills by means of written tests, as well as practical and project work.

SLOVENIA

No. of 13-year-olds in country	30,243
% of 13-year-olds in IAEP frame	97%
Per Capita GNP (US $)	$7,233
% of GNP spent on education	3.4%

Located at the juncture of three major European cultures, Germanic, Romance, and Slavic, Slovenia's educational system for centuries followed Germanic traditions. This pattern abruptly changed during the 19th century occupation by Napoleon's forces and again in 1918 when Slovenia merged with other nations to become Yugoslavia. The first transformation was characterized by Romance influences and the second introduced a Byzantine flavor.

The end of World War II brought with it a Soviet influence in all areas of Slovenia's life, including education. During that time, a number of scholars devoted a great deal of energy to liberalizing those stringent educational concepts and practices.

Education is a strong value among Slovenia's homogeneous and largely Roman Catholic population, and schooling is mandatory until age 15. The objectives of elementary and secondary education include basic and higher-level skills as well as moral values and employment preparation.

Teachers at all levels of education are required to have university degrees and at the secondary level are specialists in their subjects. Teachers are now able to select their own teaching materials and textbooks from local and international sources. Currently there is no national testing or assessment program.

THE SOVIET UNION

No. of 13-year-olds in country	4,485,000
% of 13-year-olds in IAEP frame	60%
Per Capita GNP (US $)	$8728
% of GNP spent on education	7.0%

Until September 1991, the Soviet Union was comprised of 15 republics, with a population of 290 million people of many different cultures and languages. New structures and relationships unfolded as the year drew to a close.

For a long time, almost all schools in the country had one common curriculum and common textbooks were provided to schools for all subjects. Secondary education was characterized by strenuous curriculum requirements and was reserved for students of strong academic ability. Since 1988, the standards for secondary education have been adjusted so that the main goals are now to provide all students a strong basic education, and to develop their personalities and creativity. Also, the years of compulsory education have been reduced from 11 to 9 years.

Instruction in the higher levels of knowledge and skills is provided only for those planning university careers. Higher education is open to all who can pass difficult entrance examinations. Achievement is viewed as the result of diligence, persistence, and intelligence.

Public opinion is that the Soviet Union has too many university graduates whose training is not considered of high quality. The trend is to improve the quality of graduates and to reduce their numbers.

No. of 13-year-olds in country	573,900
% of 13-year-olds in IAEP frame	80%
Per Capita GNP (US $)	$8,078
% of GNP spent on education	3.2%

Spain's 39.5 million people are unevenly distributed throughout the country. During the past decade, its demographics have changed significantly as a declining birth rate has resulted in an increasing percentage of retired workers within the society. The workforce has moved from agricultural, to industrial, and currently is moving to the service sector of the economy. One of the country's severest problems is a high unemployment rate, especially among the young. This has resulted in higher expectations for better educated and better trained graduates from educational institutions.

The most striking feature of the educational scene in Spain today is the deliberate transfer of responsibility for education to the autonomous communities. A vital issue is the liberation of educational institutions from excessive rules and regulations and the encouragement of local community support and involvement. In 1990, the new federal education law established the sharing of authority and funding of public education by the federal government and the autonomous communities. Its provisions take effect in 1992.

The national administration defines the content of the curriculum for all Spanish schools. However, there are no national examinations; schools evaluate achievement in their own way. Those who wish to teach at any level in the public or private school systems must have a university degree and appropriate pedagogical training.

Education is highly valued in the culture and many families privately fund a variety of educational enrichment activities for their children.

No. of 13-year-olds in country	73,800
% of 13-year-olds in IAEP frame	76%
Per Capita GNP (US $)	$27,693
% of GNP spent on education	4.8%

A small country of 7 million in the heart of Europe, Switzerland is made up of 26 democratic and independent cantons. Sixty-five percent of its population speak German, 18 percent speak French, 9 percent speak Italian, and less than 1 percent, Romansch. The remaining people speak other languages. The economy is moving from an industrial- to a service-centered base. Not currently part of the European Economic Community (EEC), the country is wrestling with decisions about its own future.

Because of its political structure, a national decision must reflect the combined wishes of the 26 cantons.

Each canton makes its own decisions concerning educational policy, teacher certification, curriculum, instructional materials, and standards. Regional ministries of education are tiny and act by convening groups of teachers and administrators and reaching consensus on issues affecting schooling. Schools tend to be small and local and are often administered by a senior teacher rather than by a full-time director.

There is growing concern over the level of preparation being provided their young citizens (only 11 percent go on to universities) as they face direct competition from their peers in neighboring countries.

TAIWAN

No. of 13-year-olds in country	392,000
% of 13-year-olds in IAEP frame	100%
Per Capita GNP (US $)	$4,355
% of GNP spent on education	3.6%

Taiwan is a mountainous, prosperous, and industrialized nation of 20 million people, 85 percent of whom are Taiwanese and 14 percent mainland Chinese.

Education is highly valued and centralized. All schools use the same set of textbooks. While basic facilities such as laboratories, computers, and instructional materials are readily available, educational experts in Taiwan feel they are not properly used in most schools. Teachers are highly regarded and there is no shortage of mathematics and science teachers.

After-school academic-enrichment programs are popular for secondary school students. Most parents provide strong home support for school programs and regularly pay for extra educational materials.

An important educational goal is to develop a sense of dignity in students by building their confidence in subjects in which they have shown potential. About one quarter of the students leave school for employment at about age 15. The others who pass competitive national entrance examinations go on for technical education or university training.

THE UNITED STATES

No. of 13-year-olds in country	3,451,000
% of 13-year-olds in IAEP frame	98%
Per Capita GNP (US $)	$19,789
% of GNP spent on education	7.5%

In the United States, public education extends through grade 12 and about three in four students graduate from high school at the expected time; about 90 percent earn their secondary diplomas by their early 20s. Half of high-school graduates enter college, and about one in four will eventually enter the full-time labor force with a four-year college degree.

At present, the nation is engaged in a concerted effort to raise educational achievement in a system that is highly decentralized. Educational authority for elementary and secondary education exists at the state level and is decentralized considerably beyond that level to about 15,000 local school districts.

The nation's 50 governors and the president have recently established six goals for education to be reached by the year 2000. One such goal is to be *Number 1* in the world in mathematics and science by that year.

The United States has been involved in an educational reform effort for more than a decade. This effort, stimulated by the report of a national Educational Excellence Commission, is being carried out by governors and legislators; mathematics particularly has been a target for improvement. However, the National Assessment of Educational Progress (NAEP), through regular assessments for more than 20 years, has found no sustained improvement in mathematics and science for that period, although there has been a recovery from declines in proficiency during the 1970s.

There are currently under discussion significant changes toward a more centralized system including voluntary national curricula, a national test, and achievement standards. Adoption of these features would constitute a major shift in the United States' educational policy.

These radical departures from traditional practice are being considered and promoted because of concerns about the country's ability to compete successfully in an increasingly technological global market place.

ALBERTA Alberta is a resource-rich province with a multicultural population of approximately 2.4 million. About 80 percent of the people live in urban centers.

All children in Alberta are entitled to public education and are required to attend school until age 16. The province supports two major school systems in Alberta: public and Catholic. Approximately 20 percent of all students attend Catholic schools.

The provincial government has primary responsibility for education and curricula but shares it with local school boards. Since 1982, student learning has been monitored through a provincial assessment program for students in grades 3, 6, and 9. Provincial examinations, which count for 50 percent of a student's final grade in selected twelfth-grade courses, have been in place since 1984. School boards are responsible for the instructional needs of their students and for individual student progress. The system strives to achieve equity, excellence, and effectiveness in meeting its students' needs.

Alberta is keen on ensuring that its students are adequately prepared to live happily and productively in an international marketplace. Its citizens consider international comparisons, such as IAEP, an important indicator of how well this goal is being achieved.

BRITISH COLUMBIA Geographically, British Columbia is Canada's third largest province and has a population of about 3 million. Greater Vancouver is home to 50 percent of the population with another 20 percent residing in the towns and cities of the extreme southwest.

British Columbia's society is becoming increasingly diverse. Twenty years ago, immigrants were easily integrated into a Eurocentric education system. Today, special school programs are needed to integrate Asian students into the schools.

The ministry of education, which is responsible for overall funding and direction of the system, plays a leading role both in the development and maintenance of curriculum and educational standards. Local boards of trustees are responsible for distribution of funding, hiring of teachers, and delivery of programs and services.

British Columbia's education system, spurred by the recommendations of the latest Royal Commission, is undergoing considerable — and very exciting — change. Based upon principles concerning the nature of learning, the curriculum and assessment process is learner-focused rather than subject matter-focused. Educational change is well underway, with significant momentum and support.

The purpose of the British Columbia school system is to enable students to develop their individual potential and to acquire the knowledge, skills, and attitudes needed to contribute to a healthy society and a prosperous and sustainable economy.

MANITOBA Sixty percent of this large province's 1 million people live in or near the capital city of Winnipeg. Brandon, the next largest city, has only 40,000 inhabitants.

All students have access to free public education until the age of 21 and attendance is compulsory until age 16. The goals of elementary education are to develop basic skills as well as to introduce students to family and societal values, while secondary schools focus on academic and vocational preparation and the development of critical thinking skills.

Curriculua are designed at the provincial level by committees that develop content descriptions and scope and sequence patterns across grades. Local adaptations are allowed but textbooks and other instructional materials are approved at the provincial level. Evaluation is the responsibility of local faculties but periodic provincial subject matter examinations are administered to 12th graders.

Teachers, who are required to have a university degree, are fairly well regarded and paid on a scale similar to other professionals. There is some concern that some of the many ethnic groups in the province are not represented among Manitoba teachers. Elementary school faculty are more child-focused while secondary teachers are more discipline-oriented. Family participation in school activities varies according to parents' educational and socioeconomic status. Pressure on students to work hard depends upon parental values.

NEW BRUNSWICK   Compared with other Canadian provinces New Brunswick is relatively small in terms of its physical size (72,515 square kilometers). It has a population of 727,000, of which almost half resides in urban areas.

New Brunswick is Canada's only officially bilingual province where about 64 percent of the total population classify themselves as English-speaking and 32 percent claim French as their first language. The remaining 4 percent are bilingual or speak different languages at home.

The provincial government finances all public schools. The curriculum is prescribed and authorized by the ministry of education. The province's schools and school boards are operated on the basis of language. There are 27 English-speaking districts and 15 French-speaking districts with a combined total of 415 schools. Those now entering the teaching profession in New Brunswick must complete a four-year degree program.

Education is deemed necessary for economic self-reliance and human development. Serious efforts are being made to improve and enhance public schooling. Just recently, a provincially financed, full-day kindergarten program was introduced for 5-year-olds. In the near future, the release of a provincially sponsored study dealing with excellence in education is expected to initiate dialogue among all the stakeholders in public education.

NEWFOUNDLAND   Newfoundland includes the island portion and a large territory on the mainland of Canada known as Labrador. Although the province is geographically large, it has a small population of just more than 500,000. The total school population, Kindergarten through grade 12, is approximately 125,000 and is decreasing rapidly because of a low birth rate and continuous emigration.

The language of instruction in almost all schools is English. There is a small population of French-speaking natives and immigrants in the province, but 98 percent of those assessed are English-speaking.

Although Newfoundland's per-pupil expenditure is among the lowest in Canada, education is highly valued and the province commits 11.5 percent of its gross national product to it, the highest percentage of the 10 provinces.

The province has a centralized curriculum and the teacher population is well educated. A system of provincial examinations sets the standard for graduation from secondary school, and an assessment program to evaluate strengths and weaknesses in the basic skills areas has been in place for more than a decade.

Although the province was not totally satisfied with its performance on the IAEP testing, the trends of its own testing programs has shown continuous improvement. This gradual improvement gives a real sense of optimism about Newfoundland's education system, and it is felt that good assessment programs with measures of accountability will further improve its education system.

NOVA SCOTIA   Nova Scotia is a small province with a total area of 54,400 square kilometers and a population of approximately 895,000. Close to half the population is of British origin and about 6 percent is French. The rest of the population includes sizable groups of Germans, Dutch, Blacks and Native people. Forestry, fishing, mining, construction and agriculture make up a major part of the economy along with service and tourist sectors.

Nova Scotia has many connections with the traditions and values of the British Isles. Education was of particular concern to the settlers, many of whom were from educated British families. Shortly after their arrival they set up schools to ensure the education of their children. The Acadian French also have a significant population and have maintained their culture and language.

All children in Nova Scotia are entitled to a free public school education to the age of 21, and attendance is compulsory from the age of 6 to 16. The provincial government has overall responsibility for the elementary and secondary schools, with 21 local school boards handling the operations of the schools. Funding is allocated on a formula basis with both provincial and local input.

Teacher training is provided at a provincially run teachers' college and at universities. All institutions have supervised practicums as part of their training programs.

Academic, vocational, and technical programs are available to meet the needs of the population. Promotion and placement are a responsibility of local school boards and no central examination system is used. The province does, however, have provincially developed achievement tests at grades 5, 9, and 12 to monitor curriculum throughout the province. These assessment instruments are not used for promotion purposes.

The province is in the process of reviewing curriculum offerings and of developing new guidelines for credit requirements for high school completion and issuance of graduation credentials.

ONTARIO In Ontario, education is the shared responsibility of the ministry of education and the local school boards. The ministry establishes the goals of education, provides broad curriculum guidelines, approves textbooks, establishes requirements for diplomas and certificates for both teachers and students, and distributes operating grants to school boards. It is the responsibility of local school boards to deliver education programs and services to their students.

All permanent residents of Ontario between the ages of 6 and 15 are required by law to attend school. Approximately 2 million students are enrolled in elementary or secondary schools. Instruction in Ontario's schools is offered in either English or French. In 1990-91, close to 98,000 students received their education with French as the language of instruction.

The last decade has seen a significant increase in immigration, and about two-thirds of these new children start school with a first language other than English or French. To serve the needs of the various cultural communities, all newcomers are given the opportunity to take courses in English or French as a second language. Elementary school students are given the opportunity to learn about the language and customs of their home country through the Heritage Languages Program.

Elementary schools attempt to shape a child's attitude toward learning and provide the basic skills and motivation for secondary studies. Secondary schools (grades 9 to 12) offer a wide variety of courses to prepare students for post-secondary education or employment.

The ministry of education does not administer any province-wide examinations. The only school examinations are those given to measure students' readiness for selected academic courses and these are reviewed by the ministry to improve the consistency of evaluation practices across the province.

QUEBEC Quebec has a population of almost 7 million people. The largest linguistic groups are the Francophones (nearly 85 percent) and the Anglophones (more than 12 percent). School attendance is compulsory for all youth from age 6 to 16. Access to the public school system — six years of elementary education, five years of secondary education — is free for all students.

The ministry of education determines the programs of study and the rules governing the organization of educational services and approves textbooks. It also administers compulsory examinations at the end of secondary school.

All elementary and secondary teachers must hold a university degree and are required to follow the same programs of study, although they have a choice of teaching methods and materials. They also have a major part of the responsibility for the summative evaluation of their students' learning.

For the next three years, the ministry's plan of action identifies the following priorities: reduction of the school drop-out rate, consolidation of vocational education reforms and of the improvements that have occurred in general education.

SASKATCHEWAN Saskatchewan, officially a province of Canada since 1905, has a population of about 1 million. Approximately one-third of the province's people live in the two urban centers of Regina and Saskatoon. Forty-four percent of the province's students are enrolled in rural areas. Ethnic diversity is a feature of Saskatchewan. In addition to the Native people, the province's ethnic makeup reflects waves of immigration from various parts of the world.

Enrollments in kindergarten through grade 12 in publicly funded schools (public and Catholic) are estimated at 200,000 with approximately 10,000 students enrolled in French language schools and French Immersion programs. The department of education issues official curriculum guides and lists of appropriate teaching resources. Alternative English and French programs are offered at the secondary level. The department of education administers provincial examinations in 18 subject areas for grade 12 students. However, only students of non-accredited teachers are obliged to take them.

The curriculum and instruction review process of the 1980s resulted in a new core curriculum. A variety of provincial initiatives in the areas of student, program, and curriculum evaluation are also being undertaken.

IAEP is the first international study in which Saskatchewan has participated in recent years. Comparative information from the project will be valuable to the province's educational community and to the public at large.

Procedural Appendix

INTRODUCTION The second International Assessment of Educational Progress (IAEP), conducted in 1991, is an international comparative study of the mathematics and science skills of samples of 9- and 13-year-old students from 20 countries. The first IAEP in 1988 provided results on the mathematics and science achievement of 13-year-olds from six countries: Canada (which conducted separate surveys in four provinces), Ireland, Korea, Spain, the United Kingdom, and the United States.[31]

The IAEP applies a technology developed for a United States project, the National Assessment of Educational Progress (NAEP), which has conducted national surveys of the educational achievement of United States' students for more than 20 years. Using reliable and uniform scientific procedures, NAEP has obtained comprehensive educational achievement data and reported trends over time on student performance. Since 1983, Educational Testing Service (ETS) has administered NAEP as well as related projects, including IAEP.

IAEP was designed to collect and report data on what students know and can do, on the educational and cultural factors associated with achievement, and on students' attitudes, backgrounds, and classroom experiences. By utilizing existing NAEP technology and procedures, the time and money required to conduct these international comparative studies was reduced and many interested countries were able to experiment with these innovative psychometric techniques.

After the first international assessment, interest from representatives of several foreign countries prompted ETS staff to develop a proposal for a second international assessment that sought to expand upon the 1988 experience. This second project was a four-part survey: a main assessment of 13-year-olds' performance in mathematics and science; an assessment of 9-year-olds' performance in mathematics and science; an experimental, performance-based assessment of 13-year-olds' ability to use equipment and materials to solve mathematics and science problems; and a short probe of the geography skills and knowledge of 13-year-olds. All countries participated in the main assessment of 13-year-olds; participation in the other assessment components was optional.

---

[31] Archie E. Lapointe, Nancy A. Mead, and Gary W. Phillips, *A World of Differences. An International Assessment of Mathematics and Science.* Princeton, NJ: Educational Testing Service, 1989.

The IAEP project was asked to provide separate, state-level results for the state of Colorado, which opted to assess its 9- and 13-year-old students in mathematics, science, and geography. The results described in this report, however, include performance statistics only for the United States as a whole and for participants from the other 19 countries. The results from the Colorado state project will be reported in a separate publication.

Each participating country was responsible for carrying out all aspects of the project, including sampling, survey administration, quality control, and data entry using standardized procedures that were developed for the project. Several training manuals were developed for the IAEP project. These comprehensive documents, discussed with participants during several international training sessions, explained in detail each step of the assessment process.[32]

The second International Assessment of Educational Progress is supported financially by the National Science Foundation and the U.S. Department of Education's National Center for Education Statistics for the expenses of overall coordination, sampling, data analysis, and reporting. The Carnegie Corporation provided additional funds to cover the travel expenses of some of the participants who could not meet the financial burdens of traveling to the project's coordination and training meetings, held in Canada, England, France, Hong Kong, and the United States. Decisions concerning the design and implementation of the project were made collaboratively by the representatives of the provinces and countries involved in the survey. The National Academy of Sciences' Board on International Comparative Studies in Education reviewed plans for IAEP at several stages of its development and made suggestions to improve the technical quality of the study. The board is responsible for reviewing the soundness of the technical procedures of international studies funded by federal agencies of the U.S. government.

DEVELOPING THE ASSESSMENT The IAEP assessment was developed through a consensus-building process that involved curriculum and measurement experts from each of the participating countries and provinces. As models, several existing NAEP frameworks were reviewed by participants and evaluated as to their appropriateness for their own countries' curriculums. Together, the participants then adapted the NAEP frameworks to reflect an international consensus of subject-specific topics and cognitive processes that they believed reasonably reflected curriculums being implemented in their own school systems.[33]

Once the participants had agreed upon common frameworks and the relative emphases that would be placed on each topic and cognitive process category of the assessment, more than one-half submitted test items from their countries' own assessment programs that they felt were appropriate and met the requirements of the IAEP assessment. Many questions from the United States' NAEP assessments were included as well. These items, more than 1,500, were then distributed to each country and each was evaluated and rated for its quality, relevance to the framework, and appropriateness for that country's culture and curricula. The items with the highest ratings across all countries were placed into a pool of acceptable questions from which a subset was selected and pilot-tested in all of the participating provinces and countries.[34]

---

[32] See the *IAEP Technical Report* for a full discussion of the standardized assessment procedures.

[33] See *The 1991 IAEP Assessment: Objectives for Mathematics, Science, and Geography* for a full discussion of the development of the frameworks and selection of questions.

[34] One participant, Slovenia, joined the project after the pilot testing had been completed.

All questions for the IAEP assessment were screened by subject-matter experts and subjected to ETS editorial and sensitivity review procedures to detect any potential bias or lack of sensitivity to any particular student group. In non-English-speaking countries, each question was translated into the appropriate language and then checked for accuracy by language experts at ETS. The IAEP assessment included 13 separate language groups among the 20 countries. All countries made minor adaptations to the items, such as changing mathematical notations (e.g., decimals points to commas), units of measurement (yards to meters), and the names of people, places, and types of plants and animals to reflect local usage. These adaptations did not alter the psychometric nature or content of the assessment questions.

In the final administration of the assessment, about 70 cognitive test questions or items were selected for each subject area and for each age level. Each assessment contained a range of questions that measured achievement of the objectives developed by the participants. The mathematics portion of the assessment for both 9- and 13-year- olds contained about one quarter constructed-response questions requiring students to generate and write their own answers, while the remaining questions required students to select from several response choices. All of the science and geography items used a multiple-choice format.

FIGURE A.1 describes the percentage distributions of questions for 9- and 13-year-old students by topic and cognitive process. The target percentages of questions within each category were established at the onset of the project. The final numbers and percentages of questions within each topic and process category represent final decisions after examination of the results of pilot-testing in the participating countries. After final data collection, responses for each question were analyzed to ensure the results could be summarized accurately for all populations. At that time, some questions were removed from the summary statistics as indicated in a later section.

Because it is particularly instructive to policymakers and educators to interpret achievement results in context, IAEP developed three separate background questionnaires including one each for the student, the school, and the country. These asked various questions about resources within the school and at home, curricular emphases, instructional practices, as well as other school and non-school factors that may influence learning. In addition, a limited set of subject-specific background questions asked students for information about the mathematics, science, and geography instruction they received and probed their own attitudes about these subjects. In this report, the answers to background questions are examined along with student performance — for example, the relationship between how much television students report watching and their performance on the IAEP assessment. Since IAEP was designed to collect only a limited amount of background information from a students at one point in time, these analyses cannot be used to establish cause-and-effect relationships, which may be impacted by a great number of variables.

Some of the countries asked other background questions in addition to those required by the project in order to evaluate issues relevant to their own cultures. These additional items appeared at the end of the commonly agreed-upon questions.

Percentage Distributions of Questions for 9- and 13-Year-Olds by Science Topic and Cognitive Process**

TOPICS	Ages	Target Percentage of Questions	Actual Number of Questions	Actual Percentage of Questions
Life Sciences	9	35	23	38
	13	35	25	35
Physical Science	9	30	19	32
	13	35	26	36
Earth and Space Sciences	9	20	10	17
	13	15	9	12
Nature of Science	9	15	8	13
	13	15	12	17
PROCESSES				
Know Facts, Concepts, and Principles	9	45	26	43
	13	40	20	28
Uses Knowledge to Solve Simple Problems	9	35	23	38
	13	35	33	46
Integrates Knowledge to Solve More Complex Problems	9	20	11	18
	13	25	19	26

** Percentages may not total 100 due to rounding.

ASSESSMENT DESIGN At each age level, two separate booklets, one for each subject area in the main assessment, were prepared. At age 13, the mathematics and science booklets also included a small number of geography items for countries that chose to assess geography. At each age, students were administered either a mathematics or a science booklet. The administration instructions and procedures for both the mathematics and science assessments were identical and permitted sampled students at a particular school to be assessed together in a single 90-minute session.

At age 9, each assessment booklet was composed of five parts called "blocks": four 15-minute blocks of cognitive questions followed by an untimed block of background questions. For age 13, students were administered four 15-minute blocks of cognitive questions, followed by 7 minutes of background questions. Those countries assessing geography also administered a final block that included 7 1/2 minutes of geography items, followed by 2 1/2 minutes of geography-related background questions at the end of the assessment.

In each subject area, one common block, "an overlap block," asked 9- and 13-year-old students to respond to the same set of items. This overlap block permitted IAEP to compare performance at the two age levels. (At age 13, the overlap block contained a few additional questions at the end of the block)

The test questions in each block were arranged in easy-to-more-difficult order and reflected a broad range of content and cognitive processes based on the frameworks described earlier.

In order to minimize the possible effects of fatigue on final results, the cognitive blocks were administered in two different sequences. Students from one-half of the schools in each country answered the four cognitive blocks sequentially (Part 1, Part 2, Part 3, Part 4) followed by the background questions (Part 5). Students in the other half of the schools responded to the four cognitive blocks in a different order (Part 3, Part 4, Part 1, Part 2) followed by the background questions (Part 5). Countries that opted for the geography assessment administered this block (Part 6) last in all schools.

SAMPLING The sampling design for the IAEP survey called for representative samples of 3,300 students from about 110 schools in each participating country at each age level. Three countries — Brazil, Korea, and Mozambique — which begin the school year in March, conducted the survey in September 1990. The remaining 17 countries conducted the assessment during an equivalent period in the school year, in March 1991. Mozambique assessed their 13-year-olds in only mathematics. They did not participate in the science portion of the assessment. School samples were drawn from public and private elementary and secondary schools. Samples of 9-and 13-year-old students were drawn from those born during calendar years 1981 and 1977, respectively. Students assessed in Brazil and Korea were six months older (born between July 1, 1976 and June 30, 1977) because they were assessed six months earlier.

The IAEP sample design was a two-stage, stratified, cluster design. The first-stage sampling units were usually individual schools, but in some instances, consisted of two or more small schools (i.e., school clusters). Typically, 110 schools or school clusters were selected with probability proportionate to the estimated number of age-eligible students in the school. At the second stage of sampling, a list of age-eligible students was prepared for each sampled school. A systematic sample of 30 to 35 students was typically drawn from each school and one-half of the sampled students were assigned the mathematics assessment and the remaining half, the science assessment. Thus, each country typically assessed 1,650 students in each subject area at each age level.

Each participating country had the option of selecting its own samples of schools and students or of having Westat, Inc., a sampling and survey design subcontractor for the project, select the samples. Five participants, including Korea, Mozambique, Ontario, Quebec, and the United States, opted to have Westat select their samples. Countries and provinces that elected to select their own samples were trained in the use of specially designed computer software created for this purpose.

Most of the participants used the IAEP design and software. Special circumstances in some of the participating countries necessitated the development and use of alternative sampling procedures. Their designs, sampling procedures, and final weights were reviewed and approved by Westat. For example, China and the Soviet Union used a three-stage sample (first selecting primary sampling units, PSUs, consisting of defined geographic areas) because centralized lists of school enrollments for the entire country did not exist. In England and Switzerland, the need to sample whole classrooms meant that alternative within-school sampling procedures using classrooms as sampling units had to be designed and implemented.[35]

---

[35] The sample designs used by each participant are described in detail in the *IAEP Technical Report*.

Some countries drew samples from virtually all children in the appropriate age group and others confined their assessments to specific geographic areas, language groups, or grade levels. The definition of populations often coincided with the structure of school systems, political divisions, and cultural distinctions. All countries limited their assessment to students in school, which for some, meant excluding significant numbers of age-eligible children.

In Brazil, two separate samples of 13-year-olds were drawn, one each from the cities of São Paulo and Fortaleza. In Mozambique, a single sample of 13-year-olds was drawn across two cities, Maputo and Beira.

In Canada, nine out of 10 provinces drew separate samples of 13-year-olds and five of these drew separate samples of English-speaking and French-speaking schools, for a total of 14 separate samples. Taken together, these samples represent 94 percent of the 13-year-olds in Canada. Four Canadian provinces — six separate samples — participated in the 9-year-old assessment, representing 74 percent of the children that age in Canada. The assessment of native English-speaking students who were enrolled in French immersion programs (where they receive all or most of their instruction in French) was not handled in a consistent way across the provinces. In Manitoba and Saskatchewan they were a part of the French samples and assessed in French. In Alberta, British Columbia, Newfoundland, Nova Scotia, and Quebec, they were part of the English samples and assessed in English. In Ontario, French-immersion students were part of the English sample and some schools assessed these students in English and others assessed them in French.

The characteristics of the sampling frame of each of the participating countries at each age level are documented in FIGURES A.2 and A.3.

The first four columns of Figures A.2 and A.3 indicate the representativeness of the sampling frames. The first column provides the number of age-eligible children in the country. The second and third columns give the estimated percentages of age-eligible children included in the sampling frame for the country as a whole and for the defined population. If the defined population is the whole country, these two percentages are the same. If the population is limited to a specific region or language group, the percentage in the third column reflects the coverage of the sampling frame within those defined limits.

Age 9
Sampling Frame

	No. of Age-eligible Children in Country[1]	Estimated Percent of Age-eligible Children in Country Included in the Sampling Frame	Estimated Percent of Age-eligible Children in Defined Population Included in the Sampling Frame	Percent of Age-eligible Children in School[2]	No. of Schools in Sampling Frame	Estimated No. of Age-eligible Students in School Frame	Estimated No. of Age-eligible Students Represented by Study
Canada[3]	364,000	74	97	96 – 99.6	5,595	267,797	238,295
England	625,400[4]	97	97	100	15,715	571,091	553,543[2]
Hungary	125,700	99	99	97.8	2,609	159,649	122,651
Ireland	65,700	94	94	99.8	2,619	66,609	60,040
Israel	98,000	71	93	98.5	1,045	61,927	52,344
Italy	599,700	4	98	99.0	290	31,680	25,794
Korea	809,800	95	95	98.9	4,990	804,500	762,161
Portugal	137,200	81	81	100	7,818	110,352	120,701
Scotland	64,900	98	98	100	2,054	64,919	63,308
Slovenia	29,279[5]	97	97	96.1	399	28,572	26,870
Soviet Union	4,645,000[6]	63	99	—	52,178	2,822,700	2,258,384
Spain	482,100	80	96	100	9,983	436,399	397,972
Taiwan	409,000[7]	97	97	98	1,754	387,021	379,881
United States	3,660,000[8]	97	97	98.9	70,405	3,460,234	3,069,620[4]

— Information is not available.
[1] *1988 Demographic Yearbook*, Fortieth Issue, New York: United Nations, 1990.
[2] Estimates were provided by project director from available data.
[3] Details of the sampling frames of the individual Canadian populations are provided in the *IAEP Technical Report*.
[4] Including Wales.
[5] *Annual Statistical Report of Slovenia*, Ljubljana, Slovenia: Central Statistics Office, 1990.
[6] Counts are based on the 1989 census.
[7] *Education Statistics of the ROC*, Taipei: Ministry of Education, 1989.
[8] *Current Population Reports, Population Estimates and Projections*, Series P-25, No. 1045. Washington, DC: U.S. Department of Commerce, n.d.

IAEP

Percentages in the third column are usually lower than 100 because some age-eligible children have been excluded from the frame. Often students in small schools, schools in remote areas, or in other types of schools that for some reason might be difficult to assess have been excluded. In some cases, students in particular grades have been excluded. Also, since the sample is school-based, children who do not attend schools have been excluded, and the magnitude of this exclusion is indicated in the fourth column, the percentage of age-eligible children attending school. If the estimated percentage of age-eligible children in the defined population included in the sampling frame (column 3) is below 90 percent, the frame is not considered to be representative of the target-age population and results from these samples are presented as populations with exclusions or low participation.

Age 13
Sampling Frame

	No. of Age-eligible Children in Country[1]	Estimated Percent of Age-eligible Children in Country Included in the Sampling Frame[2]	Estimated Percent of Age-eligible Children in Defined Population Included in the Sampling Frame[2]	Percent of Age-eligible Children in School[3]	No. of Schools in Sampling Frame	Estimated No. of Age-eligible Students in Schools	Estimated No. of Age-eligible Students Represented by Study
Brazil, São Paulo	3,383,600	3	80	92	1,565	126,053	97,652
Brazil, Fortaleza	3,383,600	<1	56	85	388	13,861	13,612
Canada[4]	361,600	94	95	94 – 100	5,555	345,827	310,274
China	18,474,000	38	45	51	60,790	7,117,960	6,388,601
England	591,900[5]	96	96	100	5,078	515,000	504,590
France	771,700	98	98	99.7	6,678	661,728	672,764
Hungary	152,000	99	99	97.8	2,609	159,649	149,647
Ireland	70,130	93	93	99.8	1,002	71,512	63,791
Israel	91,900	71	90	95.5	651	66,777	55,348
Italy	669,600	6	98	98.2	391	38,127	36,817
Jordan	83,000	96	96	98.5	1,462	77,947	74,290
Korea	811,700	97	97	95.9	2,258	709,903	671,867
Portugal	151,400	68	79	86.1	1,364	110,992	149,228
Scotland	62,100	99	99	100	458	60,265	55,398
Slovenia	30,243[6]	97	97	95.4	407	28,150	26,640
Soviet Union	4,485,000[7]	60	99	—	49,491	2,619,300	2,374,694
Spain	573,900	80	96	100	9,663	524,567	440,322
Switzerland	73,800	76	92	100	classes only	52,819	52,726
Taiwan	392,000[8]	100	100	90	669	346,619	338,249
United States	3,451,000[9]	98	98	99.0	73,769	3,518,390	3,028,386

— Information is not available.

[1] *1988 Demographic Yearbook*, Fortieth Issue, New York: United Nations, 1990.

[2] Estimates for Fortaleza, Brazil, China, Mozambique, and Portugal take into account the age-eligible children who have dropped out of school; estimates for other populations (those with at least 90 percent of age-eligible children in school) do not take into account age-eligible children who have dropped out of school.

[3] Estimates were provided by project director from available data.

[4] Details of the sampling frames of the individual Canadian populations are provided in the *IAEP Technical Report.*

[5] Including Wales.

[6] *Annual Statistical Report of Slovenia*, Ljubljana, Slovenia: Central Statistics Office, 1990.

[7] Counts are based on the 1989 census.

[8] *Education Statistics of the ROC*, Taipei: Ministry of Education, 1989.

[9] *Current Population Reports, Population Estimates and Projections*, Series P-25, No. 1045, Washington, DC: U.S. Department of Commerce, n.d.

The last three columns of Figures A.2 and A.3 document the characteristics of the sampling frame and the achieved samples of each participant. The fifth column indicates the number of schools in the sampling frame and the sixth column, the estimated number of age-eligible students in those schools used to draw the school sample (i.e., the estimated measure of size). The last column shows the estimated number of age-eligible students represented by those who actually took the assessment (i.e., the sum of the student sampling weights).

Some inconsistencies can be seen in Figures A.2 and A.3 because data are drawn from different sources, cover different time frames, and in some cases reflect estimates. For example, estimated numbers of age-eligible students are often based on grade data rather than age data. On occasion, the estimated number of age-eligible students in the school frame or represented by the study is larger than the total number of age-eligible children in the country. Also, the estimated percentage of age-eligible children in the country included in the sampling frame is not always derived directly from the total number of age-eligible students in the school frame or represented by the study and the total number of age-eligible children in the country. The numbers presented represent the best available data for each characteristic of the sampling frames.

The numbers of schools and students assessed and the school and student cooperation rates for each participant at each age level are provided in FIGURES A.4 and A.5 that follow. Typically, if more than 5 percent of the originally sampled schools or school clusters refused to cooperate in the survey, alternate schools were selected. The total number of schools assessed (column 1) includes both originally selected and alternate schools that actually participated in the assessment. The total number of students assessed (column 2) includes all students assessed in science in those schools.

Science, Age 9
Numbers of Schools and Students Assessed and School and Student Cooperation Rates

	Number of Schools Assessed	Number of Students Assessed	Weighted School Response Ratess	Student Completion Rate in Participating Schools	Combined Overall Response Rates
Canada[1]	797	9,362	97	95	92
England	89	1,086	56	94	53
Hungary	144	1,607	100	93	93
Ireland	126	1,282	94	98	92
Israel	116	1,627	100	96	96
Italy	70	1,157	65	95	62
Korea	114	1,638	100	98	98
Portugal	128	1,439	89	98	87
Scotland	90	1,154	62	93	58
Slovenia	113	1,593	100	93	93
Soviet Union	139	1,853	98[2]	93	85
Spain	110	1,620	89	95	85
Taiwan	110	1,799	100	98	98
United States	105	1,464	80	92	74

IAEP

[1] Details of participation in individual Canadian populations are provided in the *IAEP Technical Report*.
[2] This is the school response rate within participating Primary Sampling Units (PSUs). The overall student response rates given in this table reflect nonresponse at all levels of sampling, including the sampling of PSUs.

The school response rates in the third column reflect only the percentage of schools that were originally sampled and that participated in the assessment. The school response rate was calculated by using weights that take into account the number of students that would have been sampled if the school had participated in the study. Thus, the cooperation of large schools (in terms of expected numbers of students) received greater weight than the cooperation of smaller schools. The student completion rate (column 4) is the percentage of sampled students that were actually assessed in both the original and alternate schools. This rate was calculated without weights. The combined overall response rate (column 5) is the product of the weighted school response rate and student completion rate.

Science, Age 13

Numbers of Schools and Students Assessed
and School and Student Cooperation Rates

	Number of Schools Assessed	Number of Students Assessed	Weighted School Response Rates	Student Completion Rate in Participating Schools	Combined Overall Response Rates
Brazil, São Paulo	108	1,469	95	93	88
Brazil, Fortaleza	118	1,505	97	93	90
Canada[1]	1,373	19,738	97	94	91
China	119	1,775	100[2]	99	96
England	83	929	52	92	48
France	103	1,787	93	98	91
Hungary	144	1,623	100	92	92
Ireland	110	1,657	96	94	90
Israel	110	1,584	98	95	93
Italy	90	1,485	82	95	78
Jordan	106	1,588	85	99	84
Korea	110	1,635	100	99	99
Portugal	89	1,520	82	94	77
Scotland	92	1,584	82	92	75
Slovenia	114	1,598	100	95	95
Soviet Union	138	1,839	97[2]	94	85
Spain	109	1,609	93	95	88
Switzerland	397	3,653	82	98	80
Taiwan	108	1,786	100	99	99
United States	96	1,404	77	92	71

[1] Details of participation in individual Canadian populations are provided in the *IAEP Technical Report*.
[2] This is the school response rate within participating Primary Sampling Units (PSUs). The overall student response rates given in this table reflect nonresponse at all levels of sampling, including the sampling of PSUs.

Populations with a combined nonresponse rate below .80 but at least .70 have been identified in all figures that show performance data with a warning that the results should be interpreted with caution because of possible nonresponse bias. Populations with a combined nonresponse rate below .70 have been identified in all figures that show performance data with a warning that results should be interpreted with extreme caution because of possible large nonresponse biases, and for that reason, these populations have been listed in a special group of populations with exclusions or low participation.

Sampling weights have been adjusted to account for school and student nonresponse. No other adjustments, such as post-stratification, have been made.[36]

Typically, most students age 9 are in their third and fourth years of schooling, and most students age 13 are in their seventh and eight years. However, because the entry age and promotion policies differ from country to country, the distributions of students by year in school vary among participants. While children in most countries begin their first year of schooling at age 6, children in England and Scotland start at age 5 and children in Brazil, parts of China, Mozambique, Slovenia, parts of the Soviet Union, and German Switzerland do not start until age 7. In Ireland, children are required to begin school at age 6 and in the distributions presented in FIGURES A.6 and A.7 this is considered to be year 1. However, almost all Irish children have had two additional years of infant school, which is available to all children and which includes academic work.

Science, Age 9

Percentage Distributions of Sampled Students
by Year of Schooling**

	Year 2	Year 3	Year 4	Year 5	Year 6
Canada	0	17	82	1	0
England[1]	0	0	39	61	0
Hungary	0	51	49	0	0
Ireland[2]	3	59	38	0	0
Israel	0	10	90	0	0
Italy	0	0	0	99	1
Korea	0	28	72	0	0
Portugal	0	12	88	0	0
Scotland[1]	0	0	1	85	15
Slovenia	2	89	8	0	0
Soviet Union	7	68	24	0	0
Spain	0	9	91	0	0
Taiwan	0	31	69	0	0
United States	2	35	62	0	0

** Percentages may not total 100 due to rounding.
[1] Since children are age 5 when they begin their first academic year of school, the majority of 9-year-olds are in their fifth year of school.
[2] Children are required to begin school at age 6 and for these distributions this is considered to be year 1. However, almost all children have had two additional years of infant school, which is available to all children and which includes academic work.

Science, Age 13
Percentage Distributions of Sampled Students by Year of Schooling**

	Year 5	Year 6	Year 7	Year 8	Year 9	Year 10
Brazil	28	29	35	8	0	0
Canada	0	0	19	80	1	0
China	0	0	72	25	3	0
England[1]	0	0	0	37	63	0
France	0	8	32	57	3	0
Hungary	0	4	39	58	0	0
Ireland[2]	0	1	63	35	0	0
Israel	0	0	10	89	0	0
Italy	0	0	9	90	0	0
Jordan	0	5	16	78	1	0
Korea	0	0	30	67	3	0
Portugal	3	6	35	56	1	0
Scotland[1]	0	0	0	0	86	13
Slovenia	0	6	81	13	0	0
Soviet Union	0	1	15	84	0	0
Spain	0	0	22	78	0	0
Switzerland	0	7	69	25	0	0
Taiwan	0	0	28	72	0	0
United States	0	3	36	60	0	0

** Percentages may not total 100 due to rounding.
[1] Since children are age 5 when they begin their first academic year of school, the majority of 13-year-olds are in their fifth year of school.
[2] Children are required to begin school at age 6 and for these distributions this is considered to be year 1. However, almost all children have had two additional years of infant school, which is available to all children and which includes academic work.

DATA COLLECTION Each participating country and Canadian province appointed a National Coordinator to administer data collection for the IAEP project. These individuals were provided with a detailed *IAEP National Coordinator's Manual* and training at one of two regional meetings. While participants strove to implement all procedures as outlined, occasionally they encountered situations where deviations were necessary. The administration procedures used by each participating country and Canadian province are summarized in FIGURE A.8.

Local school personnel or external administrators conducted the assessments at the selected schools, using standardized procedures provided in the *IAEP School Coordinator's Manual* during the specified assessment period (see Figure A.8). The administration script read aloud to students and the time limits for each part of the test were the same in all countries.

In addition to providing administrators with the *IAEP School Coordinator's Manual*, IAEP recommended that each country train each administrator in the procedures for conducting the assessment. To facilitate the training process, IAEP developed a training package that included a script for the trainers, suggested overhead transparencies, and simulations on how to complete the forms and implement the procedures. Based on their own testing programs, participants determined which method of training would be most helpful and efficient. Some of the countries conducted regional training sessions or used telephone conferences and audiotapes to supplement the *IAEP School Coordinator's Manual* (see Figure A.8).

Countries were provided with a practice test that students could take a day or two prior to the assessment to help them prepare for the assessment. It was designed particularly for students who were unfamiliar with multiple-choice formats. Countries were not required to use the practice test if they felt it was unnecessary (see Figure A.8).

QUALITY CONTROL AND ON-SITE OBSERVATIONS In order to ensure that the assessments had been conducted uniformly in all locations, each country was required to develop and follow a quality-control plan approved by ETS. The participants were encouraged to conduct unannounced site visits to a random number of participating schools on the day of the assessment to determine if the standardized procedures of the assessment were being followed. Observation of 20 percent on the assessments was recommended. Because of limited resources, some countries conducted fewer visits (see Figure A.8). Some countries felt that making unannounced site visits would jeopardize their relationship with schools and instead implemented informal monitoring systems.

The quality control visits were typically conducted by officials from the ministry, research center, or by external staff hired and trained in IAEP test administration procedures. An *IAEP Quality Control Observers Manual* was developed as a guide for observation visits. The main purpose of the visits was to document that the test administrator had maintained test security and correctly followed the administration script, time limits, and rules for answering student questions.

Overall Summary of Test Administration by Country and Canadian Province

	Scheduled Assessment Month	Who Gave Test	Test Administrator Trained	Practice Test Used	Percent of Site Visits	Percent of Accurate Scores***
Brazil, Fortaleza and São Paulo	Sept. '90	External Administrators	Yes	No	23	99.5
Canada, Alberta	March '91	School Personnel	No	No	20	99.7
British Columbia	March '91	School Personnel	No	No	Informal	99.5
Manitoba	March '91	School Personnel	Yes	No	18	99.6
New Brunswick, English	March '91	School Personnel	Yes	Optional	15	99.8
New Brunswick, French	March '91	School Personnel	Yes	Yes	39	Not Done
Newfoundland	March '91	School Personnel	No	No	21	99.0
Nova Scotia	March '91	School Personnel	No	No	21	99.9
Ontario	March '91	School Personnel	Yes	Yes (9) Optional (13)	19	98.1
Quebec	March '91	School Personnel	Yes	Yes	22	98.2
Saskatchewan	March '91	School Personnel	No	No	Informal	99.3
China	March '91	School Personnel	Yes	No	19	99.3
England	March '91	School Personnel	No	No	Informal	99.6
France	March '91	School Personnel	Yes	Yes	21	99.4
Hungary	March '91	External Adminstrators	Yes	No	16	99.5
Ireland	March '91	School Personnel	No	No	Informal	99.6
Israel	March '91	School Personnel	Yes	No	19	100
Italy	March '91	School Personnel	Yes	No	21	98.0
Jordan	March '91	School Personnel	Yes	Yes	24	99.3
Korea	Sept. '90	School Personnel	Yes	Yes	20	99.5
Portugal	March '91	External Administrators	Yes	Yes (9) No (13)	20	99.8
Scotland	March '91	School Personnel	No	Optional (9) No (13)	Informal	99.2
Slovenia	March '91	External Administrators	Yes	Optional	10	99.8
Soviet Union	March '91 (9) April '91 (13)	School Personnel	Yes	Yes	52	99.3
Spain	March '91	External Administrators	Yes	Optional (9) No (13)	20	99.7
Switzerland	March '91	School Personnel	Yes	No	Informal	99.5
Taiwan	March '91	School Personnel	Yes	No	20	99.8
United States	March '91	School Personnel	No	No	16	99.8

*** This number represents the mean of the percents of accurate scores for mathematics constructed-response questions.
— Information is not available.

The project considered quality control of administration crucial to the validity and reliability of assessment results, and therefore, a second, independent group of observers was hired by ETS to make site visits within each of the countries. These observers, trained in the same procedures were fluent, in most cases, in the language of the assessment and familiar with the cultural idiosyncrasies of the populations being assessed. They visited testing sessions and interviewed project personnel on the management of the assessment in all participating countries except Brazil and Mozambique.

DATA PROCESSING   Once the assessments had been completed, the booklets were returned to a central location within each country and checked for completeness. The constructed-response items for the mathematics assessment were hand-scored, using standardized scoring guides. Ten percent of these booklets were scored by a second scorer. The average of the percentage of accurate scores across all questions is given in Figure A.8. Afterwards, all responses were either key-entered or scanned into a database.

Each country was responsible for developing a preliminary data file that followed standard formats and contained student responses and other demographic information for each population assessed. Requirements for the data files, including 100 percent verification of key entry, were specified in the *IAEP Data Processing Manual*. Specially designed software was created for data entry and verification, and data processing personnel from each country received training in these procedures at one of five regional meetings. All participants were required to use the verification program, which checked for duplicate identification numbers and responses that fell outside the expected ranges, and to resolve inconsistencies in the data.

All database management and data analysis activities were conducted by a Canadian Data Analysis Group consisting of individuals from Educan, Inc., GRICS, the Quebec Ministry of Education, and the University of Montreal.

Completed data files were sent to the IAEP Data Processing Center where files were verified a second time and item analyses were conducted to identify other problems in the data files. In several cases, responses to a specific item from a specific population had to be removed from the master data file because of a printing or translation error. Each participant also sent 10 samples (selected at random) of each type of test booklet and questionnaire so that the data files could be re-checked against the original source documents. If the student response portion of the records that were checked contained one percent or more errors, participants were required to rekey the entire data file. This happened in one instance and the data file was rekeyed.

ITEM PERCENTS CORRECT   The first stage of analysis involved the calculation of the percentage of correct answers and standard errors for individual questions. For each population, the weighted percentage of correct answers was calculated for each question. The results of students who omitted questions at the ends of sections because they did not reach them were excluded from the calculations for those questions. For each percent correct, an estimate of its standard error was calculated using the jackknife procedure. Percentages and standard errors were calculated for subgroups within each population, including gender and grade. Statistics for Canada were calculated using an appropriately weighted sample of responses drawn from the individual Canadian populations.

CLUSTER ANALYSIS To be most useful, survey results should provide educators, policymakers, and the public at large with an easily understood summary of performance in a specific content area, while taking into account country-to-country differences in performance within sub-areas of the subject being assessed. For example, it is possible that a certain topic within a subject might be more difficult for some populations than for others. This country-by-topic interaction, due to a large extent to differences in curricular emphasis, might affect the relative performance standings of the various populations depending upon the relative importance assigned to each of the topics in the overall summary measure.

To meet these dual needs, IAEP conducted a series of analyses before deciding which questions could be combined into a summary measure of science. These analyses began with a matrix with rows corresponding to the countries and with columns corresponding to the cells in the topic by process matrix (e.g., one cell consisted of questions measuring the Life Sciences topic and the Knowledge of Science process). The entries in the table were the average percent correct for a given country for questions in the topic-by-process cell. These average percents correct were transformed into normal deviates and then converted into country-by-cell interactions by removing the overall country and topic-by-process main effects. The interaction matrix was then analyzed using the interactive K-Means cluster-analysis technique.[37] The aim of the analysis was to obtain aggregate sets of questions where the country-by-cell type interaction within an aggregate set was negligible. Solutions involving one, two, three, and sometimes more clusters were examined in order to define legitimate groups of items for summary analyses. These analyses confirmed the reasonableness of summarizing across all questions in science at each age level except for two items at age 9 and eight at age 13 that were identified in the differential item functioning (DIF) analyses described in the following section.

DIFFERENTIAL ITEM FUNCTIONING While cluster analyses focus on differences in performance across groups of questions defined by topics and processes, differential item functioning (DIF) analyses identify differences in performance on a single item. These latter analyses are likely to pick up the effects of cultural and linguistic differences as well as curricular differences. A generalized Mantel-Haenszel statistic was used for these analyses.[38] A test question was identified as functioning differentially across populations if students of equal ability but from different populations had different probabilities of answering it correctly.

[37] J.A. Hartigan and M.A. Wong, A K-Means Clustering Algorithm, *Applied Statistics*, Vol. 28, No. 1, 1979.

[38] Grant W. Somes, The Generalized Mantel-Haenszel Statistic, *The American Statistician*, Vol. 40, No. 2, 1986.

Differential item functioning analyses were conducted for each question for each country. For countries assessing in more than one language, items within language groups were considered separately. The questions were then ranked in terms of their across-population DIF statistics and the magnitude of their ordered DIF statistics was compared with reference values that would be expected to be obtained if there were no differential item functioning for any question. Questions with across-population DIF statistics that were significantly larger than the reference values were identified as outliers. These questions were deemed to be exhibiting differential item functioning and were therefore inappropriate for inclusion in summary statistics.

The differential item functioning analyses identified two science questions at age 9 and eight questions at age 13 that were outliers. These questions were removed from subsequent summary analyses. Although the two science questions at age 9 did exhibit differential item functioning, their magnitude of DIF was not considered significantly larger than the reference values and these two questions could have been included in the overall summary measures. However, the results of the items were excluded from this report because it was determined through the K-Means analyses that exclusion of these two items would reduce the population-by-item type interaction. The two questions removed at age 9 were both categorized as Physical Science, Knowledge items. The questions removed at age 13 included five Life Sciences Knowledge items, one Life Sciences Utilization item, one Physical Sciences Utilization item, and one Nature of Science Integration item.

SUMMARY MEASURES Weighted average percentages of correct responses were computed for each topic and process area and across all science questions for each population. They were computed by averaging across the individual weighted percents correct for the items included in each category. For each average, an estimate of its standard error was calculated using the jackknife procedure. Average percentages and standard errors were calculated for subgroups within each population including gender and grade. Statistics for Canada were calculated using an appropriately weighted sample of responses drawn from the individual Canadian populations.

TESTS OF SIGNIFICANCE A Bonferroni multiple comparison procedure was used to determine the statistical significance of differences in performance between participating countries. This procedure holds the probability of falsely declaring a significant difference to 5 percent across the entire set of possible pairwise comparisons between the comprehensive populations, populations with exclusions or low participation, and Canadian populations.

The procedure used to determine the statistical significance of differences in the performance between males and females was to divide the difference between the two averages by the square root of the sum of the two variances. Values of 2 or larger were cited as statistically significant.

The procedure used to determine the statistical significance of differences in performance of a population on a particular topic or process area and on the science test as a whole looked at the difference between a population's deviation from the average for the topic or process and its deviation from the overall average. Values greater than 0 indicated performance in the category was relatively higher than performance overall and values less than 0 indicated performance was relatively lower than performance overall. If the absolute value of the difference in those deviations was equal to or greater than twice the standard error of that difference, it was cited as statistically significant.

The linear relationship between levels of a background variable and average performance was estimated by applying a set of orthogonal contrasts to the set of average performance by level of the background variable. The linear component was estimated by the sum of $b = \sum c_j x_j$, where the x_j are the average percent correct for students with level j on the background variable and the c_j are defined so that b corresponds to the slope of the unweighted regression of the average percents correct on the levels of the background variable. The statistical significance of b was evaluated by comparison with its standard error, computed as the square root of the sum $\sum c_j^2 SE_j^2$, where SE_j is the standard error of x_j. Values of b that were equal to or greater than twice the standard error were considered to be statistically significant.

Data Appendix

Science: Age 13

Average Percents Correct and Standard Errors

IAEP AVERAGE	TOTAL 66.9	MALE	FEMALE	Canadian Populations	TOTAL	MALE	FEMALE
Populations							
BRAZIL, FORTALEZA	46.4 (0.6)	49.1 (0.7)	44.3 (0.8)	ALBERTA	74.1 (0.4)	76.4 (0.6)	71.8 (0.5)
BRAZIL, SÃO PAULO	52.7 (0.6)	56.3 (0.8)	49.6 (0.7)	BRITISH COLUMBIA	72.4 (0.5)	73.5 (0.6)	71.4 (0.6)
CANADA	68.8 (0.4)	70.5 (0.5)	67.1 (0.4)	MANITOBA-ENGLISH	68.6 (0.6)	70.3 (0.7)	66.9 (0.7)
CHINA	67.2 (1.1)	69.4 (1.2)	64.8 (1.1)	MANITOBA-FRENCH	66.6 (0.7)	69.5 (1.1)	64.2 (0.8)
ENGLAND	68.7 (1.2)	70.3 (1.6)	67.1 (1.8)	NEW BRUNSWICK-ENGLISH	66.3 (0.4)	67.9 (0.5)	64.8 (0.5)
FRANCE	68.6 (0.6)	70.7 (0.7)	66.5 (0.7)	NEW BRUNSWICK-FRENCH	63.6 (0.3)	64.2 (0.6)	63.1 (0.5)
HUNGARY	73.4 (0.5)	75.6 (0.6)	71.4 (0.7)	NEWFOUNDLAND	66.1 (0.5)	68.7 (0.7)	63.7 (0.6)
IRELAND	63.3 (0.6)	66.1 (0.9)	60.8 (0.8)	NOVA SCOTIA	68.7 (0.4)	70.2 (0.7)	67.0 (0.6)
ISRAEL	69.7 (0.7)	71.6 (0.8)	68.0 (0.8)	ONTARIO-ENGLISH	67.0 (0.6)	68.6 (0.8)	65.5 (0.5)
ITALY	69.9 (0.7)	72.2 (0.8)	67.6 (0.8)	ONTARIO-FRENCH	60.3 (0.7)	62.2 (0.7)	58.5 (0.7)
JORDAN	56.6 (0.7)	57.1 (0.8)	55.9 (1.3)	QUEBEC-ENGLISH	69.2 (0.5)	71.2 (0.7)	67.1 (0.7)
KOREA	77.5 (0.5)	79.6 (0.6)	75.0 (0.7)	QUEBEC-FRENCH	71.4 (0.5)	73.1 (0.6)	69.5 (0.6)
PORTUGAL	62.6 (0.8)	65.0 (1.0)	60.3 (0.8)	SASKATCHEWAN-ENGLISH	70.1 (0.6)	72.0 (0.7)	68.2 (0.6)
SCOTLAND	67.9 (0.6)	69.6 (0.7)	66.3 (0.9)	SASKATCHEWAN-FRENCH	64.8 (0.8)	66.2 (1.1)	63.4 (1.3)
SLOVENIA	70.3 (0.5)	72.5 (0.7)	68.2 (0.6)				
SOVIET UNION	71.3 (1.0)	72.9 (1.1)	69.6 (1.0)				
SPAIN	67.5 (0.6)	69.2 (0.8)	66.0 (0.7)				
SWITZERLAND	73.7 (0.9)	76.4 (1.1)	70.9 (0.8)				
TAIWAN	75.6 (0.4)	76.3 (0.6)	74.9 (0.6)				
UNITED STATES	67.0 (1.0)	69.4 (1.2)	64.5 (0.9)				

Percentile Scores and Standard Errors

	1ST	5TH	10TH	90TH	95TH	99TH
Populations						
BRAZIL, FORTALEZA	21.8 (2.1)	27.3 (1.1)	31.3 (0.0)	67.2 (0.6)	73.4 (0.1)	85.9 (2.5)
BRAZIL, SÃO PAULO	23.4 (1.2)	29.7 (0.7)	33.3 (0.8)	74.5 (3.9)	81.3 (1.7)	92.2 (2.7)
CANADA	32.8 (0.0)	43.8 (0.0)	48.4 (1.7)	87.5 (0.0)	90.6 (0.0)	95.3 (0.0)
CHINA	28.1 (3.5)	40.6 (0.6)	45.3 (1.6)	87.5 (1.6)	92.2 (2.2)	96.9 (1.6)
ENGLAND	31.3 (0.0)	39.1 (0.0)	44.3 (3.3)	89.1 (0.0)	92.2 (0.0)	98.4 (3.5)
FRANCE	31.3 (1.8)	40.6 (2.1)	45.3 (1.7)	89.1 (0.0)	92.2 (0.0)	96.9 (0.0)
HUNGARY	33.3 (1.9)	45.3 (1.0)	51.6 (0.0)	92.2 (0.0)	95.3 (0.0)	98.4 (0.0)
IRELAND	27.4 (2.3)	35.9 (0.0)	40.6 (2.3)	84.4 (3.2)	89.1 (0.0)	95.3 (0.0)
ISRAEL	34.4 (0.1)	42.2 (0.0)	47.6 (3.9)	89.1 (0.0)	92.2 (0.0)	96.9 (0.0)
ITALY	31.3 (2.7)	43.8 (4.4)	48.4 (0.0)	89.1 (0.8)	92.2 (0.0)	95.3 (0.0)
JORDAN	23.4 (0.0)	30.2 (2.9)	35.9 (0.0)	78.1 (1.6)	84.4 (2.1)	92.2 (3.5)
KOREA	35.9 (0.0)	50.0 (0.0)	57.8 (3.8)	93.8 (0.0)	95.3 (0.0)	98.4 (0.0)
PORTUGAL	28.1 (2.7)	37.3 (1.6)	42.2 (3.1)	84.4 (0.0)	89.1 (0.0)	93.8 (1.6)
SCOTLAND	28.6 (2.5)	39.1 (0.0)	45.3 (0.0)	87.5 (2.6)	90.6 (5.4)	96.9 (5.2)
SLOVENIA	34.4 (2.2)	43.8 (0.0)	50.0 (0.0)	89.1 (0.0)	92.2 (0.0)	96.9 (3.8)
SOVIET UNION	31.3 (0.6)	43.8 (1.0)	50.8 (1.9)	89.1 (2.3)	92.2 (2.7)	96.9 (0.0)
SPAIN	35.1 (0.5)	42.6 (1.3)	48.4 (0.2)	85.9 (2.6)	89.1 (0.0)	95.3 (0.0)
SWITZERLAND	35.9 (2.9)	50.0 (5.7)	57.8 (0.6)	92.2 (0.0)	95.3 (0.0)	98.4 (0.0)
TAIWAN	28.6 (3.6)	42.2 (0.0)	51.6 (0.0)	93.8 (0.0)	95.3 (0.0)	98.4 (0.0)
UNITED STATES	28.1 (2.0)	39.3 (2.9)	43.8 (5.1)	85.9 (0.0)	90.6 (0.0)	95.3 (0.0)
Canadian Populations						
ALBERTA	35.9 (0.5)	48.4 (0.0)	54.7 (0.0)	90.6 (0.0)	93.8 (0.0)	96.9 (0.0)
BRITISH COLUMBIA	35.9 (1.6)	46.9 (0.0)	53.1 (0.0)	89.1 (0.0)	92.2 (0.0)	95.3 (0.0)
MANITOBA-ENGLISH	29.7 (4.1)	39.1 (1.6)	45.3 (2.3)	87.5 (2.2)	92.2 (0.0)	95.3 (1.6)
MANITOBA-FRENCH	32.8 (2.2)	42.2 (2.7)	46.9 (0.0)	85.9 (0.0)	89.1 (0.0)	93.8 (3.1)
NEW BRUNSWICK-ENGLISH	29.6 (0.3)	39.1 (0.0)	45.3 (0.0)	85.9 (0.0)	89.1 (0.0)	95.3 (3.5)
NEW BRUNSWICK-FRENCH	29.7 (0.0)	37.5 (0.0)	43.8 (0.0)	82.8 (3.5)	87.5 (0.0)	93.8 (0.0)
NEWFOUNDLAND	31.3 (0.0)	39.1 (0.0)	45.3 (0.0)	87.5 (2.2)	90.6 (0.0)	95.3 (0.0)
NOVA SCOTIA	31.3 (4.7)	42.2 (7.0)	48.4 (1.6)	87.5 (0.0)	90.6 (0.0)	95.3 (0.0)
ONTARIO-ENGLISH	31.3 (1.1)	42.2 (4.8)	46.9 (0.0)	85.9 (2.2)	90.6 (2.7)	95.3 (0.0)
ONTARIO-FRENCH	29.0 (2.6)	37.5 (0.0)	40.6 (1.8)	81.3 (0.6)	84.4 (0.0)	92.2 (0.0)
QUEBEC-ENGLISH	32.8 (0.0)	43.8 (0.0)	48.4 (2.2)	87.5 (0.0)	92.2 (0.0)	96.9 (3.8)
QUEBEC-FRENCH	34.4 (3.1)	46.9 (1.6)	53.1 (1.3)	89.1 (0.0)	92.2 (0.0)	96.9 (1.6)
SASKATCHEWAN-ENGLISH	32.8 (1.6)	43.8 (0.0)	50.0 (0.0)	89.1 (0.0)	92.2 (0.0)	96.9 (0.0)
SASKATCHEWAN-FRENCH	32.8 (3.5)	45.3 (3.8)	50.0 (3.8)	82.8 (3.0)	87.5 (2.7)	92.2 (1.6)

Science: Age 13

	LIFE SCIENCES	PHYSICAL SCIENCES	EARTH AND SPACE SCIENCES	NATURE OF SCIENCE	KNOWS	USES	INTEGRATES
IAEP TOPIC AVERAGE	**68.0**	**64.4**	**66.9**	**70.9**	**72.6**	**65.4**	**64.9**
Populations							
BRAZIL, FORTALEZA	51.3 (0.7)	42.6 (0.6)	48.6 (0.7)	44.8 (0.9)	55.5 (0.8)	45.4 (0.5)	40.5 (0.8)
BRAZIL, SÃO PAULO	56.3 (0.8)	48.8 (0.5)	55.8 (0.7)	52.5 (0.8)	60.4 (0.9)	51.9 (0.5)	47.5 (0.7)
CANADA	68.5 (0.4)	64.9 (0.4)	67.9 (0.4)	79.0 (0.5)	71.7 (0.4)	66.1 (0.4)	71.0 (0.5)
CHINA	63.8 (1.1)	67.6 (1.1)	70.2 (1.4)	69.7 (1.1)	68.2 (1.1)	67.1 (1.1)	66.6 (1.1)
ENGLAND	68.2 (1.2)	66.6 (1.2)	65.9 (1.5)	76.5 (1.4)	72.1 (1.2)	66.8 (1.2)	69.0 (1.5)
FRANCE	67.5 (0.6)	66.8 (0.6)	66.8 (0.6)	75.7 (0.7)	71.4 (0.6)	66.3 (0.6)	70.1 (0.8)
HUNGARY	77.3 (0.5)	70.1 (0.6)	72.2 (0.6)	75.3 (0.7)	82.5 (0.5)	71.1 (0.5)	69.9 (0.7)
IRELAND	61.0 (0.6)	60.7 (0.7)	65.5 (0.8)	71.4 (0.7)	66.0 (0.7)	62.0 (0.6)	63.4 (0.7)
ISRAEL	65.4 (0.7)	69.8 (0.7)	67.5 (0.8)	78.5 (0.7)	70.5 (0.7)	68.4 (0.6)	71.1 (0.8)
ITALY	71.8 (0.7)	67.0 (0.7)	70.8 (0.7)	72.7 (0.7)	76.7 (0.7)	66.9 (0.7)	69.6 (0.8)
JORDAN	58.6 (0.7)	53.8 (0.8)	60.7 (0.9)	56.1 (0.9)	65.3 (0.7)	56.6 (0.8)	49.2 (0.9)
KOREA	80.3 (0.5)	75.8 (0.5)	74.8 (0.6)	78.8 (0.6)	83.9 (0.5)	77.2 (0.4)	72.7 (0.6)
PORTUGAL	65.9 (0.8)	58.4 (0.7)	61.1 (0.9)	67.7 (1.2)	69.8 (0.8)	60.9 (0.7)	59.5 (1.1)
SCOTLAND	67.3 (0.7)	65.7 (0.7)	64.1 (0.8)	76.8 (0.7)	72.3 (0.7)	65.8 (0.6)	67.7 (0.8)
SLOVENIA	73.1 (0.6)	67.3 (0.5)	70.1 (0.6)	72.5 (0.6)	80.2 (0.5)	68.0 (0.5)	66.0 (0.6)
SOVIET UNION	73.0 (1.0)	70.8 (1.0)	73.0 (0.9)	68.0 (1.2)	78.8 (1.1)	69.8 (0.8)	67.6 (1.3)
SPAIN	70.3 (0.6)	64.1 (0.7)	68.5 (0.7)	70.0 (0.7)	76.3 (0.7)	65.2 (0.6)	64.3 (0.8)
SWITZERLAND	74.3 (0.9)	70.3 (0.9)	74.5 (0.8)	79.8 (1.0)	77.1 (0.9)	71.6 (0.8)	74.6 (1.1)
TAIWAN	77.9 (0.5)	74.8 (0.4)	72.2 (0.5)	76.4 (0.6)	81.4 (0.5)	74.7 (0.4)	72.3 (0.5)
UNITED STATES	69.1 (1.0)	61.6 (1.1)	67.0 (0.9)	75.6 (1.3)	72.8 (1.0)	65.1 (0.9)	65.4 (1.3)
Canadian Populations							
ALBERTA	72.3 (0.5)	71.3 (0.5)	73.7 (0.5)	84.0 (0.5)	75.7 (0.5)	72.0 (0.4)	76.4 (0.6)
BRITISH COLUMBIA	70.2 (0.5)	70.7 (0.5)	72.1 (0.6)	80.7 (0.6)	76.4 (0.5)	69.6 (0.5)	74.0 (0.6)
MANITOBA-ENGLISH	67.5 (0.6)	64.9 (0.6)	70.5 (0.6)	77.3 (0.7)	72.6 (0.6)	66.8 (0.5)	68.3 (0.7)
MANITOBA-FRENCH	65.2 (0.8)	64.4 (0.8)	67.4 (0.7)	73.3 (0.9)	69.7 (0.8)	64.1 (0.7)	68.2 (1.0)
NEW BRUNSWICK-ENGLISH	66.2 (0.4)	62.8 (0.4)	65.8 (0.5)	74.9 (0.4)	69.7 (0.4)	64.6 (0.4)	66.5 (0.5)
NEW BRUNSWICK-FRENCH	62.0 (0.4)	62.2 (0.4)	64.5 (0.4)	69.0 (0.5)	63.5 (0.5)	63.4 (0.3)	64.1 (0.5)
NEWFOUNDLAND	64.8 (0.6)	62.4 (0.5)	68.5 (0.7)	75.1 (0.6)	69.9 (0.6)	64.6 (0.5)	65.7 (0.6)
NOVA SCOTIA	68.0 (0.5)	65.8 (0.4)	68.9 (0.5)	76.4 (0.9)	71.8 (0.4)	67.7 (0.4)	67.8 (0.8)
ONTARIO-ENGLISH	66.4 (0.6)	63.0 (0.7)	65.8 (0.6)	78.1 (0.7)	69.8 (0.6)	64.2 (0.6)	69.4 (0.8)
ONTARIO-FRENCH	60.7 (0.6)	56.2 (0.6)	61.2 (0.6)	68.1 (0.8)	62.1 (0.7)	58.8 (0.5)	61.2 (0.7)
QUEBEC-ENGLISH	69.0 (0.5)	64.8 (0.6)	68.1 (0.6)	80.6 (0.6)	72.9 (0.6)	66.4 (0.5)	71.1 (0.7)
QUEBEC-FRENCH	72.5 (0.5)	67.1 (0.6)	70.4 (0.6)	80.2 (0.6)	74.3 (0.6)	68.8 (0.5)	73.5 (0.7)
SASKATCHEWAN-ENGLISH	70.5 (0.6)	65.1 (0.7)	71.5 (0.7)	79.8 (0.6)	74.0 (0.6)	68.2 (0.5)	70.2 (0.8)
SASKATCHEWAN-FRENCH	63.9 (1.1)	59.8 (1.1)	68.7 (0.9)	74.4 (1.1)	67.8 (1.1)	62.1 (0.8)	67.0 (1.2)

Percents Reporting, Average Percents Correct, and Standard Errors

Populations		Amounts of Weekly Science Homework		
		0-1 HR	2-3 HRS	4 HRS/MORE
BRAZIL, FORTALEZA	%	59 (1.6)	33 (1.7)	8 (0.9)
	P	47 (0.7)	47 (0.8)	51 (1.6)
BRAZIL, SÃO PAULO	%	68 (1.1)	24 (1.2)	8 (0.8)
	P	53 (0.6)	53 (1.1)	55 (1.9)
CANADA	%	83 (0.8)	13 (0.8)	4 (0.3)
	P	69 (0.3)	70 (1.1)	70 (1.1)
CHINA	%	57 (2.5)	27 (1.8)	16 (1.5)
	P	68 (1.1)	68 (1.8)	67 (1.5)
ENGLAND	%	75 (2.5)	24 (2.3)	2 (0.4)
	P	67 (1.3)	73 (2.1)	77 (4.3)
FRANCE	%	88 (0.8)	12 (0.7)	1 (0.2)
	P	69 (0.6)	67 (1.4)	56 (4.7)
HUNGARY	%	55 (1.3)	32 (1.4)	13 (0.8)
	P	71 (0.7)	76 (0.7)	78 (1.1)
IRELAND	%	74 (1.6)	21 (1.2)	5 (0.7)
	P	62 (0.7)	67 (0.9)	70 (1.5)
ISRAEL	%	72 (1.6)	23 (1.3)	4 (0.5)
	P	70 (0.7)	69 (1.0)	67 (1.8)
ITALY	%	75 (1.4)	22 (1.4)	2 (0.4)
	P	70 (0.8)	70 (1.0)	66 (2.9)
JORDAN	%	60 (1.6)	28 (1.3)	12 (1.0)
	P	58 (0.7)	54 (1.2)	59 (1.7)
KOREA	%	56 (1.8)	34 (1.6)	9 (1.0)
	P	78 (0.6)	78 (0.6)	75 (1.2)
PORTUGAL	%	75 (1.6)	19 (1.4)	6 (0.7)
	P	63 (0.8)	63 (1.5)	62 (1.8)
SCOTLAND	%	90 (1.2)	8 (1.1)	2 (0.4)
	P	67 (0.7)	73 (1.8)	69 (3.3)
SLOVENIA	%	63 (1.3)	30 (1.2)	7 (0.7)
	P	71 (0.6)	69 (0.8)	73 (1.4)
SOVIET UNION	%	3 (0.7)	37 (0.8)	59 (0.8)
	P	66 (1.5)	73 (0.8)	71 (1.2)
SPAIN	%	58 (1.6)	30 (1.3)	12 (0.9)
	P	67 (0.7)	68 (1.0)	71 (1.0)
SWITZERLAND	%	89 (1.2)	9 (1.0)	1 (0.4)
	P	74 (0.8)	70 (1.7)	70 (1.2)
TAIWAN	%	64 (1.1)	25 (1.1)	10 (0.8)
	P	74 (0.4)	77 (0.9)	86 (1.1)
UNITED STATES	%	76 (1.7)	17 (1.2)	7 (0.8)
	P	67 (0.9)	70 (1.9)	66 (2.1)

Canadian Populations

Populations		0-1 HR	2-3 HRS	4 HRS/MORE
ALBERTA	%	74 (1.2)	20 (1.2)	6 (0.7)
	P	73 (0.4)	76 (1.0)	74 (1.7)
BRITISH COLUMBIA	%	69 (1.4)	24 (1.1)	7 (0.9)
	P	72 (0.5)	74 (0.8)	74 (1.4)
MANITOBA-ENGLISH	%	82 (1.1)	14 (1.0)	4 (0.6)
	P	68 (0.6)	70 (1.1)	70 (1.8)
MANITOBA-FRENCH	%	74 (1.8)	19 (1.8)	7 (1.0)
	P	67 (0.8)	66 (1.4)	61 (2.5)
NEW BRUNSWICK-ENGLISH	%	82 (0.9)	14 (0.8)	3 (0.4)
	P	66 (0.4)	68 (0.9)	68 (2.8)
NEW BRUNSWICK-FRENCH	%	85 (0.8)	12 (0.8)	4 (0.5)
	P	64 (0.4)	63 (1.2)	57 (2.2)
NEWFOUNDLAND	%	68 (1.6)	25 (1.4)	7 (0.9)
	P	66 (0.6)	67 (0.8)	64 (1.7)
NOVA SCOTIA	%	72 (1.3)	22 (1.3)	6 (0.6)
	P	69 (0.5)	69 (0.7)	68 (2.0)
ONTARIO-ENGLISH	%	85 (1.1)	12 (1.0)	3 (0.5)
	P	67 (0.5)	68 (2.0)	70 (1.7)
ONTARIO-FRENCH	%	82 (1.4)	14 (1.1)	4 (0.7)
	P	61 (0.5)	60 (1.3)	62 (1.8)
QUEBEC-ENGLISH	%	75 (1.3)	20 (1.2)	6 (0.7)
	P	68 (0.6)	73 (0.9)	73 (1.8)
QUEBEC-FRENCH	%	83 (1.0)	13 (0.9)	4 (0.5)
	P	71 (0.5)	74 (1.1)	69 (2.3)
SASKATCHEWAN-ENGLISH	%	85 (0.9)	12 (0.7)	3 (0.5)
	P	70 (0.6)	69 (1.2)	71 (1.9)
SASKATCHEWAN-FRENCH	%	79 (3.3)	18 (2.8)	4 (1.6)
	P	65 (1.0)	66 (2.1)	59 (3.2)

Populations		Amounts of Daily Homework		
		NO HMWK	1 HR/LESS	2 HRS/MORE
BRAZIL, FORTALEZA	%	9 (0.8)	41 (2.0)	50 (2.0)
	P	42 (1.4)	45 (0.7)	50 (0.8)
BRAZIL, SÃO PAULO	%	5 (0.9)	46 (1.6)	48 (1.9)
	P	50 (2.7)	53 (0.7)	54 (0.8)
CANADA	%	8 (0.8)	65 (1.0)	26 (0.9)
	P	72 (1.0)	69 (0.4)	67 (0.8)
CHINA	%	6 (0.7)	57 (2.1)	35 (2.1)
	P	64 (1.7)	68 (1.3)	68 (1.1)
ENGLAND	%	3 (0.9)	71 (2.7)	26 (2.8)
	P	56 (3.6)	69 (1.2)	70 (2.1)
FRANCE	%	0 (0.1)	44 (1.5)	55 (1.6)
	P	52 (3.8)	68 (0.7)	69 (0.7)
HUNGARY	%	0 (0.1)	39 (1.6)	61 (1.5)
	P	62 (4.8)	73 (0.8)	73 (0.6)
IRELAND	%	1 (0.6)	33 (1.4)	66 (1.6)
	P	41 (4.6)	62 (0.9)	65 (0.7)
ISRAEL	%	1 (0.3)	49 (1.4)	49 (1.4)
	P	66 (4.3)	72 (0.8)	67 (0.8)
ITALY	%	0 (0.1)	21 (1.1)	78 (1.2)
	P	70 (2.5)	68 (1.3)	71 (0.6)
JORDAN	%	7 (0.8)	39 (1.7)	54 (2.0)
	P	52 (1.3)	55 (1.0)	58 (0.9)
KOREA	%	3 (0.5)	58 (1.3)	38 (1.5)
	P	78 (1.7)	77 (0.5)	78 (0.7)
PORTUGAL	%	5 (0.9)	65 (1.5)	30 (1.7)
	P	61 (2.1)	64 (0.9)	60 (1.2)
SCOTLAND	%	17 (1.4)	68 (1.5)	15 (1.5)
	P	66 (1.3)	68 (0.6)	70 (1.5)
SLOVENIA	%	1 (0.2)	72 (1.4)	27 (1.4)
	P	69 (6.0)	72 (0.6)	67 (0.6)
SOVIET UNION	%	0 (0.1)	48 (1.6)	52 (1.6)
	P	46 (3.0)	70 (0.9)	72 (1.0)
SPAIN	%	1 (0.4)	36 (1.9)	62 (1.9)
	P	65 (2.5)	66 (0.9)	69 (0.6)
SWITZERLAND	%	1 (0.2)	78 (1.3)	21 (1.3)
	P	68 (4.9)	74 (0.9)	73 (1.1)
TAIWAN	%	5 (0.6)	51 (1.3)	44 (1.3)
	P	68 (1.8)	73 (0.6)	80 (0.6)
UNITED STATES	%	11 (1.2)	58 (1.5)	31 (1.6)
	P	68 (1.7)	67 (1.1)	67 (1.1)

Canadian Populations

Populations		NO HMWK	1 HR/LESS	2 HRS/MORE
ALBERTA	%	9 (1.0)	71 (1.1)	20 (1.1)
	P	79 (1.3)	74 (0.4)	72 (0.9)
BRITISH COLUMBIA	%	9 (0.7)	63 (1.5)	27 (1.6)
	P	74 (1.0)	73 (0.6)	72 (0.9)
MANITOBA-ENGLISH	%	16 (1.1)	67 (1.3)	16 (1.1)
	P	70 (1.3)	69 (0.6)	65 (1.2)
MANITOBA-FRENCH	%	9 (1.0)	70 (1.6)	21 (1.5)
	P	71 (2.3)	67 (0.7)	63 (1.1)
NEW BRUNSWICK-ENGLISH	%	10 (0.6)	71 (1.1)	19 (1.0)
	P	70 (1.0)	66 (0.4)	65 (0.9)
NEW BRUNSWICK-FRENCH	%	8 (0.6)	72 (1.1)	19 (0.8)
	P	67 (1.4)	64 (0.5)	63 (0.8)
NEWFOUNDLAND	%	6 (0.9)	67 (1.3)	27 (1.6)
	P	69 (2.3)	67 (0.6)	64 (0.8)
NOVA SCOTIA	%	7 (0.9)	72 (1.2)	20 (1.4)
	P	72 (2.5)	69 (0.6)	67 (0.9)
ONTARIO-ENGLISH	%	10 (1.2)	62 (1.6)	27 (1.4)
	P	71 (1.4)	67 (0.6)	65 (1.2)
ONTARIO-FRENCH	%	10 (1.1)	67 (1.9)	22 (1.5)
	P	62 (1.1)	60 (0.6)	59 (1.0)
QUEBEC-ENGLISH	%	5 (0.8)	61 (1.5)	33 (1.7)
	P	69 (2.3)	69 (0.6)	69 (0.7)
QUEBEC-FRENCH	%	4 (0.7)	70 (1.8)	25 (1.7)
	P	74 (1.8)	71 (0.5)	71 (0.9)
SASKATCHEWAN-ENGLISH	%	20 (1.5)	66 (1.3)	13 (1.0)
	P	74 (0.7)	70 (0.7)	66 (1.2)
SASKATCHEWAN-FRENCH	%	11 (1.7)	71 (3.0)	17 (2.8)
	P	64 (2.1)	65 (1.0)	66 (2.0)

% = Percentages of Students
P = Average Percent Correct

Science: Age 13

Populations		Amounts of Daily Television Viewing		
		0-1 HR	2-4 HRS	5 HRS/MORE
BRAZIL, FORTALEZA	%	29 (1.2)	52 (1.8)	20 (1.5)
	P	44 (0.7)	49 (0.8)	46 (1.0)
BRAZIL, SÃO PAULO	%	27 (1.3)	56 (1.6)	18 (1.1)
	P	51 (0.8)	55 (0.7)	53 (1.0)
CANADA	%	17 (0.9)	68 (0.8)	15 (0.7)
	P	72 (0.8)	69 (0.4)	65 (0.9)
CHINA	%	82 (1.6)	16 (1.5)	2 (0.4)
	P	68 (1.2)	66 (1.2)	57 (2.5)
ENGLAND	%	12 (1.8)	66 (2.4)	23 (1.7)
	P	70 (3.5)	70 (1.2)	66 (1.7)
FRANCE	%	48 (1.6)	48 (1.5)	4 (0.5)
	P	71 (0.7)	67 (0.7)	59 (1.8)
HUNGARY	%	10 (0.8)	75 (1.1)	16 (1.1)
	P	73 (1.4)	75 (0.6)	67 (1.3)
IRELAND	%	26 (1.3)	65 (1.2)	9 (0.9)
	P	65 (1.0)	63 (0.6)	57 (1.3)
ISRAEL	%	11 (0.9)	69 (1.0)	20 (1.2)
	P	66 (1.5)	71 (0.8)	69 (0.9)
ITALY	%	23 (1.0)	70 (1.2)	7 (0.8)
	P	69 (1.2)	70 (0.8)	68 (2.0)
JORDAN	%	34 (1.2)	56 (1.4)	10 (0.9)
	P	56 (1.1)	58 (0.8)	53 (1.4)
KOREA	%	22 (1.3)	68 (1.4)	10 (0.8)
	P	81 (0.7)	77 (0.5)	73 (1.3)
PORTUGAL	%	22 (1.2)	67 (1.2)	11 (0.9)
	P	58 (1.2)	64 (0.9)	65 (1.3)
SCOTLAND	%	9 (1.0)	68 (1.4)	23 (1.3)
	P	71 (2.3)	68 (0.7)	65 (0.9)
SLOVENIA	%	30 (1.4)	66 (1.2)	5 (0.6)
	P	71 (0.7)	70 (0.7)	67 (2.0)
SOVIET UNION	%	12 (0.5)	69 (1.3)	19 (1.3)
	P	68 (1.6)	72 (0.9)	70 (1.7)
SPAIN	%	23 (1.4)	66 (1.4)	11 (0.9)
	P	69 (1.1)	68 (0.6)	66 (1.1)
SWITZERLAND	%	41 (1.4)	52 (1.4)	7 (0.6)
	P	75 (0.8)	73 (1.1)	68 (1.3)
TAIWAN	%	41 (1.5)	53 (1.5)	7 (0.7)
	P	80 (0.6)	73 (0.7)	67 (1.6)
UNITED STATES	%	15 (1.0)	63 (1.8)	22 (1.7)
	P	71 (1.3)	68 (1.0)	62 (1.3)

Canadian Populations		Amounts of Daily Television Viewing		
		0-1 HR	2-4 HRS	5 HRS/MORE
ALBERTA	%	16 (1.3)	70 (1.4)	14 (0.9)
	P	77 (1.0)	74 (0.5)	70 (1.0)
BRITISH COLUMBIA	%	23 (1.3)	64 (1.3)	13 (1.1)
	P	75 (1.0)	73 (0.5)	68 (1.1)
MANITOBA-ENGLISH	%	15 (1.1)	66 (1.2)	19 (1.2)
	P	71 (1.5)	69 (0.5)	64 (0.9)
MANITOBA-FRENCH	%	16 (1.4)	70 (2.0)	14 (1.2)
	P	71 (1.3)	66 (0.8)	62 (1.8)
NEW BRUNSWICK-ENGLISH	%	12 (0.8)	66 (1.3)	22 (1.0)
	P	68 (1.0)	68 (0.5)	62 (0.8)
NEW BRUNSWICK-FRENCH	%	13 (0.8)	72 (0.9)	16 (0.7)
	P	65 (1.2)	65 (0.4)	59 (1.0)
NEWFOUNDLAND	%	8 (0.7)	68 (1.3)	23 (1.2)
	P	66 (1.7)	67 (0.6)	63 (0.9)
NOVA SCOTIA	%	12 (0.9)	66 (1.1)	22 (0.9)
	P	71 (1.6)	69 (0.5)	65 (1.1)
ONTARIO-ENGLISH	%	16 (1.1)	67 (1.2)	17 (1.1)
	P	70 (1.3)	67 (0.6)	64 (1.2)
ONTARIO-FRENCH	%	14 (1.1)	68 (1.3)	18 (1.2)
	P	64 (1.3)	60 (0.6)	57 (1.0)
QUEBEC-ENGLISH	%	23 (2.0)	63 (1.8)	15 (1.2)
	P	73 (1.4)	69 (0.6)	65 (1.3)
QUEBEC-FRENCH	%	19 (1.3)	69 (1.2)	12 (0.9)
	P	73 (1.0)	71 (0.5)	69 (1.1)
SASKATCHEWAN-ENGLISH	%	14 (0.9)	69 (1.1)	17 (1.0)
	P	72 (1.2)	71 (0.6)	66 (1.0)
SASKATCHEWAN-FRENCH	%	22 (2.6)	68 (2.7)	10 (2.1)
	P	67 (1.8)	65 (1.0)	63 (3.1)

% = Percentages of Students
P = Average Percent Correct

Science: Age 13

Populations		Amounts of Experimenting on Own				
		EVR/DAY	SEV/WK	1/WEEK	<1/WEEK	NEVER
BRAZIL, FORTALEZA	%	2 (0.6)	9 (1.2)	20 (1.0)	25 (1.4)	44 (1.9)
	P	40 (2.1)	45 (1.7)	44 (0.8)	51 (1.1)	47 (0.7)
BRAZIL, SAO PAULO	%	2 (0.4)	7 (0.6)	17 (1.4)	40 (2.2)	35 (1.6)
	P	43 (2.7)	49 (1.6)	51 (1.4)	55 (1.0)	53 (0.8)
CANADA	%	3 (0.3)	25 (1.3)	23 (1.0)	35 (1.4)	13 (0.7)
	P	67 (1.7)	71 (0.6)	70 (0.6)	69 (0.6)	64 (0.8)
CHINA	%	2 (0.5)	15 (1.4)	27 (1.3)	26 (2.3)	29 (2.4)
	P	63 (4.4)	69 (1.7)	68 (1.7)	72 (1.3)	63 (0.9)
ENGLAND	%	3 (0.7)	50 (2.9)	30 (2.7)	15 (2.0)	2 (0.6)
	P	56 (7.2)	70 (1.3)	67 (1.7)	71 (1.9)	57 (3.8)
FRANCE	%	2 (0.3)	10 (0.8)	26 (1.3)	42 (1.4)	20 (1.7)
	P	63 (2.8)	64 (1.4)	67 (0.8)	72 (0.8)	67 (0.9)
HUNGARY	%	0 (0.2)	4 (0.6)	12 (0.9)	53 (1.7)	31 (1.7)
	P	55 (4.9)	72 (2.6)	70 (1.2)	76 (0.6)	71 (0.8)
IRELAND	%	1 (0.2)	11 (1.0)	31 (1.6)	31 (1.8)	27 (2.1)
	P	56 (2.5)	63 (1.3)	65 (1.1)	66 (0.8)	59 (0.9)
ISRAEL	%	1 (0.2)	12 (0.9)	19 (1.0)	34 (1.0)	35 (1.4)
	P	59 (3.7)	72 (1.7)	68 (1.0)	72 (0.9)	68 (0.9)
ITALY	%	0 (0.1)	5 (0.9)	5 (0.5)	30 (1.8)	59 (1.9)
	P	58 (7.6)	68 (1.7)	64 (1.4)	73 (0.8)	69 (0.9)
JORDAN	%	3 (0.5)	19 (1.0)	22 (1.4)	30 (1.4)	26 (1.4)
	P	41 (1.9)	54 (1.8)	57 (1.0)	60 (1.0)	57 (0.8)
KOREA	%	1 (0.3)	6 (0.7)	19 (1.1)	39 (1.3)	35 (1.7)
	P	63 (3.9)	72 (2.2)	75 (1.0)	80 (0.6)	77 (0.8)
PORTUGAL	%	2 (0.4)	8 (0.9)	12 (1.2)	30 (1.4)	48 (1.7)
	P	39 (3.8)	52 (2.0)	57 (2.0)	66 (0.9)	65 (0.9)
SCOTLAND	%	7 (0.9)	60 (1.6)	19 (1.2)	11 (1.2)	3 (0.3)
	P	63 (1.6)	70 (0.8)	67 (1.2)	64 (1.3)	60 (2.6)
SLOVENIA	%	1 (0.3)	10 (0.8)	23 (1.3)	44 (1.6)	22 (1.5)
	P	58 (5.3)	67 (1.6)	69 (0.9)	73 (0.6)	69 (0.8)
SOVIET UNION	%	11 (1.2)	20 (0.8)	22 (1.5)	25 (0.9)	13 (0.8)
	P	67 (1.7)	70 (1.3)	75 (0.8)	75 (0.9)	68 (2.0)
SPAIN	%	1 (0.3)	6 (1.1)	10 (1.0)	31 (1.7)	51 (2.3)
	P	62 (3.7)	66 (2.3)	65 (1.2)	70 (0.8)	68 (0.7)
SWITZERLAND	%	2 (0.3)	7 (0.7)	15 (1.5)	41 (1.9)	36 (1.7)
	P	73 (2.1)	73 (1.4)	74 (1.4)	76 (0.9)	71 (1.2)
TAIWAN	%	0 (0.2)	11 (0.9)	25 (1.2)	38 (1.3)	25 (1.3)
	P	61 (8.7)	71 (1.1)	75 (0.9)	80 (0.6)	72 (0.8)
UNITED STATES	%	2 (0.7)	11 (1.6)	19 (1.6)	42 (2.0)	25 (1.9)
	P	50 (4.4)	67 (2.2)	69 (1.3)	69 (0.8)	64 (1.4)
Canadian Populations						
ALBERTA	%	2 (0.4)	23 (1.9)	25 (1.4)	37 (1.9)	14 (1.2)
	P	71 (3.0)	73 (0.8)	74 (0.9)	76 (0.5)	72 (1.0)
BRITISH COLUMBIA	%	4 (0.7)	26 (1.8)	25 (1.3)	30 (1.8)	14 (1.0)
	P	68 (2.5)	73 (0.8)	72 (0.8)	74 (0.6)	69 (0.9)
MANITOBA-ENGLISH	%	2 (0.3)	14 (1.7)	16 (1.0)	45 (1.7)	23 (1.4)
	P	59 (3.3)	70 (1.4)	67 (1.1)	70 (0.6)	66 (0.8)
MANITOBA-FRENCH	%	8 (1.0)	20 (1.8)	19 (1.6)	42 (1.9)	10 (0.9)
	P	64 (2.0)	63 (1.2)	69 (1.3)	67 (1.0)	68 (1.7)
NEW BRUNSWICK-ENGLISH	%	2 (0.3)	10 (0.8)	19 (0.9)	45 (1.4)	24 (0.9)
	P	50 (3.8)	66 (1.3)	67 (0.8)	68 (0.5)	63 (0.7)
NEW BRUNSWICK-FRENCH	%	4 (0.5)	22 (0.9)	23 (0.9)	37 (1.1)	14 (0.7)
	P	56 (2.2)	61 (0.6)	65 (0.9)	66 (0.5)	63 (1.0)
NEWFOUNDLAND	%	2 (0.4)	30 (2.0)	22 (1.4)	32 (1.7)	13 (1.2)
	P	60 (3.2)	67 (0.9)	67 (0.9)	67 (0.7)	63 (1.5)
NOVA SCOTIA	%	2 (0.4)	14 (1.3)	21 (1.1)	45 (1.6)	18 (1.4)
	P	60 (3.6)	69 (1.3)	68 (1.1)	71 (0.7)	64 (1.1)
ONTARIO-ENGLISH	%	2 (0.4)	22 (2.2)	22 (1.6)	41 (2.2)	14 (1.2)
	P	59 (4.9)	69 (1.0)	67 (0.9)	68 (0.8)	62 (1.0)
ONTARIO-FRENCH	%	6 (0.7)	32 (1.7)	26 (1.3)	31 (1.8)	5 (0.7)
	P	59 (1.7)	61 (1.0)	60 (0.8)	62 (0.8)	55 (2.1)
QUEBEC-ENGLISH	%	3 (0.9)	22 (1.9)	23 (1.5)	31 (1.7)	21 (1.3)
	P	71 (2.7)	71 (0.9)	69 (1.1)	71 (0.8)	64 (1.1)
QUEBEC-FRENCH	%	5 (0.6)	34 (1.9)	25 (1.6)	25 (1.7)	10 (1.3)
	P	74 (1.2)	74 (0.6)	73 (0.9)	71 (1.0)	63 (1.5)
SASKATCHEWAN-ENGLISH	%	1 (0.2)	6 (0.8)	13 (1.4)	45 (1.9)	34 (2.0)
	P	63 (5.4)	66 (1.6)	69 (1.2)	72 (0.7)	69 (0.8)
SASKATCHEWAN-FRENCH	%	5 (1.4)	16 (2.5)	25 (2.5)	42 (3.1)	12 (2.2)
	P	59 (4.0)	62 (2.2)	66 (1.6)	66 (1.4)	64 (2.4)

% = Percentages of Students
P = Average Percent Correct

Science: Age 13

Percents Reporting, Average Percents Correct, and Standard Errors

Populations		Science Attitudes POSITIVE	UNDECIDED	NEGATIVE
BRAZIL, FORTALEZA	%	74 (1.3)	24 (1.2)	2 (0.5)
	P	47 (0.7)	47 (0.8)	48 (2.8)
BRAZIL, SÃO PAULO	%	69 (1.3)	29 (1.2)	2 (0.4)
	P	53 (0.7)	53 (1.0)	58 (4.0)
CANADA	%	62 (1.0)	33 (0.8)	6 (0.5)
	P	71 (0.4)	66 (0.5)	65 (1.0)
CHINA	%	74 (1.7)	24 (1.5)	1 (0.4)
	P	69 (1.3)	64 (0.9)	62 (2.0)
ENGLAND	%	66 (2.9)	31 (2.8)	3 (0.8)
	P	70 (1.3)	67 (1.8)	62 (3.3)
FRANCE	%	55 (1.3)	37 (1.2)	8 (0.6)
	P	70 (0.7)	67 (0.7)	65 (1.1)
HUNGARY	%	69 (1.2)	28 (1.2)	2 (0.5)
	P	75 (0.6)	69 (0.8)	70 (2.1)
IRELAND	%	57 (1.4)	34 (1.2)	9 (0.9)
	P	66 (0.7)	61 (0.8)	58 (1.4)
ISRAEL	%	62 (1.6)	33 (1.6)	5 (0.5)
	P	70 (0.8)	69 (0.8)	68 (1.5)
ITALY	%	73 (1.4)	25 (1.3)	2 (0.4)
	P	71 (0.8)	67 (0.7)	62 (3.0)
JORDAN	%	82 (1.0)	16 (1.0)	2 (0.3)
	P	58 (0.8)	51 (1.0)	44 (3.0)
KOREA	%	27 (1.3)	54 (1.3)	19 (1.0)
	P	80 (0.7)	77 (0.6)	76 (0.9)
PORTUGAL	%	71 (1.4)	27 (1.4)	2 (0.4)
	P	63 (1.0)	60 (1.0)	66 (2.4)
SCOTLAND	%	66 (1.2)	29 (1.1)	4 (0.5)
	P	71 (0.7)	63 (0.8)	59 (2.1)
SLOVENIA	%	78 (1.2)	20 (1.2)	1 (0.3)
	P	71 (0.5)	68 (1.0)	62 (2.4)
SOVIET UNION	%	66 (1.4)	32 (1.4)	2 (0.4)
	P	73 (1.1)	68 (1.0)	68 (3.1)
SPAIN	%	78 (1.4)	20 (1.1)	2 (0.5)
	P	68 (0.6)	68 (0.9)	64 (1.9)
SWITZERLAND	%	59 (1.5)	34 (1.3)	7 (0.5)
	P	75 (0.9)	73 (1.1)	70 (1.1)
TAIWAN	%	51 (1.2)	44 (1.2)	5 (0.6)
	P	78 (0.7)	73 (0.5)	72 (2.3)
UNITED STATES	%	57 (2.1)	36 (1.9)	7 (0.9)
	P	69 (1.2)	64 (0.8)	64 (1.8)

Canadian Populations		Science Attitudes POSITIVE	UNDECIDED	NEGATIVE
ALBERTA	%	62 (1.2)	32 (1.3)	6 (0.6)
	P	76 (0.5)	71 (0.7)	67 (1.6)
BRITISH COLUMBIA	%	60 (1.7)	34 (1.5)	6 (0.8)
	P	75 (0.5)	69 (0.9)	67 (1.4)
MANITOBA-ENGLISH	%	55 (1.4)	36 (1.3)	9 (0.8)
	P	71 (0.7)	66 (0.7)	61 (1.3)
MANITOBA-FRENCH	%	58 (2.0)	34 (1.9)	8 (1.0)
	P	69 (0.9)	64 (1.0)	62 (2.0)
NEW BRUNSWICK-ENGLISH	%	56 (1.1)	36 (1.1)	8 (0.7)
	P	69 (0.4)	64 (0.6)	61 (1.2)
NEW BRUNSWICK-FRENCH	%	63 (1.2)	31 (1.2)	6 (0.5)
	P	66 (0.5)	61 (0.6)	60 (1.4)
NEWFOUNDLAND	%	67 (1.4)	30 (1.2)	4 (0.5)
	P	68 (0.6)	63 (0.8)	58 (1.9)
NOVA SCOTIA	%	59 (1.5)	35 (1.4)	6 (0.7)
	P	71 (0.6)	66 (0.7)	62 (1.4)
ONTARIO-ENGLISH	%	62 (1.3)	33 (1.1)	5 (0.6)
	P	69 (0.7)	64 (0.8)	63 (1.9)
ONTARIO-FRENCH	%	71 (1.3)	25 (1.1)	4 (0.6)
	P	62 (0.6)	57 (0.8)	55 (1.4)
QUEBEC-ENGLISH	%	56 (1.6)	35 (1.4)	10 (0.9)
	P	72 (0.7)	67 (0.8)	64 (1.4)
QUEBEC-FRENCH	%	61 (1.5)	32 (1.4)	6 (0.8)
	P	73 (0.6)	69 (0.6)	69 (1.4)
SASKATCHEWAN-ENGLISH	%	55 (1.5)	38 (1.3)	7 (0.8)
	P	73 (0.7)	68 (0.7)	63 (1.5)
SASKATCHEWAN-FRENCH	%	57 (3.1)	37 (3.1)	6 (1.3)
	P	68 (1.0)	61 (1.3)	57 (4.8)

% = Percentages of Students
P = Average Percent Correct

Science Age 13

Percentages of Students Responding Correctly to IAEP Assessment Items

Topic: Life Sciences	IAEP Item Average
Food webs	80
Insect and plant interactions – pollination	79
Classification by physical form	79
Body structure – relating form and function	79
Organisms and environments – bacteria	78
Human anatomy – digestion	76
Classification of animals – mammals	75
Food chains	71
Human anatomy – nervous system	70
Experimental design and conclusions – plants and light	69
Identification of animals with description of body	69
Plant structure – flowers	69
Human anatomy – identifying internal organs by function	68
Classification of animals – common characteristics	67
Life cycles – birds	65
Organisms and environments – fish	62
Life cycles – insects	54
Experimental design – plants and water	45
Adaptation – leaf size in plants	44

Topic: Physical Sciences	IAEP Item Average
Conductors and insulators	89
Conductors and insulators	87
Conservation of mass	83
Lever and fulcrum principles	77
Chemical processes – dissolving	77
Combustion – oxygen requirements	76
Conservation of mass	74
Physical properties of air	72
Conservation of mass	70
Measuring volume	67
Chemical processes – dissolving	66
Newton's first law	64
Soil changes – evaporation	64
Magnetic poles	64
Reflection from plain mirror	61
Circuits	61
Friction and heating	59
Measuring mass	58
Chemical changes – dissolving	58
Physical vs. chemical change	57
Understanding heating curve	52
Phases of matter	52
Phases of matter	49
Circuits	46
Physical changes – freezing	37

Topic: Earth and Space Sciences	IAEP Item Average
Compass directions	88
Earth's rotation – night and day	81
Solar system structure	80
Reflectivity of the Moon	78
Interpreting geologic evidence – limestone	77
Water cycle	72
Eclipses	54
Interpreting geologic evidence – oil	41
Barometric pressure vs. height	33

Topic: Nature of Science	IAEP Item Average
Reading data	84
Reading charts	84
Graphing data	83
Inferences vs. observations	82
Experimental design – selecting the correct controls	77
Understanding purpose of experiment from description	74
Estimating – interpolating data	65
Drawing experimental conclusions – absorbency	60
Drawing experimental conclusion – larvae	57
Choosing correct experiment to test a hypothesis	57
Understanding purpose of experiment from description	54

Science: Age 9

Average Percents Correct and Standard Errors

	TOTAL	MALE	FEMALE
IAEP AVERAGE	62.1		
Populations			
CANADA	62.8 (0.4)	63.6 (0.4)	62.0 (0.5)
ENGLAND	62.9 (0.9)	63.8 (1.3)	62.0 (1.2)
HUNGARY	62.5 (0.5)	63.4 (0.6)	61.6 (0.6)
IRELAND	56.5 (0.7)	58.2 (1.0)	54.8 (0.9)
ISRAEL	61.2 (0.7)	63.0 (0.9)	59.4 (0.7)
ITALY	66.9 (0.9)	67.9 (1.0)	65.8 (1.0)
KOREA	67.9 (0.5)	70.4 (0.7)	65.1 (0.5)
PORTUGAL	54.8 (0.7)	56.3 (0.9)	53.3 (0.9)
SCOTLAND	62.2 (0.7)	61.9 (0.7)	62.5 (1.0)
SLOVENIA	57.7 (0.5)	58.3 (0.6)	57.0 (0.6)
SOVIET UNION	61.5 (1.2)	62.7 (1.4)	60.4 (1.2)
SPAIN	61.7 (0.7)	63.4 (0.9)	59.7 (0.7)
TAIWAN	66.7 (0.5)	68.5 (0.6)	64.6 (0.7)
UNITED STATES	64.7 (0.9)	65.5 (1.1)	63.8 (0.8)
Canadian Populations			
BRITISH COLUMBIA	65.9 (0.6)	66.1 (0.8)	65.6 (0.6)
NEW BRUNSWICK-ENGLISH	61.6 (0.4)	61.9 (0.5)	61.3 (0.6)
ONTARIO-ENGLISH	62.5 (0.5)	63.6 (0.6)	61.4 (0.7)
ONTARIO-FRENCH	56.3 (0.5)	56.5 (0.7)	56.1 (0.5)
QUEBEC-ENGLISH	63.0 (0.7)	64.3 (0.9)	61.7 (0.8)
QUEBEC-FRENCH	62.8 (0.5)	63.2 (0.7)	62.4 (0.5)

Science: Ages 9 & 13

Averages and Standard Errors for Common Items

	AGE 9	AGE 13
Populations		
CANADA	58.9(0.5)	79.1(0.4)
ENGLAND	59.0(1.1)	77.7(1.0)
HUNGARY	60.5(0.7)	81.6(0.5)
IRELAND	52.8(0.8)	74.1(0.6)
ISRAEL	59.6(0.8)	78.3(0.6)
ITALY	63.9(1.1)	80.0(0.6)
KOREA	63.6(0.7)	85.0(0.5)
PORTUGAL	52.6(1.0)	76.2(0.8)
SCOTLAND	56.6(0.7)	77.4(0.6)
SLOVENIA	56.8(0.6)	81.9(0.4)
SOVIET UNION	57.7(1.4)	80.2(0.9)
SPAIN	61.1(0.8)	80.8(0.6)
TAIWAN	64.1(0.7)	83.1(0.4)
UNITED STATES	60.5(1.0)	77.7(1.0)
Canadian Populations		
BRITISH COLUMBIA	61.8(0.8)	81.6(0.4)
NEW BRUNSWICK-ENGLISH	57.7(0.5)	76.3(0.4)
ONTARIO-ENGLISH	58.5(0.6)	76.9(0.6)
ONTARIO-FRENCH	51.5(0.6)	70.6(0.6)
QUEBEC-ENGLISH	59.8(0.8)	79.5(0.5)
QUEBEC-FRENCH	59.0(0.7)	83.0(0.5)

Science: Age 9

Percentile Scores and Standard Errors

	1ST	5TH	10TH	90TH	95TH	99TH
Populations						
CANADA	27.6 (0.5)	37.9 (1.1)	43.1 (0.0)	81.0 (0.0)	84.5 (0.0)	91.4 (0.0)
ENGLAND	24.1 (4.1)	36.2 (0.9)	41.4 (0.0)	82.8 (0.0)	86.2 (2.8)	93.1 (0.0)
HUNGARY	26.9 (1.7)	38.5 (0.7)	44.8 (0.0)	79.3 (0.0)	84.2 (2.9)	89.7 (0.0)
IRELAND	22.9 (1.4)	29.3 (1.6)	36.2 (1.3)	75.9 (0.0)	81.0 (1.8)	89.7 (5.2)
ISRAEL	27.6 (0.3)	36.2 (1.4)	41.4 (0.0)	81.0 (0.0)	86.2 (0.0)	93.1 (0.0)
ITALY	31.0 (1.7)	41.4 (3.3)	48.3 (0.3)	86.2 (1.7)	89.7 (1.7)	94.8 (0.0)
KOREA	32.8 (4.9)	44.8 (0.4)	50.0 (0.0)	84.5 (0.0)	87.9 (0.0)	93.1 (3.4)
PORTUGAL	26.3 (3.8)	33.3 (3.2)	37.9 (0.0)	72.4 (0.0)	79.0 (5.6)	86.2 (3.9)
SCOTLAND	27.6 (0.0)	36.8 (3.0)	43.1 (0.0)	81.0 (3.5)	84.5 (0.0)	89.7 (0.0)
SLOVENIA	27.8 (0.8)	35.1 (0.2)	40.4 (0.4)	75.4 (0.0)	79.0 (0.0)	86.0 (1.5)
SOVIET UNION	29.3 (4.2)	39.7 (1.5)	43.1 (1.4)	79.3 (4.8)	86.2 (2.4)	93.1 (2.4)
SPAIN	27.6 (3.1)	36.2 (1.0)	41.8 (1.6)	81.0 (0.0)	84.5 (0.0)	89.7 (0.0)
TAIWAN	27.6 (1.3)	39.7 (0.0)	44.8 (7.2)	86.2 (0.0)	89.7 (0.0)	94.8 (0.0)
UNITED STATES	25.9 (0.3)	36.2 (1.7)	43.1 (5.1)	84.5 (0.0)	87.9 (0.0)	93.1 (0.0)
Canadian Populations						
BRITISH COLUMBIA	29.3 (4.6)	41.4 (0.0)	46.6 (3.6)	82.8 (0.0)	86.2 (0.0)	91.4 (0.0)
NEW BRUNSWICK-ENGLISH	24.1 (0.0)	34.5 (3.2)	41.4 (0.0)	81.0 (0.0)	84.5 (0.0)	91.4 (0.0)
ONTARIO-ENGLISH	27.6 (0.0)	36.2 (2.6)	43.1 (3.1)	81.0 (0.0)	86.2 (3.4)	91.4 (0.0)
ONTARIO-FRENCH	28.9 (3.5)	34.5 (0.0)	39.7 (0.0)	74.1 (0.0)	79.3 (1.8)	86.2 (0.0)
QUEBEC-ENGLISH	29.3 (2.0)	37.9 (0.0)	43.1 (2.0)	82.8 (0.0)	86.2 (0.0)	91.4 (0.0)
QUEBEC-FRENCH	32.8 (5.2)	40.7 (3.6)	44.8 (0.6)	79.3 (0.0)	84.5 (0.0)	89.7 (4.9)

Science: Age 9

Topic and Process Averages and Standard Errors

	LIFE SCIENCES	PHYSICAL SCIENCES	EARTH AND SPACE SCIENCES	NATURE OF SCIENCE	KNOWS	USES	INTEGRATES
IAEP TOPIC AVERAGE	63.3	58.6	64.1	63.9	63.9	62.7	56.9
Populations							
CANADA	63.3 (0.4)	57.7 (0.4)	66.8 (0.4)	67.3 (0.5)	63.4 (0.4)	65.3 (0.4)	56.4 (0.4)
ENGLAND	62.4 (0.9)	60.1 (0.9)	66.3 (1.1)	66.0 (1.1)	64.5 (1.0)	63.6 (0.9)	58.2 (1.0)
HUNGARY	64.7 (0.6)	56.3 (0.6)	68.2 (0.5)	62.0 (0.6)	66.1 (0.5)	61.1 (0.5)	57.4 (0.7)
IRELAND	54.7 (0.8)	53.8 (0.7)	62.9 (0.8)	59.5 (0.8)	57.2 (0.8)	57.4 (0.7)	53.0 (0.8)
ISRAEL	61.4 (0.8)	59.8 (0.6)	60.6 (0.7)	64.1 (0.9)	61.0 (0.8)	63.0 (0.6)	57.7 (0.8)
ITALY	71.3 (0.9)	61.0 (0.9)	66.8 (0.9)	66.9 (1.1)	71.6 (0.9)	66.1 (0.9)	58.2 (1.1)
KOREA	69.1 (0.5)	68.2 (0.5)	62.4 (0.6)	70.7 (0.6)	67.3 (0.5)	70.1 (0.5)	64.5 (0.5)
PORTUGAL	58.1 (0.8)	50.0 (0.6)	57.3 (0.9)	52.4 (1.1)	58.4 (0.9)	54.1 (0.7)	48.5 (0.8)
SCOTLAND	61.3 (0.7)	59.1 (0.8)	65.1 (0.7)	67.7 (1.0)	62.5 (0.6)	62.7 (0.7)	60.4 (0.8)
SLOVENIA	59.4 (0.5)	56.6 (0.5)	58.3 (0.7)	54.1 (0.6)	60.3 (0.5)	57.0 (0.5)	52.9 (0.7)
SOVIET UNION	63.8 (1.4)	58.1 (0.9)	63.1 (1.4)	60.2 (1.4)	63.9 (1.4)	62.3 (1.1)	54.7 (1.4)
SPAIN	65.7 (0.7)	54.1 (0.7)	62.7 (0.7)	65.1 (1.0)	66.7 (0.7)	60.3 (0.7)	53.8 (0.8)
TAIWAN	65.3 (0.6)	68.1 (0.5)	66.6 (0.7)	67.4 (0.6)	65.3 (0.6)	69.5 (0.6)	63.6 (0.6)
UNITED STATES	65.2 (0.9)	57.5 (0.8)	70.6 (1.1)	70.7 (1.0)	67.0 (1.0)	65.5 (0.9)	57.9 (0.8)
Canadian Populations							
BRITISH COLUMBIA	66.4 (0.7)	59.6 (0.7)	72.1 (0.6)	69.9 (0.8)	68.2 (0.6)	66.9 (0.6)	58.6 (0.8)
NEW BRUNSWICK-ENGLISH	61.3 (0.4)	56.9 (0.4)	67.2 (0.5)	65.4 (0.5)	63.1 (0.4)	63.4 (0.4)	54.5 (0.5)
ONTARIO-ENGLISH	63.0 (0.6)	56.6 (0.5)	68.4 (0.6)	66.2 (0.7)	64.3 (0.6)	64.1 (0.5)	55.1 (0.5)
ONTARIO-FRENCH	54.9 (0.5)	53.7 (0.5)	60.5 (0.5)	60.3 (0.7)	55.1 (0.5)	59.7 (0.5)	51.7 (0.6)
QUEBEC-ENGLISH	63.9 (0.8)	57.3 (0.6)	66.8 (0.8)	67.9 (0.8)	65.1 (0.8)	64.4 (0.6)	55.7 (0.8)
QUEBEC-FRENCH	63.3 (0.6)	59.1 (0.6)	63.0 (0.6)	69.0 (0.7)	61.1 (0.5)	66.9 (0.6)	57.9 (0.6)

Percents Reporting, Average Percents Correct, and Standard Errors

Amounts of Weekly Science Homework

Populations		0-1 HR	2-3 HRS	4 HRS/MORE
CANADA	%	80 (0.9)	14 (0.7)	6 (0.5)
	P	64 (0.3)	59 (0.8)	60 (1.2)
ENGLAND	%	87 (1.3)	10 (1.1)	3 (0.6)
	P	64 (0.9)	57 (1.9)	51 (4.0)
HUNGARY	%	62 (1.6)	26 (1.2)	12 (1.1)
	P	63 (0.6)	62 (0.8)	63 (1.3)
IRELAND	%	82 (1.5)	12 (1.2)	6 (0.9)
	P	58 (0.7)	51 (1.7)	46 (2.3)
ISRAEL	%	70 (1.3)	23 (1.1)	7 (0.6)
	P	62 (0.7)	59 (1.0)	55 (1.7)
ITALY	%	71 (2.2)	21 (1.7)	8 (0.9)
	P	68 (0.8)	66 (1.9)	67 (1.5)
KOREA	%	69 (1.5)	24 (1.0)	7 (0.9)
	P	69 (0.4)	66 (0.9)	66 (1.6)
PORTUGAL	%	64 (1.9)	22 (1.3)	15 (1.4)
	P	56 (0.8)	53 (1.0)	55 (1.8)
SCOTLAND	%	92 (1.2)	5 (0.8)	3 (0.6)
	P	63 (0.6)	55 (2.8)	57 (4.0)
SLOVENIA	%	68 (1.7)	21 (1.2)	11 (1.0)
	P	58 (0.5)	58 (0.9)	58 (1.3)
SOVIET UNION	%	75 (1.5)	19 (1.3)	6 (0.5)
	P	62 (1.3)	61 (1.3)	58 (2.2)
SPAIN	%	51 (2.0)	29 (1.5)	20 (1.6)
	P	61 (0.8)	62 (0.8)	63 (1.2)
TAIWAN	%	58 (1.4)	32 (1.1)	9 (1.0)
	P	67 (0.6)	66 (0.7)	66 (1.8)
UNITED STATES	%	78 (1.4)	15 (1.3)	7 (0.8)
	P	66 (0.8)	62 (1.8)	57 (2.5)
Canadian Populations				
BRITISH COLUMBIA	%	80 (1.5)	15 (1.2)	6 (0.6)
	P	67 (0.6)	61 (1.3)	62 (2.5)
NEW BRUNSWICK-ENGLISH	%	83 (1.0)	12 (0.7)	5 (0.5)
	P	63 (0.4)	57 (1.3)	51 (2.2)
ONTARIO-ENGLISH	%	82 (1.3)	13 (1.0)	5 (0.6)
	P	64 (0.4)	58 (1.3)	58 (2.0)
ONTARIO-FRENCH	%	78 (1.0)	17 (0.9)	6 (0.6)
	P	57 (0.5)	54 (0.7)	52 (1.6)
QUEBEC-ENGLISH	%	83 (1.4)	12 (1.0)	5 (0.8)
	P	64 (0.6)	57 (1.3)	62 (1.6)
QUEBEC-FRENCH	%	77 (1.2)	14 (1.0)	8 (0.7)
	P	64 (0.5)	61 (1.0)	61 (1.6)

Amounts of Daily Homework

Populations		NO HMWK	1 HR/LESS	2 HRS/MORE
CANADA	%	29 (1.0)	58 (1.1)	12 (0.6)
	P	65 (0.5)	63 (0.4)	60 (0.8)
ENGLAND	%	55 (3.2)	34 (2.8)	10 (1.1)
	P	64 (1.0)	63 (1.5)	55 (1.8)
HUNGARY	%	4 (0.6)	67 (1.5)	29 (1.5)
	P	63 (2.4)	63 (0.6)	63 (0.7)
IRELAND	%	2 (0.4)	82 (1.4)	16 (1.3)
	P	46 (3.5)	57 (0.8)	55 (1.2)
ISRAEL	%	5 (0.6)	60 (1.7)	36 (1.7)
	P	53 (2.0)	62 (0.9)	61 (0.7)
ITALY	%	6 (0.9)	66 (1.5)	27 (1.2)
	P	67 (3.3)	68 (0.9)	65 (1.3)
KOREA	%	3 (0.5)	77 (1.3)	20 (1.2)
	P	64 (2.4)	68 (0.5)	70 (0.8)
PORTUGAL	%	2 (0.2)	76 (1.6)	22 (1.6)
	P	56 (4.0)	56 (0.7)	53 (1.1)
SCOTLAND	%	16 (2.1)	78 (2.3)	5 (0.8)
	P	63 (2.3)	63 (0.6)	53 (2.9)
SLOVENIA	%	5 (0.8)	79 (1.2)	15 (1.2)
	P	57 (1.8)	58 (0.5)	56 (0.7)
SOVIET UNION	%	2 (0.4)	71 (1.6)	27 (1.8)
	P	59 (3.6)	62 (1.4)	61 (1.2)
SPAIN	%	15 (1.5)	57 (1.9)	28 (1.6)
	P	61 (1.3)	62 (0.8)	62 (0.8)
TAIWAN	%	3 (0.4)	68 (1.4)	29 (1.4)
	P	54 (2.6)	66 (0.6)	69 (0.8)
UNITED STATES	%	21 (1.6)	61 (1.8)	19 (1.4)
	P	67 (1.1)	65 (0.8)	61 (1.6)
Canadian Populations				
BRITISH COLUMBIA	%	35 (2.1)	53 (2.0)	12 (1.1)
	P	67 (0.8)	66 (0.7)	63 (1.1)
NEW BRUNSWICK-ENGLISH	%	7 (0.7)	80 (1.0)	13 (0.8)
	P	60 (1.8)	63 (0.4)	57 (1.0)
ONTARIO-ENGLISH	%	46 (1.7)	42 (1.6)	12 (1.0)
	P	65 (0.5)	62 (0.8)	58 (1.2)
ONTARIO-FRENCH	%	15 (1.0)	76 (1.3)	9 (0.9)
	P	60 (0.9)	56 (0.5)	52 (1.1)
QUEBEC-ENGLISH	%	6 (1.0)	73 (1.4)	20 (1.3)
	P	60 (2.1)	64 (0.8)	62 (0.9)
QUEBEC-FRENCH	%	2 (0.4)	84 (1.2)	13 (1.2)
	P	56 (3.3)	63 (0.5)	61 (0.9)

% = Percentages of Students
P = Average Percents Correct

Science: Age 9

Amounts of Daily Television Viewing

Populations		0-1 HR	2-4 HRS	5 HRS/MORE
CANADA	%	26 (0.8)	52 (0.8)	22 (0.7)
	P	63 (0.6)	64 (0.4)	60 (0.6)
ENGLAND	%	28 (1.9)	50 (1.9)	22 (1.9)
	P	61 (1.7)	66 (1.0)	59 (1.3)
HUNGARY	%	26 (1.6)	60 (1.7)	15 (1.2)
	P	62 (1.0)	64 (0.5)	59 (1.0)
IRELAND	%	23 (1.4)	55 (1.7)	22 (1.6)
	P	57 (1.1)	57 (0.8)	54 (1.1)
ISRAEL	%	20 (1.2)	56 (1.5)	24 (1.2)
	P	58 (0.9)	62 (0.8)	61 (0.9)
ITALY	%	44 (1.3)	47 (1.2)	9 (1.1)
	P	67 (0.9)	67 (0.9)	66 (1.7)
KOREA	%	30 (1.1)	60 (1.1)	10 (0.8)
	P	69 (0.7)	68 (0.5)	65 (1.4)
PORTUGAL	%	34 (1.9)	48 (1.7)	18 (1.6)
	P	53 (0.9)	56 (0.8)	55 (1.4)
SCOTLAND	%	19 (1.1)	57 (1.7)	24 (1.4)
	P	64 (1.7)	63 (0.6)	60 (1.3)
SLOVENIA	%	34 (1.6)	56 (1.4)	10 (0.8)
	P	58 (0.7)	59 (0.6)	55 (1.3)
SOVIET UNION	%	24 (1.5)	59 (1.5)	17 (1.1)
	P	62 (1.8)	62 (1.2)	60 (1.3)
SPAIN	%	29 (1.8)	51 (1.7)	20 (1.8)
	P	61 (0.8)	63 (0.7)	60 (1.1)
TAIWAN	%	37 (1.4)	51 (1.5)	12 (0.8)
	P	67 (0.8)	67 (0.7)	63 (0.9)
UNITED STATES	%	25 (1.3)	49 (1.6)	25 (1.6)
	P	63 (1.5)	67 (0.9)	60 (0.9)
Canadian Populations				
BRITISH COLUMBIA	%	27 (1.5)	51 (1.3)	22 (1.2)
	P	67 (1.0)	67 (0.5)	62 (1.0)
NEW BRUNSWICK-ENGLISH	%	23 (1.0)	50 (1.1)	26 (1.0)
	P	61 (0.8)	63 (0.5)	59 (0.9)
ONTARIO-ENGLISH	%	22 (1.2)	51 (1.3)	27 (1.1)
	P	62 (1.1)	64 (0.6)	60 (0.8)
ONTARIO-FRENCH	%	26 (1.4)	54 (1.4)	20 (1.0)
	P	57 (0.8)	57 (0.6)	54 (0.7)
QUEBEC-ENGLISH	%	29 (1.6)	50 (1.6)	21 (1.6)
	P	64 (1.1)	64 (0.9)	59 (0.9)
QUEBEC-FRENCH	%	32 (1.3)	53 (1.4)	14 (0.8)
	P	63 (0.8)	64 (0.6)	59 (0.9)

Amounts of Experimenting on Own

Populations		OFTEN	SOMETIMES	NEVER
CANADA	%	17 (0.8)	57 (1.1)	27 (1.0)
	P	62 (0.7)	63 (0.4)	63 (0.6)
ENGLAND	%	30 (2.4)	59 (2.4)	11 (1.3)
	P	63 (1.3)	64 (0.9)	60 (1.9)
HUNGARY	%	15 (0.9)	45 (1.3)	40 (1.3)
	P	56 (1.1)	62 (0.7)	65 (0.6)
IRELAND	%	13 (1.2)	37 (1.7)	50 (2.0)
	P	53 (1.5)	56 (1.0)	58 (0.8)
ISRAEL	%	36 (1.9)	50 (1.6)	14 (1.1)
	P	61 (0.9)	61 (0.9)	62 (1.0)
ITALY	%	7 (0.8)	43 (1.8)	50 (1.8)
	P	61 (2.0)	67 (1.0)	68 (1.0)
KOREA	%	20 (1.2)	62 (1.4)	19 (1.1)
	P	68 (0.9)	68 (0.5)	66 (0.9)
PORTUGAL	%	9 (1.0)	68 (1.9)	22 (1.6)
	P	48 (1.3)	56 (0.9)	56 (1.1)
SCOTLAND	%	19 (1.9)	53 (1.8)	28 (2.6)
	P	60 (1.3)	64 (0.9)	61 (1.0)
SLOVENIA	%	26 (1.5)	53 (1.6)	21 (1.1)
	P	54 (1.0)	59 (0.5)	61 (0.7)
SOVIET UNION	%	14 (1.0)	42 (0.9)	44 (1.2)
	P	56 (2.4)	63 (1.3)	62 (1.2)
SPAIN	%	12 (1.0)	48 (2.0)	40 (2.2)
	P	58 (1.5)	63 (0.8)	62 (0.7)
TAIWAN	%	23 (1.2)	66 (1.1)	10 (0.8)
	P	67 (0.9)	67 (0.6)	64 (1.3)
UNITED STATES	%	23 (1.3)	55 (1.4)	22 (1.3)
	P	63 (1.3)	66 (0.9)	63 (1.0)
Canadian Populations				
BRITISH COLUMBIA	%	21 (1.4)	59 (1.6)	21 (1.7)
	P	64 (1.1)	66 (0.7)	67 (0.9)
NEW BRUNSWICK-ENGLISH	%	17 (1.1)	54 (1.4)	29 (1.2)
	P	58 (0.9)	63 (0.5)	62 (0.8)
ONTARIO-ENGLISH	%	18 (1.2)	57 (1.5)	26 (1.5)
	P	61 (0.9)	63 (0.6)	61 (0.9)
ONTARIO-FRENCH	%	29 (1.7)	59 (1.6)	12 (1.0)
	P	57 (0.8)	57 (0.5)	54 (1.1)
QUEBEC-ENGLISH	%	17 (1.1)	53 (1.6)	31 (1.5)
	P	61 (1.3)	64 (0.7)	63 (0.9)
QUEBEC-FRENCH	%	14 (1.3)	56 (1.7)	30 (1.7)
	P	62 (1.0)	63 (0.6)	64 (0.9)

% = Percentages of Students
P = Average Percent Correct

Science: Age 9

Percentages of Students Responding Correctly to IAEP Assessment Items

Topic: Life Sciences	IAEP Item Average
Bird anatomy – form and function	87
Human anatomy – identify organ by function	86
Human anatomy – identifying organ by function	83
Classification of animals – insects	82
Adaptation – camouflage	79
Classification of animals – mammals	77
Plants – identifying structures by function	76
Classification of animals	71
Human anatomy – identifying organ by function	65
Genetics – inherited traits	65
Plant life cycle	65
Classification of animals	63
Bird anatomy – form and function	62
Insects and pollination	56
Plants – identifying structures by function	55
Adaptation – desert ecosystem	55
Human anatomy – digestion	51
Oxygen and life	50
Classification of animals – mammals	50
Causes of disease	48
Life cycle – insects	47
Plant growth	40
Plants – identifying structures by function	38

Topic: Physical Sciences	IAEP Item Average
Volume	82
Electrical conductivity	79
Lever and fulcrum principles	71
Collisions	70
Gravity	65
Weighing objects – comparisons of weights	63
Conservation of mass	63
Newton's first law	58
Magnetic properties of iron	56
Conservation of mass	55
Stored energy	53
Chemical changes – dissolving	53
Gravity	52
Physical changes – freezing	48
Expansion of gases	45
Vibrations on string	44
Shadows vs. light source	38

Topic: Earth and Space Sciences	IAEP Item Average
Weather – wind	91
Fuels	79
Stars – production of light	73
Solar System structure	70
Reflectivity of the Moon	66
Solar System structure	62
Weather – lightning	56
Earth – Moon physical properties	54
Water cycle	45
Phases of the Moon	40

Topic: Nature of Science	IAEP Item Average
Linking description with observation	85
Reading scales	81
Linking description with observation	78
Reading charts	60
Experimental design – selecting the correct controls	54
Reading graphs	51
Experimental conclusions	49
Understanding experimental purpose from description	49

Canadian Data

Science: Age 13, Percent of Students Reporting

Canadian Populations	SCIENCE IS FOR BOYS AND GIRLS	LISTEN TO TEACHER EVERY DAY	NEVER DO EXPERIMENTS	TAKE TESTS 1/WEEK	4/MORE HRS SCI HMWK EACH WEEK	SAME LANGUAGE HOME/SCH	4/MORE BROTHERS OR SISTERS	LESS 25 BOOKS IN HOME
ALBERTA	94 (0.6)	44 (1.7)	14 (1.2)	24 (1.5)	6 (0.7)	91 (0.8)	11 (1)	11 (0.8)
BRITISH COLUMBIA	94 (0.7)	29 (2.1)	14 (1.0)	33 (2.0)	7 (0.9)	88 (1.3)	9 (0.8)	9 (1.1)
MANITOBA-ENGLISH	92 (0.7)	45 (1.6)	23 (1.4)	27 (2.1)	4 (0.6)	89 (1.0)	10 (1.1)	12 (1.2)
MANITOBA-FRENCH	93 (1.0)	19 (1.5)	10 (0.9)	55 (1.5)	7 (1.0)	19 (1.2)	9 (0.9)	15 (1.4)
NEW BRUNSWICK-ENGLISH	94 (0.6)	37 (1.3)	24 (0.9)	27 (1.1)	3 (0.4)	96 (0.6)	10 (0.8)	14 (0.8)
NEW BRUNSWICK-FRENCH	93 (0.6)	24 (0.8)	14 (0.7)	44 (1.1)	4 (0.5)	89 (0.6)	7 (0.6)	31 (1.2)
NEWFOUNDLAND	94 (0.6)	38 (1.6)	13 (1.2)	17 (1.2)	7 (0.9)	98 (0.4)	11 (0.9)	18 (1.1)
NOVA SCOTIA	94 (1.0)	47 (1.7)	18 (1.4)	19 (1.4)	6 (0.6)	98 (0.4)	9 (0.8)	12 (0.9)
ONTARIO-ENGLISH	95 (0.6)	22 (1.6)	14 (1.2)	14 (1.4)	3 (0.5)	86 (1.6)	8 (0.9)	10 (1.0)
ONTARIO-FRENCH	93 (0.7)	14 (1.0)	5 (0.7)	38 (1.6)	4 (0.7)	52 (2.3)	5 (0.6)	26 (1.1)
QUEBEC-ENGLISH	95 (0.5)	36 (1.8)	21 (1.3)	34 (1.8)	6 (0.7)	79 (1.7)	7 (0.8)	7 (0.9)
QUEBEC-FRENCH	98 (0.3)	12 (1.0)	10 (1.3)	51 (1.9)	4 (0.5)	92 (0.7)	5 (0.5)	21 (1.3)
SASKATCHEWAN-ENGLISH	93 (0.8)	22 (1.5)	34 (2.0)	14 (1.4)	3 (0.5)	95 (0.5)	11 (0.7)	12 (0.8)
SASKATCHEWAN-FRENCH	92 (2.1)	14 (2.1)	12 (2.2)	30 (3.3)	4 (1.6)	11 (1.8)	12 (2.1)	12 (2.1)

Canadian Populations	PARENTS INTERESTED IN SCIENCE	SOMEONE TALKS ABOUT SCIENCE	SOMEONE HELPS WITH SCI HMWK	READ FOR FUN EVERY DAY	2/MORE HRS ALL HMWK EVERY DAY	5/MORE HRS TELEVISION EVERY DAY	POSITIVE SCIENCE ATTITUDES
ALBERTA	39 (1.3)	52 (1.5)	59 (1.4)	37 (1.6)	20 (1.1)	14 (0.9)	62 (1.2)
BRITISH COLUMBIA	39 (1.3)	57 (1.3)	56 (1.6)	38 (1.2)	27 (1.6)	13 (1.1)	60 (1.7)
MANITOBA-ENGLISH	33 (1.3)	44 (1.3)	47 (1.6)	37 (1.4)	16 (1.1)	19 (1.2)	55 (1.4)
MANITOBA-FRENCH	33 (1.7)	50 (2.0)	42 (1.6)	43 (1.7)	21 (1.5)	14 (1.2)	58 (2.0)
NEW BRUNSWICK-ENGLISH	34 (1.1)	44 (1.3)	51 (1.3)	38 (1.1)	19 (1.0)	22 (1.0)	56 (1.1)
NEW BRUNSWICK-FRENCH	28 (1.2)	45 (1.2)	49 (1.0)	28 (1.2)	19 (0.8)	16 (0.7)	63 (1.2)
NEWFOUNDLAND	39 (1.4)	53 (1.6)	62 (1.5)	39 (1.3)	27 (1.6)	23 (1.2)	67 (1.4)
NOVA SCOTIA	39 (1.2)	48 (1.6)	60 (1.4)	36 (1.4)	20 (1.4)	22 (0.9)	59 (1.5)
ONTARIO-ENGLISH	38 (1.3)	45 (1.4)	50 (1.4)	37 (1.4)	27 (1.4)	17 (1.1)	62 (1.3)
ONTARIO-FRENCH	36 (1.4)	44 (1.5)	49 (1.4)	33 (1.3)	22 (1.5)	18 (1.2)	71 (1.3)
QUEBEC-ENGLISH	41 (1.4)	46 (1.6)	38 (1.6)	40 (1.4)	33 (1.7)	15 (1.2)	56 (1.6)
QUEBEC-FRENCH	31 (1.2)	47 (1.8)	40 (1.7)	32 (1.2)	25 (1.7)	12 (0.9)	61 (1.5)
SASKATCHEWAN-ENGLISH	34 (1.3)	43 (1.4)	51 (1.7)	36 (1.3)	13 (1.0)	17 (1.0)	55 (1.5)
SASKATCHEWAN-FRENCH	37 (3.5)	53 (3.5)	52 (3.9)	45 (3.9)	17 (2.8)	10 (2.1)	57 (3.1)

Science: Age 9, Percent of Students Reporting

Canadian Populations	5/MORE HRS TELEVISION EVERY DAY	READ FOR FUN EVERY DAY	2/MORE HRS ALL HMWK EVERY DAY	SCIENCE IS FOR BOYS AND GIRLS	READ SCIENCE OFTEN	NEVER DO EXPER
BRITISH COLUMBIA	22 (1.2)	55 (1.6)	12 (1.1)	86 (1.4)	24 (1.4)	21 (1.7)
NEW BRUNSWICK-ENGLISH	26 (1.0)	47 (1.2)	13 (0.8)	84 (0.9)	23 (1.1)	29 (1.2)
ONTARIO-ENGLISH	27 (1.1)	44 (1.2)	12 (1.0)	82 (1.2)	20 (1.0)	26 (1.5)
ONTARIO-FRENCH	20 (1.0)	46 (1.4)	9 (0.9)	67 (1.6)	18 (1.1)	12 (1.0)
QUEBEC-ENGLISH	21 (1.6)	53 (1.7)	20 (1.3)	87 (1.2)	28 (1.5)	31 (1.5)
QUEBEC-FRENCH	14 (0.8)	53 (1.3)	13 (1.2)	84 (1.1)	19 (0.9)	30 (1.7)

Canadian Data

Science: Age 13, Percent of Schools Reporting

	EMPHASIZE PLANTS	EMPHASIZE ANIMALS	EMPHASIZE HUMANS	EMPHASIZE ELECTRICITY	EMPHASIZE MASS	EMPHASIZE CHEMICALS	EMPHASIZE LIGHT	EMPHASIZE SOLIDS
Canadian Populations								
ALBERTA	26 (5.2)	8 (3.0)	4 (2.4)	7 (2.6)	15 (3.3)	4 (1.8)	4 (2.2)	33 (4.5)
BRITISH COLUMBIA	4 (1.7)	10 (2.6)	31 (7.1)	6 (2.3)	24 (5.6)	17 (6.9)	37 (6.3)	83 (5.5)
MANITOBA-ENGLISH	18 (4.2)	21 (4.6)	62 (6.2)	21 (5.0)	16 (3.6)	34 (5.1)	11 (2.5)	40 (6.3)
MANITOBA-FRENCH	44 (0.0)	44 (0.0)	56 (0.0)	40 (0.0)	29 (0.0)	47 (0.0)	27 (0.0)	71 (0.0)
NEW BRUNSWICK-ENGLISH	33 (5.6)	43 (5.4)	3 (1.9)	46 (6.0)	14 (4.2)	42 (6.9)	8 (2.9)	34 (6.3)
NEW BRUNSWICK-FRENCH	24 (6.9)	27 (6.4)	0 (0.0)	6 (3.5)	26 (6.2)	16 (4.9)	3 (2.4)	66 (6.7)
NEWFOUNDLAND	6 (2.4)	27 (5.7)	48 (6.2)	42 (7.4)	2 (0.2)	10 (4.3)	1 (0.1)	46 (6.7)
NOVA SCOTIA	20 (6.3)	38 (6.7)	1 (0.9)	55 (8.7)	27 (6.7)	55 (8.5)	2 (1.2)	18 (4.2)
ONTARIO-ENGLISH	27 (7.4)	25 (7.5)	3 (2.1)	21 (6.0)	45 (5.3)	19 (4.9)	8 (3.0)	55 (6.5)
ONTARIO-FRENCH	47 (7.4)	31 (7.0)	16 (4.2)	30 (5.3)	69 (7.1)	34 (5.4)	19 (4.0)	71 (8.5)
QUEBEC-ENGLISH	3 (0.4)	5 (0.6)	5 (1.1)	2 (1.0)	13 (8.8)	11 (6.8)	9 (8.6)	60 (***)
QUEBEC-FRENCH	6 (2.9)	6 (2.9)	2 (1.2)	6 (2.9)	27 (6.4)	6 (2.1)	4 (2.5)	83 (4.4)
SASKATCHEWAN-ENGLISH	10 (3.2)	9 (3.3)	5 (2.0)	4 (1.6)	13 (3.4)	4 (1.7)	3 (1.4)	10 (2.6)
SASKATCHEWAN-FRENCH	11 (0.0)	19 (0.0)	12 (0.0)	21 (0.0)	34 (0.0)	10 (0.0)	21 (0.0)	17 (0.0)

	EMPHASIZE ROCKS	EMPHASIZE WEATHER	EMPHASIZE STARS	EMPHASIZE PROCESSES	EMPHASIZE EXPERIMENTS	SCIENCE MIN/WEEK	NO LABS	SEPARATE LABS
Canadian Populations								
ALBERTA	67 (5.2)	30 (6.2)	26 (6.1)	68 (5.9)	48 (6.1)	194 (1.9)	2 (1.4)	88 (3.9)
BRITISH COLUMBIA	36 (7.6)	12 (3.5)	10 (4.1)	71 (8.6)	22 (4.9)	188 (4.2)	4 (3.9)	96 (3.9)
MANITOBA-ENGLISH	32 (4.4)	12 (4.0)	29 (5.3)	62 (5.5)	58 (4.6)	201 (4.8)	9 (4.9)	77 (5.9)
MANITOBA-FRENCH	20 (0.0)	20 (0.0)	49 (0.0)	78 (0.0)	59 (0.0)	205 (0.0)	5 (0.0)	90 (0.0)
NEW BRUNSWICK-ENGLISH	15 (4.6)	11 (3.4)	5 (2.3)	60 (7.5)	34 (4.9)	180 (4.1)	24 (4.8)	68 (5.6)
NEW BRUNSWICK-FRENCH	0 (0.0)	3 (2.5)	0 (0.0)	60 (6.5)	49 (6.8)	180 (4.3)	8 (4.0)	71 (6.6)
NEWFOUNDLAND	28 (4.0)	3 (2.0)	0 (0.0)	67 (8.1)	58 (7.7)	198 (7.3)	7 (3.5)	83 (5.4)
NOVA SCOTIA	51 (8.3)	12 (4.9)	5 (4.0)	77 (4.3)	55 (6.4)	204 (5.7)	9 (2.5)	75 (3.8)
ONTARIO-ENGLISH	7 (2.5)	9 (2.9)	8 (3.2)	92 (3.1)	85 (4.6)	123 (2.6)	47 (6.2)	37 (5.8)
ONTARIO-FRENCH	6 (2.4)	28 (6.3)	3 (1.8)	94 (2.0)	88 (4.1)	141 (5.0)	15 (4.6)	49 (5.7)
QUEBEC-ENGLISH	68 (4.4)	71 (4.4)	5 (3.6)	84 (4.2)	39 (5.3)	178 (8.0)	18 (9.5)	81 (9.4)
QUEBEC-FRENCH	77 (5.8)	91 (3.5)	16 (4.7)	79 (4.9)	60 (7.2)	176 (5.1)	0 (0.0)	85 (5.7)
SASKATCHEWAN-ENGLISH	73 (4.6)	58 (4.4)	55 (5.2)	52 (4.2)	37 (4.5)	166 (3.1)	11 (3.0)	81 (4.6)
SASKATCHEWAN-FRENCH	79 (0.0)	45 (0.0)	72 (0.0)	64 (0.0)	52 (0.0)	133 (0.0)	13 (0.0)	52 (0.0)

	NUMBER OF COMPUTERS	TEACH ONLY SCIENCE	ALL HAVE P-SEC SCI	SCI CLASS BY ABILITY	INSTRUCTION DAY/YEAR	INSTRUCTION MIN/DAY	AVERAGE CLASS SIZE	1/MORE PROBLEMS
Populations								
ALBERTA	26 (1.7)	51 (6.0)	66 (6.4)	0 (0.0)	190 (0.3)	315 (2.8)	23 (0.7)	5 (1.8)
BRITISH COLUMBIA	37 (2.8)	78 (8.3)	84 (5.6)	8 (2.8)	190 (1.2)	304 (4.1)	25 (1.5)	19 (6.8)
MANITOBA-ENGLISH	15 (1.0)	45 (5.2)	65 (4.9)	1 (0.4)	192 (0.4)	312 (1.7)	21 (0.7)	10 (3.3)
MANITOBA-FRENCH	18 (0.0)	47 (0.0)	51 (0.0)	0 (0.0)	194 (0.0)	313 (0.0)	20 (0.0)	13 (0.0)
NEW BRUNSWICK-ENGLISH	13 (0.8)	28 (4.3)	38 (6.2)	0 (0.0)	185 (1.3)	296 (2.3)	23 (0.4)	11 (3.0)
NEW BRUNSWICK-FRENCH	8 (0.9)	21 (5.5)	52 (8.7)	18 (6.4)	188 (0.8)	303 (2.3)	24 (0.4)	27 (5.5)
NEWFOUNDLAND	7 (1.0)	49 (5.2)	61 (5.8)	2 (1.4)	187 (0.3)	289 (1.7)	24 (0.9)	35 (5.5)
NOVA SCOTIA	12 (0.9)	77 (4.3)	60 (7.1)	8 (2.8)	187 (0.5)	293 (1.7)	24 (1.1)	18 (3.3)
ONTARIO-ENGLISH	15 (2.0)	21 (6.8)	40 (6.7)	2 (1.5)	187 (0.3)	304 (1.4)	27 (0.5)	11 (2.8)
ONTARIO-FRENCH	14 (1.4)	9 (1.7)	10 (2.4)	6 (2.0)	187 (0.5)	300 (2.4)	22 (0.6)	20 (3.7)
QUEBEC-ENGLISH	15 (1.6)	61 (5.6)	86 (2.9)	7 (3.6)	181 (0.5)	302 (7.2)	26 (5.0)	14 (7.9)
QUEBEC-FRENCH	18 (1.5)	81 (6.9)	49 (7.2)	21 (5.5)	181 (0.2)	303 (2.0)	28 (1.0)	11 (3.5)
SASKATCHEWAN-ENGLISH	14 (0.8)	19 (4.0)	58 (5.1)	4 (1.8)	194 (0.5)	297 (1.5)	21 (0.6)	11 (3.2)
SASKATCHEWAN-FRENCH	10 (0.0)	14 (0.0)	43 (0.0)	17 (0.0)	195 (0.0)	309 (0.0)	20 (0.0)	21 (0.0)

ACKNOWLEDGMENTS

PARTICIPANTS

BRAZIL

Rubens Murillo Marques, Carlos Chagas Foundation
Heraldo Marelim Vianna, Carlos Chagas Foundation

CANADA

ALBERTA

Dennis Belyk, Alberta Education
Chantey MacKay, Alberta Education

BRITISH COLUMBIA

Bill Postl, Ministry of Education and Ministry Responsible
for Multiculturalism and Human Rights
Daina Watson, Ministry of Education and Ministry Responsible
for Multiculturalism and Human Rights

MANITOBA

Kim Browning, Department of Education
Norman Mayer, Department of Education

NEW BRUNSWICK, ENGLISH

Mark Holland, Department of Education
Carolyn Jones, Department of Education

NEW BRUNSWICK, FRENCH

Robert Chouinard, Ministry of Education

NEW FOUNDLAND

Russ Blagdon, Department of Education
Lenora Fagan, Department of Education

NOVA SCOTIA

Bette Kelly, Department of Education
Turney Manzer, Department of Education

ONTARIO

Michael Kozlow, Ministry of Education
André Vézina, Ministry of Education

QUEBEC

Sylvie Mazur, Ministry of Education
Allan Patenaude, Ministry of Education

SASKATCHEWAN

Richard Jones, Saskatchewan Education
Beverley Mazer, Saskatchewan Education

CHINA

Liu Yuan-tu, Central Institute for Educational Research
Teng Chun, Central Institute for Educational Research

ENGLAND

Clare Burstall, National Foundation for Educational Research
Derek Foxman, National Foundation for Educational Research

FRANCE

Pierre Jouvanceau, Ministry of Education
Martine Le Guen, Ministry of Education

HUNGARY

Peter Vari, National Institute of Education

IRELAND

Michael Martin, Educational Research Center, St. Patrick's College, Dublin

ISRAEL

Naomi Gafni, National Institute for Testing and Evaluation
Zehava Sass, The Van Leer Jerusalem Institute

ITALY

Alberta De Flora, IRRSAE/ER, Ministry of Education

JORDAN

Victor Billeh, National Center for Educational Research and Development
Bahjeh Bitar, Ministry of Education

KOREA

Kil-Ho Jang, National Board of Educational Evaluation
Yong-Ki Kim, National Board of Educational Evaluation

PORTUGAL

Fernanda Queirós, Ministry of Education
Maria Odete Valente, University of Lisbon

SCOTLAND

Cathy MacGregor, Moray House College of Education
Brian Semple, Scottish Education Department

SLOVENIA

Marjan Šetinc, Educational Research Institute

SOVIET UNION

Galina Kovalyova, Academy of Pedagogical Sciences
Vasily Razumovsky, Academy of Pedagogical Sciences

SPAIN

Mariano Alvaro, Ministry of Education
Reyes Hernandez, Ministry of Education

SWITZERLAND

Urs Moser, Office of Educational Research of Public Instruction for Bern Canton
Erich Ramseier, Office of Educational Research of Public Instruction for Bern Canton

TAIWAN

Jong Hsiang Yang, National Taiwan Normal University

UNITED STATES

Janice Askew, Educational Testing Service
Tillie Kennel, National Computer Systems

INTERNATIONAL COORDINATION

CANADIAN DATA ANALYSIS GROUP

Jean Guy Blais, University of Montreal
Maurice Dalois, GRICS
Michel Frechette, GRICS
Leo Laroche, Quebec Ministry of Education
Solange Paquet, Educan, Inc.

EDUCATIONAL TESTING SERVICE

Archie Lapointe
Nancy Mead

WESTAT

Adam Chu
Leslie Wallace